MW00583488

1 AND 2 CORINTHIANS

1 AND 2 CORINTHIANS

YUNG SUK KIM, EDITOR

Fortress Press

Minneapolis

1 AND 2 CORINTHIANS

Texts @ Contexts

Copyright © 2013 Fortress Press. All rights reserved. Except for brief quotations in critical articles or reviews, no part of this book may be reproduced in any manner without prior written permission from the publisher. Visit http://www.augsburgfortress.org/copyrights/ or write to Permissions, Augsburg Fortress, Box 1209, Minneapolis, MN 55440.

Scripture quotations, unless otherwise noted, are from the New Revised Standard Version Bible, copyright © 1989 by the Division of Christian Education of the National Council of the Churches of Christ in the USA. Used by permission. All rights reserved.

"Identity and Privilege in Corinth," by Love Sechrest, is from the forthcoming book *Race Relations and the New Testament* (Grand Rapids: Eerdmans). Used by permission of the publisher. All rights reserved.

Cover image: Christian Hugo Martin, *Las flores y las plantas de nuestro jardín*, Burn paper work, 103, 5×153,5 cm. 2010

Cover design: Laurie Ingram

Library of Congress Cataloging-in-Publication Data

ISBN: 978-0-8006-9935-2

The paper used in this publication meets the minimum requirements of American National Standard for Information Sciences — Permanence of Paper for Printed Library Materials, ANSI Z329.48-1984.

Manufactured in the U.S.A.

CONTENTS

Other Books in the Series

texts ⊕ contexts

SERIES PREFACE, UPDATED: TEXTS IN/
AT LIFE CONTEXTS

Myth cannot be defined but as an empty screen, a structure. . . . A
myth is but an empty screen for transference.[1]

שבעים פנים לתורה ("The Torah has seventy faces")[2]

The discipline of biblical studies emerges from a particular cultural context; it is
profoundly influenced by the assumptions and values of the Western European
and North Atlantic, male-dominated, and largely Protestant environment in
which it was born. Yet like the religions with which it is involved, the critical
study of the Bible has traveled beyond its original context. Its presence in
a diversity of academic settings around the globe has been experienced as
both liberative and imperialist, sometimes simultaneously. Like many travelers,
biblical scholars become aware of their own cultural rootedness only in contact
with, and through the eyes of, people in other cultures.

The way any one of us closes a door seems in Philadelphia nothing at all
remarkable, but in Chiang Mai, it seems overly loud and emphatic—so very
typically American. In the same way, Western biblical interpretation did not
seem tied to any specific context when only Westerners were reading and
writing it. Since so much economic, military, and consequently cultural power
has been vested in the West, the West has had the privilege of maintaining this
cultural closure for two centuries. Those who engaged in biblical studies—even
when they were women or men from Africa, Asia, and Latin
America—nevertheless had to take on the Western context along with the
discipline.

But much of recent Bible scholarship has moved toward the recognition that considerations not only of the contexts of assumed, or implied, biblical authors but also the contexts of the interpreters are valid and legitimate in an inquiry into biblical literature. We use *contexts* here as an umbrella term covering a wide range of issues: on the one hand, social factors (such as location, economic situation, gender, age, class, ethnicity, color, and things pertaining to personal biography) and, on the other hand, ideological factors (such as faith, beliefs, practiced norms, and personal politics).

Contextual readings of the Bible are an attempt to redress the previous longstanding and grave imbalance that says that there is a kind of "plain," unaligned biblical criticism that is somehow "normative," and that there is another, distinct kind of biblical criticism aligned with some social location: the writing of Latina/o scholars advocating liberation, the writing of feminist scholars emphasizing gender as a cultural factor, the writings of African scholars pointing out the text's and the readers' imperialism, the writing of Jews and Muslims, and so on. The project of recognizing and emphasizing the role of context in reading freely admits that we all come from somewhere: no one is native to the biblical text; no one reads only in the interests of the text itself. North Atlantic and Western European scholarship has focused on the Bible's characters as individuals, has read past its miracles and stories of spiritual manifestations, or "translated" them into other categories. These results of Euro-American contextual reading would be no problem if they were seen as such; but they have become a chain to be broken when they have been held up as the one and only "objective," plain truth of the text itself.

The biblical text, as we have come to understand in the postmodern world and as pre-Enlightenment interpreters perhaps understood more clearly, does not speak in its own voice. It cannot read itself. *We* must read it, and in reading it, we must acknowledge that our own voice's particular pitch and timbre and inflection affect the meaning that emerges. Biblical scholars usually read the text in the voice of a Western Protestant male. When interpreters in the Southern Hemisphere and in Asia have assumed ownership of the Bible, it has meant a recognition that this Euro-American male voice is not the voice of the text itself; it is only one reader's voice, or rather, the voice of one context—however familiar and authoritative it may seem to all who have been affected by Western political and economic power. Needless to say, it is not a voice suited to bring out the best meaning for every reading community. Indeed, as biblical studies tended for so long to speak in this one particular voice, it may be the case that that voice has outlived its meaning-producing usefulness: we may have heard all that this voice has to say, at least for now. Nevertheless, we have included that voice in this series, in part in an effort to hear it as emerging from its specific context, in order to put that previously authoritative voice quite literally in its place.

The trend of acknowledging readers' contexts as meaningful is already, inter alia, recognizable in the pioneering volumes of *Reading from This Place* (Segovia and Tolbert 1995; 2000; 2004), which indeed move from the center to the margins and back and from the United States to the rest of the world. More recent publications along this line also include *Her Master's Tools?* (Vander Stichele and Penner 2005), *From Every People and Nation: The Book of Revelation in Intercultural Perspective* (Rhoads 2005), *From Every People and Nation: A Biblical Theology of Race* (Hays and Carson 2003), and the *Global Bible Commentary* (*GBC*; Patte et al. 2004).

The editors of the *GBC* have gone a long way toward this shift by soliciting and admitting contributions from so-called third-, fourth-, and fifth-world scholars alongside first- and second-world scholars, thus attempting to usher the former and their perspectives into the *center* of biblical discussion. Contributors to the *GBC* were asked to begin by clearly stating their context before proceeding. The result was a collection of short introductions to the books of the Bible (Hebrew Bible/Old Testament and New Testament), each introduction from one specific context and, perforce, limited in scope. At the Society of Biblical Literature's (SBL) annual meeting in Philadelphia in 2005, during the two *GBC* sessions and especially in the session devoted to pedagogical implications, it became clear that this project should be continued, albeit articulated further and redirected.

On methodological grounds, the paradox of a deliberately inclusive policy that foregrounds differences in the interpretation of the Bible could not be addressed in a single- or double-volume format because in most instances those formats would allow for only one viewpoint for each biblical issue or passage (as in previous publications) or biblical book (as in the *GBC*) to be articulated. The acceptance of such a limit may indeed lead to a decentering of traditional scholarship, but it would definitely not usher in multivocality on any single topic. It is true that, for pedagogical reasons, a teacher might achieve multivocality of scholarship by using various specialized scholarship types together; for instance, the *GBC* has been used side-by-side in a course with historical introductions to the Bible and other focused introductions, such as the *Women's Bible Commentary* (Newsom and Ringe 1998). But research and classes focused on a single biblical book or biblical corpus need another kind of resource: volumes exemplifying a broad multivocality in themselves, varied enough in contexts from various shades of the confessional to various degrees of the secular, especially since in most previous publications, the contexts of communities of faith overrode all other contexts.

On the practical level, then, we found that we could address some of these methodological, pedagogical, and representational limitations evident in previous projects in contextual interpretation through a book series in which each volume introduces multiple contextual readings of the same biblical texts. This is what the SBL's Contextual Biblical Interpretation Consultation has already been promoting since 2005 during the American annual meeting; and since 2011 also at the annual international SBL conference. The consultation serves as a testing ground for a multiplicity of readings of the same biblical texts by scholars from different contexts.

These considerations led us to believe that a book series focusing specifically on contextual multiple readings for specific topics, of specific biblical books, would be timely. We decided to construct a series, including at least eight to ten volumes, divided between the Hebrew Bible (HB/OT) and the New Testament (NT). Each of the planned volumes would focus on one or two biblical books: Genesis, Exodus and Deuteronomy, Leviticus and Numbers, Joshua and Judges, and later books for the HB/OT; Mark, Luke-Acts, John, and Paul's letters for the NT.[3] The general HB/OT editor is Athalya Brenner, with Archie Lee and Gale Yee as associate editors. The general NT editor is Nicole Duran, with Daniel Patte and Teresa Okure as associate editors. Other colleagues have joined as editors for specific volumes.

Each volume focuses on clusters of contexts and of issues or themes, as determined by the editors in consultation with potential contributors. A combination of topics or themes, texts, and interpretive contexts seems better for our purpose than a text-only focus. In this way, more viewpoints on specific issues will be presented, with the hope of gaining a grid of interests and understanding. The interpreters' contexts will be allowed to play a central role in choosing a theme: we do not want to impose our choice of themes upon others, but as the contributions emerge, we will collect themes for each volume under several headings.

While we were soliciting articles for the first volumes (and continue to solicit contributions for future volumes), contributors were asked to foreground their own multiple "contexts" while presenting their interpretation of a given issue pertaining to the relevant biblical book(s). We asked that the interpretation be firmly grounded in those contexts and sharply focused on the specific theme, as well as in dialogue with "classical" informed biblical scholarship. Finally, we asked for a concluding assessment of the significance of this interpretation for the contributor's contexts (whether secular or in the framework of a faith community).

Our main interest in this series is to examine how formulating the content-specific, ideological, and thematic questions from life contexts will focus the reading of the biblical texts. The result is a two-way process of reading that (1) considers the contemporary life context from the perspective of the chosen themes in the given biblical book as corrective lenses, pointing out specific problems and issues in that context as highlighted by the themes in the biblical book; and (2) conversely, considers the given biblical book and the chosen theme from the perspective of the life context.

The word *contexts*, like *identity*, is a blanket term with many components. For some, their geographical context is uppermost; for others, the dominant factor may be gender, faith, membership in a certain community, class, and so forth. The balance is personal and not always conscious; it does, however, dictate choices of interpretation. One of our interests as editors is to present the personal beyond the autobiographical as pertinent to the wider scholarly endeavor, especially but not only when *grids of consent* emerge that supersede divergence. Consent is no guarantee of Truthspeak; neither does it necessarily point at a sure recognition of the biblical authors' elusive contexts and intentions. It does, however, have cultural and political implications.

Globalization promotes uniformity but also diversity, by shortening distances, enabling dissemination of information, and exchanging resources. This is an opportunity for modifying traditional power hierarchies and reallocating knowledge, for upsetting hegemonies, and for combining the old with the new, the familiar with the unknown—in short, for a fresh mutuality. This series, then, consciously promotes the revision of biblical myths into new reread and rewritten versions that hang on many threads of welcome transference. Our contributors were asked, decidedly, to be responsibly nonobjective and to represent only themselves on the biblical screen. Paradoxically, we hope, the readings here offered will form a new tapestry or, changing the metaphor, new metaphorical screens on which contemporary life contexts and the life of biblical texts in those contexts may be reflected and refracted.

The Editors

Notes

1. Mieke Bal 1993: 347, 360.

2. This saying indicates, through its usage of the stereotypic number seventy, that the Torah—and, by extension, the whole Bible—intrinsically has many meanings. It is therefore often used to indicate the multivalence and variability of biblical interpretation, and does not appear in this formulation in traditional Jewish biblical interpretation before the Middle Ages. Its earliest appearances are in the medieval commentator Ibn Ezra's introduction to his commentary on the Torah, toward the introduction's end (as in printed versions), in Midrash *Numbers Rabbah* (13:15–16), and in later Jewish mystical literature.

3. At this time, no volume on Revelation is planned, since Rhoads's volume *From Every People and Nation: The Book of Revelation in Intercultural Perspective* (2005) is readily available, with a concept similar to ours.

Contributors

Yung Suk Kim, editor, is associate professor of New Testament and early Christianity at the Samuel DeWitt Proctor School of Theology, Virginia Union University, in Richmond, Virginia. His books include *Christ's Body in Corinth: The Politics of a Metaphor* (Fortress Press, 2008); *A Theological Introduction to Paul's Letters: Exploring a Threefold Theology of Paul* (2011). Kim's forthcoming books include *Biblical Interpretation: Theory, Process and Criteria* (2013), *A Transformative Reading of the Bible* (2013), and *Truth, Testimony, and Transformation: A New Reading of the "I Am" Sayings in John's Gospel* (2013). He is a recipient of the 2010–11 Lilly Theological Scholars Grant. He is editor of the *Journal of Bible and Human Transformation*.

CONTRIBUTORS

Ayodeji Adewuya is professor of New Testament at the Pentecostal Theological Seminary, in Cleveland, Tennessee. His books include *Holiness and Community in 2 Cor. 6:14–7:1: A Study of Paul's View of Communal Holiness in the Corinthian Correspondence* (2001); *Transformed by Grace: Paul's View of Holiness in Romans 6–8* (2004). He has also published academic articles in various journals and written essay chapters in books. He is a regular contributor to Precepts for Living, a Sunday School Commentary for African Americans published by Urban Ministries, Inc., Chicago and the Evangelical Commentaries of the Church of God, Cleveland, Tennessee.

Efrain Agosto is professor of New Testament studies at New York Theological Seminary. Formerly he was academic dean at Hartford Seminary as well as professor of New Testament and director of the Hispanic Ministries Program. He is the author of *Servant Leadership: Jesus and Paul* (2005) and *Corintios*, a Spanish-language commentary on 1 and 2 Corinthians in the Conosca Su Biblia (Know Your Bible) series (Fortress Press, 2008).

Menghun Goh is a Ph.D. candidate in New Testament and early Christianity at Vanderbilt University. He was born, raised, and educated in the Chinese education system in Kuala Lumpur, Malaysia, and graduated from the University of California and the Graduate Theological Union in Berkeley. He served as a full-time Christian minister before embarking on his Ph.D. studies. He is interested in semiotics, apophaticism, phenomenology, deconstruction, and postcolonial theories.

Ma. Marilou S. Ibita holds a doctoral degree from the Katholieke Universiteit Leuven (2012). Her dissertation is titled, "'If Anyone Hungers, He/She Must Eat in the House' (1 Cor 11:34): A Narrative-Critical, Socio-Historical and Grammatical-Philological Analysis of the Story of the Lord's Supper in Corinth (1 Cor 11:17–34)." Her research interests include meal themes in the New Testament, particularly in Paul and the Gospels, the relationship of material evidence and the New Testament, as well as issues in New Testament interpretation, especially using narrative-critical, sociohistorical, ecological, liberationist, and feminist hermeneutics of the New Testament.

Luis Menéndez Antuña is a Ph.D. candidate in New Testament and early Christianity at Vanderbilt University. A Fulbright student, he was born and educated in Spain. Before enrolling in doctoral studies, he taught theology at Loyola College in Maryland, in Alcalá de Henares (Madrid), and Hebrew Bible at Saint Louis University in Madrid. His research interests include ideological criticism (more specifically, queer and postcolonial studies), critical theory, and philosophy. He has published articles on Thecla (Estudios Eclesiasticos) and postcolonial and liberation criticism (Theologica Xaveriana).

Janelle Peters is a Ph.D. candidate at Emory University. Her dissertation situates the veils and athletic metaphors of 1 Corinthians within cultural discourses on the construction of the citizen and religious participation. She has written several articles on topics in the Hebrew Bible, New Testament, and Greco-Roman milieu. She is interested in the intersection of visual and literary cultures, the ecology of individual and corporate bodies, and the prophetic economy.

Jeremy Punt is professor of New Testament in the theology faculty at Stellenbosch University, South Africa. His work is on New Testament hermeneutics past and present, as he is interested in understanding the use of the Scriptures of Israel in the New Testament (and Pauline letters in particular) as well as in contemporary cultural criticism, especially in postcolonial interpretation. His recent publications include "Hermeneutics in Identity Formation: Paul's Use of Genesis in Galatians 4" (2011) and "Pauline Agency in Postcolonial Perspective: Subverter of or Agent for Empire?" (in *The Colonized Apostle: Paul through Postcolonial Eyes*, ed. C. D. Stanley [Minneapolis: Fortress Press, 2011]).

Love Sechrest is associate professor of New Testament at Fuller Theological Seminary. Sechrest is co-chair of the African American Biblical Hermeneutics section in the Society of Biblical Literature, and gives presentations on race, ethnicity, and Christian thought in a variety of academic, business, and church contexts. She is the author of *A Former Jew: Paul and the Dialectics of Race* (2009) and other articles and book chapters in New Testament studies, critical race theory, and ethics, and is currently working on a book titled *Race Relations and the New Testament,* as well as a commentary on 2 Corinthians.

K. K. Yeo is Harry R. Kendall Professor of New Testament at Garrett-Evangelical Theological Seminary (Evanston, Ill.) and academic director of the Christian Studies program at Peking University, China. He has authored over twenty Chinese books and seven English books on cross-cultural biblical interpretation and Christian spirituality, including *What Has Jerusalem to Do with Beijing?* (1995) and *Musing with Confucius and Paul* (2008).

Abbreviations

AB   Anchor Bible
ABR   Australian Biblical Review
AJA   American Journal of Archaeology
AJP   American Journal of Philology
ANTC   Abingdon New Testament Commentaries
Bib   Biblica
BibInt   Biblical Interprtetation
BR   Biblical Research
BTB   Biblical Theology Bulletin
BZNW   Beihefte zur Zeitschrift für die neutestamentliche Wissenschaft
CBQ   Catholic Biblical Quarterly
ETL   Ephemerides theologicae lovanienses
EvT   Evangelische Theologie
HBT   Horizons in Biblical Theology
HR   History of Religions
HTR   Harvard Theological Review
HvTSt   Hervormde Teologiese Studies
IBC   Interpretation: A Bible Commentary for Teaching and Preaching
JAAR   Journal of the American Academy of Religion
JBL   Journal of Biblical Literature
JSNT   Journal for the Study of the New Testament
JSNTSup   Journal for the Study of the New Testament: Supplement Series
JRE   Journal of Religious Ethics
JTS   Journal of Theological Studies
List   Listening: Journal of Religion and Culture
Neot   Neotestamentica
NIGTC   New International Greek Testament Commentary
NovT   Novum Testamentum
NovTSup   Novum Testamentum Supplements
NTL   New Testament Library

NTM The New Testament Message

NTS *New Testament Studies*

R&T *Religion and Theology*

ResQ *Restoration Quarterly*

RTR *Reformed Theological Review*

SBLDS Society of Biblical Literature Dissertation Series

SJT *Scottish Journal of Theology*

Spec *Speculum*

TANZ Texte und Arbeiten zum neutestamentlichen Zeitalter

TJ *Trinity Journal*

TynBul *Tyndale Bulletin*

WUNT Wissenschaftliche Untersuchungen zum Neuen Testament

ZNW *Zeitschrift für die neutestamentliche Wissenschaft und die Kunde der älteren Kirche*

Introduction

YUNG SUK KIM

The books of 1 and 2 Corinthians reveal a vast array of issues in Corinth, ranging from divisive ideologies to resurrection. As Corinth is well known among scholars for its thriving commerce with a vast influx of immigrants from elsewhere in the Roman Empire, the Corinthian community appears to reflect divergent social realities due to its diverse membership from lower to upper classes. Accordingly, it is not surprising for us to see the storehouse of problems in the Corinthian community—a battleground of competing voices coming from the strong and the weak, the rich and the poor, men and women. The current volume of *First and Second Corinthians* in the Texts @ Contexts series features an intercultural reading of the Corinthian correspondence from the diverse cultural perspectives/contexts of the contributors—Africa, Asia, Latin America, Europe, and the United States. It is intercultural at several levels. First, as culture is broadly understood to encompass all kinds of ideologies and the way of life, we in the twenty-first century engage in intercultural conversations with the first-century Corinthian culture. *Intercultural* here means a conversation between those of two different time periods. Second, since most of the Corinthian issues are specifically cultural, our contributors easily find common cultural issues between themselves and the Corinthians such as identity, ritual, and community. *Intercultural* here means intercontextual discussion of cultural issues in Corinth and in our day. Third, since our contributors represent diverse cultural perspectives, they can provide unique interpretations that stem from their personal experiences in their respective environments. *Intercultural* here means a cross-cultural understanding of the given topic; for example, as will be explained later, each of our contributors approaches and discusses the topic of identity differently.

This volume is divided into three parts, arranged according to the various topics of intercultural reading. The overarching theme for part 1 is identity, which includes issues of race relations and privileges in the United States, postapartheid identity in South Africa, and Latino/a identity in the United States. The major theme for part 2 is ritual, which includes purification rites in Africa, ancestor veneration in Chinese culture, and the Lord's Supper in Filipino lowlands. The key word for part 3 is *community*, which includes hermeneutics of love in the community from a classical Daoist perspective, head veil community in America, and a community of sexual minority in Spain. A brief introduction to each essay follows.

In part 1, Love Sechrest ("Identity and the Embodiment of Privilege in Corinth") discusses identity and privileges in Corinth and in America. Stimulated by concerns about race relations and privileges in America, she seeks to deconstruct and reconstruct identity and privileges through the embodiment of Paul's gospel—specifically in "his likeness to a common, humble, disposable, and fragile piece of clay pottery." According to Sechrest, while keeping cultural heritage or sense of privilege may be important, just as Paul himself is confident in his ethnic religious heritage, Christian identity ultimately comes from the embodiment of a Christlike life, especially when remembered through Christ's crucifixion, through which God's power is revealed. Therefore, what matters is what constitutes privilege and how such privilege is perceived, gained, and practiced. Sechrest's reading challenges modern Christians across the board to envision a new model of Christian identity rooted in selfless love and sacrifice.

Jeremy Punt ("Identity and Human Dignity amid Power and Liminality in 1 Corinthians 7:17-24") similarly handles issues of identity in postapartheid South Africa in light of slavery and God's calling in 1 Cor. 7:17-24, in which Paul encourages his audience to remain in the calling in which they were called (circumcision or slavery). According to Punt, it is difficult to know Paul's firm stance on slavery, because, on one hand, he asks the Corinthians to stay where they were called, and, on the other hand, he asks them to remain with God without becoming slaves of human masters. Is Paul socially conservative, or is he implicitly challenging slavery in society? Or does he stand somewhere in between these extremes? Punt believes that Paul leaves room for his audience to challenge the world with their own interpretations of God's calling, thinking about how to live sensibly with the power of God. Punt's study implies the importance of interpreting God's calling and moving toward the step-by-step improvement of race relations, economic justice, and desirable multiethnic society.

Efrain Agosto ("An Intercultural Latino Reading of Paul: The Example of 1 Corinthians 9:19-23") juxtaposes the context of Latino/a presence in the United States with that of Paul's mission. Rather than presenting Paul as a border-eraser or a kind of imperial colonialist, he interprets Paul in 1 Cor. 9:19-23 as a person who crosses the border not to invade but to engage others in the truth of God's gospel. Using Fernando Segovia's "hermeneutics of otherness and engagement," Agosto argues that Paul's attitude toward others can be helpful for Latinos/as in America because they can identify with Paul in his passion for sharing the gospel to all through the spirit of "otherness and engagement." As

Paul becomes "all things to all people" in his sharing of the good news, Latino people also become "all things to all people" in a new world for sharing the good news of God. He suggests that borders do not signify isolation, separation, or marginalization; rather, they constitute a hermeneutical space for negotiation, engagement, or solidarity with others.

In part 2, Ayodeji Adewuya ("2 Corinthians 7:1 against the Backdrop of African Purification Rites") helps us understand holiness in Paul's text through the lens of purification rites in African tradition. Adewuya, defying the Western notion of purification in Africa as an empty myth, argues that purification rites are holistic and govern all aspects of life, personal and communal, psychological and spiritual, realistic and ideal at the same time. He goes on to say that Paul's exhortation to the Corinthians emphasizes the cleansing of all aspects of life in serving God and neighbors so that they too can be holy. The implication of this study is that purification or holiness affects every aspect of our lives as we engage in the community, neighbors, and ourselves.

Menghun Goh ("The Issue of *Eidōlothyta*: An Inter(con)textual Interpretation of 1 Corinthians 8:1—11:1 and Chinese Ancestor Veneration") addresses ancestor veneration in Chinese culture and the issue of food offered to idols in 1 Corinthians 8–10. Goh warns that ancestor veneration must not be misunderstood as an evil practice that involves elevating ancestors to idol status. Rather, the ritual of ancestor veneration is a cultural practice that honors deceased ancestors. Through ancestor veneration, members of the community find a symbolic space of unity and solidarity with one another. According to Goh, the problem of food offerings to idols in Corinth was not the idol or the food itself but the will of the strong people who ignored the conscience of the weak by consuming the food offered to idols. The implication of this study is that rituals, such as ancestor veneration, can be examined by their context. In Chinese culture, ancestor veneration serves the community in a positive way. In Corinth, meal culture (in this case, eating the food offered to idols) did not serve the whole community very well.

Ma. Marilou Ibita ("A Conversation with the Story of the Lord's Supper in 1 Corinthians 11:17-34: Engaging the Scripture Text and the Filipino Christians' Context") constructs a conversation between the story of the abuses of the Lord's Supper in Corinth and the story of meal culture in the lowland Filipino context, which emphasizes mutual care, growth, unity, and shared identity. This contextual study implies that ritual activity such as the Lord's Supper should not be limited as a practice in service but rather represent an integral part of one's life through inviting and embracing all the members of the community in the poor area. At the Lord's Supper, people find their identity in community strengthened because of the mutual care and love they feel as they remember both Jesus' feeding of the multitudes and his death. In the end, Ibita seems to ask how we can participate in the Lord's Supper while billions of people are in hunger or in poverty.

In part 3, K. K. Yeo ("Pauline Theological Counseling of Love in the Language of the *Zhuangzi*: A Reading of Love in 1 Corinthians in a Chinese Philosophical Context") opens discussion about Paul's concept of love in 1 Corinthians and the Chinese reading of love in Zhuangzi's language. Through the study of intertextual and intercultural aspects of love, Yeo suggests that Paul's concept of love and his counseling of the church can be well understood through the lens of classical Daoism, where love is other-centered wisdom and action toward others. Despite cultural-linguistic differences between Paul and Zhuangzi, Yeo argues that Chinese Christians easily understand Paul's exhortation of love to the Corinthians. The implication of Yeo's essay is that a comparative literature study can be beneficial in deepening our understanding of Paul's text and enriching our cultural heritage. Both Paul and Zhuangzi share the wisdom of deconstruction by seeking selfless communal spirit rather than self-centered pride.

Janelle Peters ("Reading 1 Corinthians 11:1-16 through Habits and Hijabs in the United States") compares the contemporary practice of women head veiling for Catholics and Muslims in America with veiling in Paul's house churches in Corinth. She argues that women's head covering in Paul's house churches was intended not for the subordination of women but for enhancing women's positive role in the church. Women in Paul's church exercised their freedom in worship, which was different from the Roman practice of worship, where only male priests wore head coverings. Paul therefore sought to establish a subculture in Corinth where women and men could find themselves in unity but yet remain separated from the dominant culture. Likewise, the modern practice of head veiling in America for Catholic and Muslim women can be understood through the lens of honor/respect or agency attached to them within their subcultures. The implication of this study is that outsiders should not judge certain religious practices because they do not like or understand them.

Luis Menendez Antuña ("What Queer Hermeneutics Can Do for us in Spain: The Case of 1 Corinthians 6:1-9") deals with the issue of homosexuality in Spain and examines a similar issue in 1 Cor. 6:1-9 and also Rom. 1:26-27. He argues that the Spanish church and the Spanish government must go beyond both the traditional conservatism of the church and the liberal position of the government so that the more-diverse or rich understanding of sexuality may be reflected in the current debate about homosexuality. Analyzing the theory of meaning with regard to sexuality and ideological issues of interpretation, Menendez warns that the Scriptures should not be easily construed for one's interests. It is the task of the reader to critically engage both the text and the world in order not only to foster a more just community but also to defy fixed definitions of community.

In closing, we are reminded that our life journey is not a solitary one. We can learn from the Corinthian struggle—the yearning for a just world and a meaningful existence in it. I hope this volume will invite Christian readers everywhere to critically reengage in the Corinthian correspondence so that the good news of God would be reinterpreted and enlivened in our day so as to benefit all—the creation of God. I thank all of our contributors for the diligence, energy, and insight they poured into this volume.

PART I

Identity, Power, and Race

1

Identity and the Embodiment of Privilege in Corinth

Love L. Sechrest

INTRODUCTION

Years ago, I learned about the seductive appeal of the "prosperity gospel" from acquaintances in a black church in a small town in the rural South. These new friends were generous and loving, and threw open the doors of their hearts and homes to me with scarcely a thought for their own scarcity. They were as open-handed in their giving to the church as they were to me, a virtual stranger. Yet, when it came to a discussion about the prosperity gospel and predatory gimmicks designed to increase contributions from people who are often poor and oppressed, we soon found ourselves at an impasse. Though I denigrated the greed that powers this movement, my friends stunned me with their passionate defense of church leaders in fine suits, fancy cars, and elaborate homes: "Who wants to follow a broke-down pastor?!" In their view, legitimate pastors must have access to the accoutrements of wealth and power; a "broke-down" pastor is simply not a compelling witness to the power of the gospel. This vignette gives insight into the complicated tangle of faith, wealth, race, and the aspirational desire for status and privilege. Though rooted in the not-too-distant past, this thinking is not that far removed from some of the problems Paul faced in Roman Corinth, problems that surface particularly in the correspondence now preserved in 2 Corinthians.

This essay explores the nature of Paul's vision of Christian ministry and the association between physical identity and privilege. Though interpreters speculate about the arguments that gave rise to Paul's responses in 2 Corinthians, many suspect that tension emerged from Paul's failure to embody then-contemporary aspirations about a leader's demeanor. Paul assumes the glory of his ministry accomplishments, heritage, and ethnic identity, but emphasizes his brokenness, humiliation, and suffering as an "earthen vessel," interpreting these qualities as the preferred expressions of participation in Christ. Here I consider the implications of this rhetorical strategy for a modern society in which white bodies signify privilege and power but which regards black and brown bodies as humble, cheap, and disposable. We shall see that Paul was, at one and the same time, both privileged and humble, occupying a position of privilege in his own culture on the one hand, while enslaving himself to recipients of his ministry on the other. We begin with a consideration of privilege and identity, before examining the way these concepts interact with the situation in 2 Corinthians.

The Embodied Nature of Social Identity

Constructs of identity are embodied; that is, they fundamentally involve the nexus of heritage, personality, physical appearance, and social connections. Educators, theologians, and critical theorists alike are exploring the ways in which we understand identity, the human person, and society (Green 2008; Westfield 2008; Tatum 1997). In racial and ethnic studies, the embodied nature of identity organically emerges from the fact that these concepts involve value judgments about skin colors, hair textures, facial features, and body types beyond the simple fact of physical difference. Recent work in the social sciences no longer focuses on the essentialist enumeration of physical characteristics that belong to particular groups, but instead explores the ways that society inscribes social meaning and privileges on particular bodies. The social history of the United States can be narrated in terms of the ways interactions in public spaces in the United States manifest embedded value judgments about bodies, ordering them by gender, ethnoracial identity, and apparent socioeconomic position.[1] In this society, white bodies signify privilege and power, while black and brown bodies are figured as either expendable or threatening, or both.

The notion of privilege is one common theoretical concept that attempts to model how persons inhabit social spaces (Feagin 2006: 33–48; Tatum 1997: 7–9). Privilege mediates position in a hierarchical ordering of ethnoracial groups by characterizing access to social resources. These resources may be material resources like wealth, credit, property, and access to safe neighborhoods and schools; alternately, resources may be immaterial and less easy to quantify, such as assumed social status, access to beneficial social networks, employment opportunity, and the presumption of innocence in the legal justice system (McIntosh 1990: 32–35). Privilege is relative, varying by the complexities of multiple identity attachments, and context sensitive, varying by social location or setting. The relative privilege may be seen in the fact that a black female college professor will enjoy the privileges of educational attainment, but that such privileges will be generally less visible than those accorded to her male colleagues from other ethnic groups (Westfield 2008). Nevertheless, context matters—if a black female professor's privilege can be positively influenced by educational achievement in certain settings, a white male professor's privilege may be diminished in some settings if, for instance, he publicly identifies as a homosexual. Though recipients of privilege are often unconscious of its influence, privilege confers advantages for both the pursuit of happiness and the cultivation of character; it not only smoothes the way for its beneficiaries, but it also confers a poise and self-possession that can function as intangible but nonetheless genuine social resources that confer competitive advantages on the bearers of privilege.

Complicating the concept of privilege is religious social location. Within the larger category of "Christian" in the U.S. scene, there is considerable ethnoracial diversity despite the disembodied, universalistic theorizing of Christian identity. Disembodied constructions of Christian identity appear in modern discourse about Christian theology, and are typically embedded in the idea that Christian identity and origins transcend ethnicity and race (Hodge 2007; Buell 2005; Sechrest 2009; Boyarin and Boyarin 1995). Such disembodied constructs of Christian identity that depict it as a nonethnic, universal group unmarked by particularity are aided by Enlightenment and modernist assumptions about the ideal objective observer, as well as the influence of body-soul dualism in the Western philosophical tradition (Douglas 2005: 3–103).[2] These constructions are not uncommon in New Testament studies, even those that self-consciously interrogate the intersection of identity theory and biblical studies (Cosgrove 2006; Duling 2008).[3]

Kelly Brown Douglas examines the interaction between racial identity and core Christian beliefs, finding among other things that the cross/crucifixion complex is a central element that has facilitated Christian oppression of the ethnic "other" inasmuch as it sanctions suffering. Indeed, Paul is sometimes mentioned as the locus of a problematic discourse about oppression that becomes racially loaded in the current context (Patterson 1998: 229–32). Douglas discusses the traditional reckoning of the crucifixion in the context of womanist thought, wherein some protest the idea of redemptive suffering as damaging for oppressed peoples, while others argue that traditional atonement categories have succored and nourished black Christians in the midst of historical oppression. Douglas steers a middle way, maintaining that when understood as a single indivisible construct, the incarnation and resurrection affirm the importance of human bodies while simultaneously participating in God's self-revelation to humanity (Douglas 2005: 89–103). According to Douglas, the incarnation/resurrection complex affirms: (1) God's identification with human suffering in the context of oppression and unjust uses of power; (2) the incarnation as a declaration of the intrinsic dignity of human flesh as a witness to and medium of God's self-revelation; and (3) God's effective rejection of the ideal of redemptive suffering by the resurrection, inasmuch as it restores Jesus to embodied life. However, contrary to Douglas and others who maintain that there is an essential collusion between Pauline theology and hyper-Platonic thought, Paul himself espouses similar values in 2 Corinthians, especially with reference to the intrinsic dignity of human flesh as a conduit of God's power. Though Paul differs from Douglas on how suffering can be redemptive, 2 Corinthians does contain Paul's conviction that the promise of the resurrection stimulates active and fearless engagement with the world. Paul's bold Christian witness is grounded in privileges that emerge from reflections on his rich ethnoracial heritage on the one hand and his identification with the embodied suffering and resurrection of Jesus on the other. Far from denigrating the body, Paul's countercultural ministry affirms the essentially embodied nature of Christian life and witness in all its messiness.

Paul's Ethnic Identity and Privilege (2 Corinthians 3–4)

Paul's extended reflection on Christian ministry in 2 Cor. 2:14—6:10 is an argument that proceeds in four moves that together address the contrast at the center of the conflict in this epistle: How can authentic ministers fail to exhibit a glory that is comparable to the glory of God in Christ? In the first move, 2:14—3:6, Paul introduces the topic of sufficiency, maintaining that God is the basis for adequacy when ministry conveys life and death to its recipients. Drawing on Roman triumphal procession imagery, Paul depicts himself as God's captive who tangibly manifests knowledge of God to others; those who accept the gospel perceive the message and its messengers as a pleasing aroma leading to salvation, while knowledge of God is the odor of death and decay for those who reject it. In the second move of the argument, Paul contrasts his ministry with Moses' ministry, the most revered leader in Israel's past (3:7—4:6), and in the third section, he develops a pottery metaphor, where he contrasts God's glorious power with the fragile and common human conduit of that power (4:7—5:10). He characterizes his work as the ministry of reconciliation in the fourth and final move, in 5:11—6:10, ending it with a *peristasis*, or catalog of suffering, offered as proof of his authenticity. Although we are here concerned with the second and third sections of this discourse, the major issue throughout 2:14—6:10 concerns a tension that we can also find at the heart of problems in race relations, and that is the clash between physical differences on the one hand and embodied social status and privilege on the other.

In 3:7—4:6, through a rereading Exod. 34:29-35, Paul introduces the new covenant ministry by contrasting the life-giving spirit with the "killing" letter, ultimately describing this as a contrast between Moses' ministry and Paul's via a series of antithetical terms.[4] Post-Shoah interpreters are understandably uncomfortable with this initial comparison and with the series of negative images used for Moses' work throughout this paragraph; including "ministry of death," "ministry of condemnation," as well as the possible references to the abolition of the old covenant (for example, 3:11, 14).[5] A closer reading suggests that these images for the Mosaic ministry were likely chosen not as a realistic or informative description of that ministry for outsiders, but instead communicates to insiders the extent to which Paul's own ministry surpasses Moses'.[6] Paul's description of Moses was intended for the consumption of insiders, and Paul seems to assume that his audience will agree with two propositions: first that Moses' ministry was glorious, and second that it is valid to compare the righteousness and life in his own ministry with the condemnation and death in Moses' (Thrall 1994: 1: 240). By contrast, when discussing the nature of the Mosaic law with outsiders in Romans 7, it is clear that he is addressing people whom he has never met; his description of the law is much more lengthy and nuanced since there he has to argue for his understanding. In the end, it is difficult to imagine a more vivid disparity than that between the description of the law as holy, just, and good in Rom. 7:12 and Moses' killing ministry of death and condemnation through the letter in 2 Cor. 3:6-9. We can reconcile these different depictions by realizing that the former careful characterization represents his core beliefs, while the latter was an ad hoc straw man never intended as a standalone exposition, for use only with colleagues in the context of a comparison.

In other words, the Mosaic ministry ministers death only inasmuch as it vividly contrasts with the resurrection life mediated through the new covenant (see 2 Cor. 4:14) (Sanders 1983: 138). Paul's esteem for the old covenant is evident in the way that he chooses to contrast "glory" with "more glory" rather than using a more negative term as a contrast to glory, such as "dishonor" (*atimia*; 1 Cor. 11:14-15; 15:43; 2 Cor. 6:8) or "humiliation" (*tapenōsis*; Phil. 3:21).[7] When Paul describes the veil over the reading of the old covenant that is only removed in Christ in 3:14-17, his reasoning seems focused on the proper interpretation of the old covenant through the Spirit versus a focus on its destruction, a conclusion that makes sense of Paul's habitual appeal to the Torah throughout the epistles. Indeed, when Paul does develop a foil to contrast with the glory of the new covenant ministry, he will not look to the old covenant but will use his own person as an illustration. The glory of the new covenant contrasts with the humble earthen vessel, lacking in all honor, privilege, or inherent power (4:7). Thus, using a *qal vahomer*, from-lesser-to-greater, argument, Paul establishes the gloriousness of the new covenant ministry by comparing it to something that was for him both self-evident and beyond argument, that is, the intrinsic glory of the Mosaic ministry and covenant (cf. Rom. 7:12).[8] Paul's purposes here are not so much to denigrate the regime of the Mosaic ministry but to establish the glory of new covenant ministry—despite Paul's own apparent lack of this quality—by showing that his ministry is more glorious than the most revered ministry in the central mythomoteur of the people of Israel. In Corinth, Paul's opponents would raise serious doubts about the authenticity of his leadership (10:1-5, 8-9; 11:20-23; 12:11-12) and person (5:12; 10:10), accusing him of poor oratory (10:10; 11:6), inconsistency (10:11; cf. 1:17), and financial fraud (11:7-9; 12:13-18; cf. 2:17; 4:2; 9:20). While we cannot know whether the charges in 2 Corinthians 10–12 had already been leveled, it seems probable that this section in 2 Corinthians 3 either responds to something similar or anticipates that such charges would soon be forthcoming.[9]

Yet one of the key messages in this section appears in the conclusion that Paul draws from his exegesis, in 2 Cor. 3:12, of Exod. 34:29-35. Here Paul infers that the upshot of the unveiled and more glorious nature of the new covenant ministry is a ministry characterized by greater boldness (*parresia*). Indeed, it seems likely that the boldness in Paul's conviction about the glorious new covenant ministry is closely akin to his confidence (*pepoithēsis*) in 3:4, which in context refers to the fact that God empowers ministry (Bultmann 1985: 75–76). Furthermore, Paul's confidence in God's empowerment and the boldness that accompanies his convictions about the surpassing glory of the new covenant ministry also issues in "freedom" (*eleutheria*; 3:17) (Bultmann 1985: 75–76; Furnish 1984: 237–38).[10] Though "freedom" in Paul is normally associated with his thinking about the role of the law for those who are in Christ (for example, Rom. 7:1-6; Gal. 4:4-5), the immediate context makes it more likely that he is using all of this language—confidence, freedom, and boldness—as a way of showing that his new covenant ministry is not only more glorious but also more powerful in its ability to overcome all kinds of obstacles. Moreover, the phrase "we do not lose heart" (*ouk enkakoumen*) in 4:1 and 4:16 simply expresses the same sentiment negatively, that the ministry of the new covenant in Christ will not be diminished by misunderstanding (4:1-4) or danger (4:16; 5:1).[11] Thus the main idea in this section and the next is that the gloriousness of the ministry of the Spirit outshines the greatest ministry in all of Israel's history, the ministry of the Lawgiver himself, and this conviction produces in Paul great confidence and boldness for the task before him (Matera 2003: 66).

In light of this discussion of the main issues in 3:7—4:6, it is necessary to pause to reflect on our earlier discussion about the notion of privilege. It will not be too much of a stretch for us to see in Paul's confidence, courage, and boldness a network of sentiments that is analogous to the fearlessness and assuredness that undergirds the modern notion of privilege in critical race theory. Here we see Paul bolstered by the idea that God has empowered his new covenant ministry so that it transcends even the most glorious ministry in his proud ethnic heritage. Though opponents point to Paul's failure to personify then-current standards of conduct for leaders in Corinth, Paul measures himself against Moses, invoking a traditional standard of leadership that was apparently still unassailable within the local community.[12] Paul's argument about the glory of his new ministry in Christ works as a source of empowerment largely because he has confidence that he and his audience share assumptions about the glory of his ethnoracial heritage.

Read another way, however, one could argue that, far from seeking strength from his ethnic heritage, Paul has actually rejected it, inasmuch as many think that he proclaims the annulment of the old covenant in this passage (3:7, 11, 13, 14; *katargoumenēn*).[13] This interpretation would not only be countercultural relative to his ancient context but would also conflict with many goals of contemporary identity theorists who seek to nurture most forms of ethnic sentiment as a way of resisting an oppressive assimilationist ideal. However, this kind of objection reduces ethnoracial identity to ancestry when identity is much more often complicated by multiple identity associations in which aspects of identity may be emphasized in one setting and subordinated in others. For many Jews of the period, ethnoracial identity included religious sentiment as a key element alongside the element of ancestry (Sechrest 2009). If Paul's religious sentiments have changed in that he now worships the God of Abraham through the new covenant, his focus on Moses affirms that he has nonetheless retained pride in his ancestry as a descendant of Abraham (see 2 Cor. 11:22). Paul does not reject his birth identity in this passage any more than he does in Phil. 3:3-6, a similar passage. In both contexts, Paul's *qal vahomer* reasoning depends on an exalted opinion of that heritage. Even more noteworthy is the fact that Paul's pride in the great example from his heritage is probably unconscious inasmuch as it is assumed rather than argued, as mentioned above. His focus is much more on the way God has empowered the new ministry of the Spirit; he takes the gloriousness of his heritage for granted, and the effectiveness of the argument rests on this shared and implicit assumption. On the other hand, Paul's attitudes do contrast with modern notions of privilege from critical race theory in that they are divorced from specifically visible markers like skin color, even though privilege is associated with particular ethnoracial cultures in both contexts. Indeed, the next sections will show that Paul reverses expectations about visible external markers of status and privilege against then current expectations.

EMBODIED MINISTRY AND THE WEAKNESS OF ETHNORACIAL STIGMA (2 CORINTHIANS 4–5)

The Corinthian correspondence does more to establish the embodied nature of Christian identity than any other section of the Pauline corpus. Much of the scholarship on this passage concerns the relationship between 2 Cor. 5:1-10 and 1 Cor. 15:35-58 and explores the question of whether Paul's views about resurrection in 2 Corinthians have shifted since he wrote the earlier document.[14] Notwithstanding the question of Paul's eschatology, this segment has important implications for contemporary race relations. In this section, we will explore the evidence about Paul's conception of embodied ministry in 2 Corinthians 4–5. Thereafter, we will connect Paul's understanding of embodiment with evidence about how the conflict in Corinth concerned rival perceptions about leadership qualities. In important ways, the opposition to Paul underlying this epistle is deeply concerned about Paul's public persona, and thus analogous to some modern identity dynamics.[15]

The focal image of 4:7—5:21 occurs in the opening verse, in the poignant description of the human body as an earthen vessel. Aune reports that this image was a common metaphor for the fragility of the human body in Greco-Roman antiquity, but the Old Testament background for this metaphor adds additional nuances—the human body is not only weak (Dan. 2:42) but also disposable (Lev. 6:28; 11.32; 15:12; cf. Isa. 30:14; Jer. 19:11), cheap (Lam. 4:2), and perhaps forgettable to boot (Ps. 31:12) (Aune 2001: 221; Thrall 1994: 322–25).[16] Paul does not evoke this image in an effort to demean human existence, but, as shown in the purpose clause in 4:7, to make the point that the human person is the conduit for the extraordinary power of God. As Paul will make even clearer in 12:1-9, the fragility and weakness of the human body is a prerequisite for the demonstration of divine power through it (Savage 1996: 166–67). The catalog of suffering in 4:8-9 shows that God's power is evident even in the midst of ostensible defeat—the minister experiences all kinds of affliction but is not crushed; she is neither perplexed nor forsaken; while struck down, she is not ultimately destroyed. Thus Pauline theology dignifies the fragility and weakness of the human body as an agent for the demonstration of divine power through ministry.

Not only does Paul link the frailty of the human body to divine power, but he goes on to link suffering in the context of Christian life and ministry with the suffering of Jesus. In 4:7-15, Paul several times refers to "Jesus" without adding "Christ," in a departure from his customary practice (4:5, 10, 11, and twice in v. 14; cf. 11:4).[17] This does not suggest, however, that Paul "separates" the Jesus of history from the Christ of faith or any similar bifurcation.[18] Indeed, Paul refers to the "Lord Jesus" in verse 14 in the midst of this particular discourse, an appellation that obviously affirms Jesus' exalted status and nature (cf. 4:5) (Lambrecht 1994: 313-14). By and large, however, interpreters do not make sense of the heavy concentration of this unusual usage in 4:5-15 beyond their insistence on what Paul does not mean.[19] Elsewhere, Paul does make occasional references to "Jesus" without the much more common addition of "Christ" in texts where he is more interested in his person rather than status: Rom. 3:26; 8:11; Gal. 6:17; Phil. 2:10; 1 Thess. 1:10; 4:14.[20] Paul also emphasizes Jesus' person over his status in 4:10, where the phrase "the death of Jesus" (literally, *nekrōsis*) emphasizes the entire network of events that led to Jesus' earthly death (Bauer 2000: 668). When Paul speaks of bearing this death process in order to manifest Jesus' life, he speaks of living a life that continues Jesus' own earthly ministry, one that is *oriented to achieve life-giving results for the benefit of others* (4:11-12, 15-16; cf. 1:6). In other words, Paul's ministry participates in the life and death of Jesus inasmuch as a life spent for others is the way of Jesus (Matera 2003: 110–12; Georgi 1986: 296). The overall message in this section is that Paul's ministry embodies Jesus' ministry; his body, like Jesus', is a concrete conduit for the expression of God's power in human society.[21]

Second Corinthians 4:16—5:10 is also a premier vehicle for Paul's dialectical eschatology, showcasing his convictions about the way a future hope impinges on present existence. The main idea in this passage is that Paul's eschatological hope of renewal provides the assurance that he can minister in confidence, notwithstanding the suffering that threatens the integrity of his physical body (4:16). As mentioned above, much of the discussion about this passage focuses on whether his views about the resurrection of the body have shifted since the writing of 1 Corinthians 15. That debate seems to spin on two axes, the first concerning whether 5:3 refers to a disembodied intermediate state, and the second surrounding the use of metaphorical language throughout the section, which may or may not refer to bodies.

Paul's eschatology in his earlier discourse in 1 Corinthians 15 is clear: First, the Christian hope is oriented toward the resurrection of the body (1 Cor. 15:12-34). Second, though different, there is nonetheless continuity between the earthly body and the resurrected body (1 Cor. 15:35-50, 53-54). Third, 1 Corinthians 15 maintains that the transformation from earthly to heavenly takes place at the Parousia (1 Cor. 15:51-52). Though some scholars think Paul's views have changed in some degree between the time he wrote 1 Cor. 15:35-57 and 2 Cor. 5:1-5, there are many similarities between these passages.[22] Paul contrasts the earthly and the heavenly in both texts (1 Cor. 15:49 vs. 2 Cor. 5:1-2). Similarly, he contrasts the perishable/imperishable on the one hand (1 Cor. 15:42, 50, 52-53) and the eternal/temporal on the other (2 Cor. 4:16—5:1). Mortality (*to thnēton*) puts on immortality in 1 Cor. 15:53-54, and mortality (*to thnēton*) is swallowed by life in 2 Cor. 5:4. He also uses clothing metaphors similarly in these texts: referring to "putting on" (*endysasthai*) imperishability and immortality in 1 Cor. 15:53, and using a similar metaphor, "clothed" (*ependysasthai*) with the heavenly in 2 Cor. 5:2, 4. In 1 Cor. 15:54, death is "swallowed up" (*katapothē*) by victory, and in 2 Cor. 5:4 mortality is "swallowed up" (*katapothē*) by life. On the one hand, Paul says that the Spirit characterizes resurrection life (1 Cor. 15:44-46), and on the other he depicts the Spirit as a down payment for being swallowed up by life (2 Cor. 5:5). Indeed, one scholar plausibly suggests that the much-debated "we know" formula in 2 Cor. 5:1 actually represents a deliberate allusion to the earlier discourse in 1 Corinthians 15 (Green 2008: 177). It seems unlikely that Paul would have significantly changed his views in 2 Cor. 5:1-5 without a more explicit signal of the change, especially given the prominence of the discourse in 1 Corinthians 15 and the significant similarities between it and 2 Cor. 5:1-5, in what is another communication to the same audience (Matera 2003: 170).

But what of the differences between the texts—do those imply that Paul changed his views? The most significant differences are those mentioned earlier, regarding the metaphorical language in 2 Cor. 5:1-5 and the specific interpretation of 5:3. While Paul uses the word "body" (*sōma*) eight times in 1 Corinthians 15 (vv. 35, 37-38, 40, 44), he does not use the word at all in 2 Cor. 5.1-5. Most agree, however, that the earthly tent (5:1; cf. 5:4) is a metaphor for the human body that reflects the same focus on fragility as the earthen vessel of 4:7.[23] Despite this consensus, opinion is divided about whether the building from God (5:1b) or the heavenly dwelling (5:4) likewise refer to the bodies of individual believers or instead to a corporate dwelling, perhaps during an intermediate state.[24] Yet these interpreters miss the import of the thrice-reiterated comparison that forms the backdrop for this imagery in 4:16—5:5, that of the contrast between the temporary and the permanent: momentary versus eternal (4:17); temporary versus eternal (4:18); an earthly house that is a tent (5:1; 5:4) versus an eternal heavenly building that is a dwelling (5:1b-2).[25]

That tent, building, dwelling, and all of the clothing metaphors in this passage symbolize bodies is reinforced in the parallel structures in 5:2-4, which vividly recall the earlier discourse in 1 Cor. 15:35-43 (Matera 2003: 121):

(2a) in this [tent] we *groan longing*	(A)
(2b) to be *clothed over with a dwelling*	(B)
(3a) If clothed[26]	(C)
(3b) then we will not be **naked**	(D)
(4a) in this tent we *groan burdened*	(A')
(4b) because we do *not* want to be *unclothed*	(B')
(4c) but clothed over	(C')
(4d) that **mortality might be swallowed by life**	(D')

Given Paul's earlier use of clothing metaphors and virtually identical sentiments in 1 Cor. 15:54d and 2 Cor. 5:4d, here we see that "nakedness" is not a reference to a corporate existence or possible intermediate state, as maintained by some,[27] but is a synonym for a death in which the believer's mortality has not been swallowed by life (see D-D'). This passage is another way of saying that the believer never has to worry about the shame of a disembodied state, even if the present home in the body is destroyed by death (Harris 1974: 384–89).[28] Indeed, far from longing for a Neoplatonic liberation of the mind from the prison of the body at death, Paul describes an abhorrence for a disembodied existence, instead groaning not to take off one body for another, but to be further embodied (*ependysasthai*; 5:4c), a sentiment that he elsewhere describes as a groaning for the redemption of our bodies (Rom. 8:23).

Thus in 4:7—5:10, Paul emphasizes the embodied nature of Christian life and ministry in three ways. First, he dignifies human somatic fragility as the preferred agency of divine power through the focal image of the earthen vessel. Second, he connects human suffering for the sake of others with the earthly suffering of Jesus as a way of manifesting Jesus' continuing ministry. Finally, he insists on the embodied nature of human life in this age and in the next. Indeed, these three elements are foundational for his argument that an apparently weak or ignoble body can manifest the glory of God and participation in Christ; the promise of a resurrection body liberates the minister from concern with the fragility of human existence to operate in a new boldness that goes beyond the great heroes of the past.

Thus the modern penchant for a Christian life that prioritizes the soul at the expense or neglect of the body is anti-Pauline, as are the associated implications for contemporary Christian ministry. It is more than wrong-headed to allow an erroneous body-soul dualism to require ministry to become segregated into relative concerns for "spiritual" evangelism versus "material" social justice, as some would have it (Green 2008: 70). Moreover, a desire for "colorblindness," that is, a goodly and pseudo-godly attempt to disregard racial difference as immaterial and perhaps even unseemly—a view rampant in Christian circles—is equally misguided. The imprudent think that a colorblind approach to encountering racial difference is godly in that it assumes difference is a flaw that generous people should overlook. It is interesting that this approach is not only politically untenable, in that it implicitly normalizes one kind of racial difference while marginalizing all others, but theologically untenable as well. What some Christians deem a handicap, Paul emphasizes as a means of participating in the work of Jesus inasmuch as racial stigmas metaphorically and literally weaken racialized bodies through social forces. In other words, colorblindness inhibits God's way of working in the world. This approach disregards the way that bodies are connected with identities and, according to the texts we have considered, sunder the connection with Christian ministry in its embodiment of Christ's suffering and glorification. From Paul's perspective, attempts to transcend the nature of earthen vessels run counter to the way of Jesus, and become attempts to subvert the power of God at work in the world, inasmuch as God uses the weak to shame the wise. That is, bodies weakened by racial and ethnic stigmas nevertheless prevail through the power of God in ministry, in ways that belie their lack of privilege.

As mentioned above, Douglas and other womanists rightly raise the concern that an emphasis on participation in the suffering of Jesus as we see here in Paul can be dangerous theology for those already occupying a demeaned position. An emphasis on suffering can be heard among those experiencing oppression as a demand to endure the evils inflicted by an unjust society, which can then have the additional negative effect of reinscribing internalized racism.[29] Yet it is important to note that Paul does not endorse all suffering, nor does he advocate that Christians should seek out suffering. Instead, Paul speaks of a suffering that is endured inasmuch as it is concomitant with service on behalf of others (Lambrecht 1994: 328). The suffering that he speaks of here is that which comes as a consequence of the Christian's fearless engagement with the world, as she flings her body into the conflict between good and evil with abandon, confident that if she loses one body, she gains something more glorious (4:16—5:10). Paul's ethic is on full display in the freedom fighters' practice of nonviolent direct engagement in the Jim Crow South, and is not the idealization of some ascetic ideal that pressures broken peoples to mute their resistance to oppression. Paul emphasizes suffering that is endured—not embraced—as part of the cost of following the way of Jesus in ministering life to others (4:11-12, 15-16; cf. 1:6). Wielding the weapons of righteousness as an agent of righteousness (5:20-21; 6:4), Paul's ministry is bold and public (3:12, 17), fearless in the face of death (5:1-5), and wholly devoted to promoting the life and well-being of those for whom Jesus has died. When it comes to encounters with the other, below we shall see that Paul's ministry philosophy is one that regards every minister and every person through a lens that penetrates stigmatized appearances.

Paul's Lack of Privilege and the Crisis in Corinth (2 Cor. 5:12-17; 11:1—12:10)

Though there is considerable debate about the identity of Paul's opposition underlying 2 Corinthians, there is broad agreement that these critics challenge Paul's leadership as an apostle and servant of Christ. In reviewing the specifics of the dispute, we will find that their charges are similar to race rhetoric in modern society. The opponents' accusations about Paul's leadership deficiencies are analogous in some ways to modern-day racist dialogue that inhibits the full participation of ethnoracial minorities in U.S. society.

The extended reflection on ministry in 2:14—6:10 seems to be an oblique answer to questions about the character of Paul's ministry and person, questions that emerge more forcefully and directly in 10:1—13:10. When Paul describes the life-and-death consequences of Christian ministry using the olfactory metaphors of aroma and fragrance, asking, "Who is sufficient?" for such a ministry (2:16), it is clear that the question of adequacy is at the heart of the opposition. Indeed, comments about letters of recommendations in 3:1-4 separate the question about adequacy in 2:16 from its response in 3:5 and following—a telling parenthesis that suggests that one of the criteria for leadership in the eyes of the opponents was evidence of support from recognized authorities (cf. 4:5; 10:2-18; 11:4). In other words, Paul faced challenges about his legitimacy with respect to a perceived lack of endorsement from key contacts. Yet we will see that in Corinth the issue of adequacy went well beyond the mere question of contacts, also encompassing the leader's total public persona, including his appearance, pedigree, finances, and public actions.

Paul may hint at some of the opposition to him again in 5:12, where he refers to those who boast *en prosōpō*—usually translated "boast in appearance" (Sumney 1990: 129).[30] Because 10:10 does indicate that his opponents malign

Paul's appearance, many interpret 5:12 similarly, an interpretation that seems strengthened by Paul's tacit admission about his own unassuming appearance in 4:7. Yet the immediate context of 5:12 suggests another possibility. Verse 13 very likely implies that some in Corinth having been boasting in appearances associated with charismatic displays. Instead, Paul says that the believers could boast in the fact that he continues the mission of Christ through self-sacrificial actions for the benefit of others (5:14-15), rather than boasting about ecstatic behavior (13; cf. 1 Cor. 14:18-19). Paul affirms that the love of Christ constrains him from offering ecstatic displays as evidence of his legitimacy when these displays do not benefit the community. Thus the opponents' boasts may indeed concern physical appearances, as some interpret 5:12, but the seamless way that Paul elaborates on the phrase "boasting in appearances" in 5:13-15 suggests that this boasting may go beyond appearances to include certain kinds of actions as well.

Several interpreters remark on the way that "knowing (or recognizing) according to the flesh" in 2 Cor. 5:16 is parallel to "boasting in appearances" in 5:12, and see in this parallelism support for the idea that these phrases refer only to appearances (O'Neill 1987: 104; Georgi 1986: 252–53).[31] However, beyond the connections between 5:12 and 5:13-15 as discussed above, the alternation in verbs of knowing in 5:16 may also support my hypothesis that "appearance" (*en prosōpō*) and "according to the flesh" (*kata sarka*) encompass more than simple physical exteriors. When Paul uses "recognize" in 5:16a (NAS; *oidamen*) and forms of "know" in the rest of verse 16 (NAS; *ginōskō*), he is using these two lexemes as synonyms for the idea of "knowing about": "Therefore, from now on we recognize [*oidamen*] no one according to the flesh; even though we have known [*egnōkamen*] Christ according to the flesh, yet now we know [*ginōskomen*] him thus no longer."

However, the alternation in these lexemes goes beyond simple stylistic variation; the tense forms of the words for "know" in these verses communicate differences in verbal aspect.[32] In the New Testament, the Greek word for "recognize" (*oida*; usually translated "know") was well on the way to being a frozen form and was thus not useful for communicating the author's perspective on the action.[33] When he uses a different word to speak of "knowing [*egnōkamen*] Christ according to the flesh" using the perfect tense, he emphasizes the complexity of the "knowing" and the stative aspect. When he says, "now we know [*ginōskomen*] him no longer in that way" with the present tense, he denies that this kind of knowledge constitutes a meaningful way of a continuing participation in Christ by using the imperfective aspect. If Paul is stressing the author's perspective on the action in this verse, then

5:16b does not at all refer to a previous encounter with the historical Jesus, as some maintain, but, as we will see, to a complex state of "knowing" that goes beyond a simple engagement with the flesh or its physical appearance.[34] It is as if Paul acknowledges that a narrative about Christ that focuses on outward appearances would produce a thoroughly unattractive judgment. If someone assesses Christ's life and status using some set of "fleshly" criteria that evaluates Christ's own earthen vessel, humble ministry, and ignoble death as contemptible, Paul maintains that Christ's resurrection nullifies these standards and inaugurates a wholly fresh way of engaging others in the new age.[35] If, according to Paul, Christians must eschew judging by fleshly superficialities even in the case of Christ's glorious status as Messiah, then it is surely appropriate to reject this kind of criteria in all lesser cases as well. Thus 5:16 indicates that in Christ, ministers have new lenses, lenses that nullify appearance and fleshly criteria as considerations that communicate the truth about persons, whether in evaluating Jesus, the minister himself, or any other person.

Paul's other uses of *kata sarka*, and especially the uses in 2 Corinthians, can help us discern the nature of the complexities associated with "knowing *kata sarka*." Paul's earliest uses of *kata sarka* may occur in Gal. 4:23, 29, where it refers to physical descent in general and a biological means of producing converts to the gospel in particular (Martyn 1997: 451–54). In that passage, the phrase stands in contrast to *kata pneuma*, which is Paul's preferred means of incorporating people into the gospel community. Uses of the phrase in other epistles are compatible with this meaning (Rom. 1:3; 4:1; 9:3; 1 Cor. 10:18),[36] but there is evidence in 2 Corinthians that Paul is responding to his opponents' usage.[37] In 2 Cor. 1:17, Paul seems to be responding to a charge that he is weak-minded, indecisive, or overly obsequious, and in 10:1-2 we see that this charge has explicitly originated from opponents ("I reckon to be bold against those who think that we are walking according to the flesh").[38] Though *kata sarka* is still ambiguous in 10:2, it seems that the phrase refers to public behavior that lacks strength of purpose and cravenly caters to public opinion. That is, though Paul aligned his demeanor with Christ's in 10:2 in rebuttal, the preceding verse reveals that he has been accused of weakness and inconsistent behavior in a way that is somewhat reminiscent of 1:17.

Paul's use of the phrase in 2 Cor. 11:18 is much more illuminating for our study of what is involved in "knowing *kata sarka*," especially since the use of *kata sarka* in this verse is most similar syntactically to the usage in 5:16.[39] Here the phrase occurs at the end of the prologue to the fool's boast in 11:1-21. The fool's boast itself begins in 11:22 and runs through 12:10 and is a discourse in which Paul depicts himself as forced to engage in the same kind of foolish boasting and self-commendation that his opponents undertake (11:1, 16, and 21). Even though Paul responds to the boasting of his opponents, he ultimately refuses to boast in kind, deftly using irony to boast in a way consistent with his theological convictions about ministry. What is revealing for our purposes is the fact that Paul names this kind of discourse "boasting according to the flesh." Thus we can expect that when Paul engages in his own boasts, however ironic the *contents* of the boasts, the *topical scope* of the boasts in the discourse will shed light on whether and how *kata sarka* goes beyond mere physical appearance to include a complex set of behaviors and demeanors as we have surmised above.

We see that when Paul boasts according to the flesh as a rebuttal to his opponents, he uses categories that suggest at least three standards of evaluation involved in assessing the legitimacy of his apostleship. First, *kata sarka* boasting includes boasting in a privileged ethnic heritage (11:22; cf. Phil. 3:3-9) (Duling 2008: 831). By way of establishing his equivalence with the "super-apostles," Paul boasts that he, too, shares language, ancestry, and nationality with them.[40] While we can only speculate about whether the opponents emphasize their service to and identity in Christ over their privileged heritage, there can be no doubt of Paul's emphasis both here and in 3:7-18. Nevertheless, the fact that Paul makes mention of these ethnic terms suggests that boasting *kata sarka* encompasses consideration of ethnoracial heritage. Second, *kata sarka* boasting includes boasting about status—here the status of being a servant of Christ. The evidence suggests that the opponents have relied in part on recommendations from outside of the community to substantiate their status as servants of Christ as well as their own self-boasting (3:1; 10:12, 18; cf. 4:2; 5:12; 6:4). Paul, however, focuses attention on the breadth, depth, and intensity of his service to Christ to speak for the legitimacy of his leadership (11:23-27). His half-hearted boast about charismatic visions in 12:1-9 (cf. 5:13) hints that the opponents have additionally relied on charismatic displays to substantiate their claims to leadership status.[41] Taken together, Paul's boasts about suffering and weaknesses in 11:23—12:9 may be intended as ironic contrasts to the opponents' boasts about a set of activities that they think substantiates their claims about being a servant of Christ. Third, boasting or walking *kata sarka* involves bearing a forceful public demeanor that contrasts with Paul's personal humility (11:30-33; cf. 10:1-2, 10; 11:20-21; 13:2-3). The comparatively numerous references to Paul's weak public persona expose this as one of the major areas of contention between Paul and the opponents. In addition, it is likely that mention of Paul's unprepossessing physical appearance and lack of eloquence also contribute to this motif (4:7-9; 5:12; 10:10; 11:6). Where opponents apparently boast in their superiority to believers in Corinth, Paul deliberately draws attention to his own weakness, among other things recounting his furtive escape from the king of Damascus (11:30-33; 12:1-9; cf. 4:7). Indeed, some in Corinth may have interpreted Paul's practice of foregoing the patronage of the Corinthians in light of legitimacy, as if the rejection of this financial support were interpreted as an admission by Paul that he had no right to support as an apostle (2:17; 11:7-11; cf. 1 Cor. 9:3-14) (Sumney 1990: 164).

Thus the uses of *kata sarka* in 2 Corinthians indicate that the term includes a broad array of social value judgments, including ethnoracial identity, social status, contacts, and a particular kind of forceful public behavior. When Paul's opponents contested his sufficiency for leadership, they were challenging him on his demeanor as a leader, including assessments of his pedigree, social contacts, actions (i.e., miracles, ecstatic utterances, etc.), and his ability to project strength in his speech and presence. In 5:16-17, then, knowing *kata sarka* likely encompasses a similar complex network of elements. In the context of the leadership crisis at Corinth, it is clear that some group or contingent in Corinth thought that Paul failed to measure up to their image of what leaders or ministers personify. Instead of someone with gravitas and social standing, exhibiting powerful deeds and all of the accoutrements of glory and wealth, they got Paul, a "broke-down" pastor, who publicly gloried in sharing the fate of a crucified Lord.

The opponents' *kata sarka* standards are analogous to judgments made in the context of contemporary race discourse. Modern identity politics involves embodied social constructs and the nexus of heritage, personality, physical appearance, and social connections, and we have seen that these same elements were in contention in Paul's defense of his ministerial identity in Corinth. Our consideration of the *kata sarka* standards operating there suggests that Paul's opponents had concepts of identity that were animated by forces not too dissimilar from modern identity dynamics. The opponents boasted in a privileged ethnic heritage and an elevated social status as servants of Christ. Ancient status privilege manifested itself in charismatic deeds, acceptance of financial support, letters of recommendation, and a boastful demeanor, behaviors that Paul considered inconsistent with his ministry of identification and participation in Christ's other-focused ministry. In Corinth, the opponents malign Paul's physical appearance and public demeanor as one who does not meet the then-current expectations associated with high status. Today, minorities often face obstacles in public life because they, too, fail to "look or act the part" due to negative stereotypes about people of color and cultural behavioral norms and status that are keyed to whiteness.

Paul's situation also exhibits the way that privilege is relative: though he shares a privileged heritage with his opponents, by refusing support and practicing manual labor, he incurs condemnation and inhabits a lower social status (11:7-9; 1 Cor 4:12; cf. Acts 18:3) (Sumney 1990: 165). The discourse on Moses in 2 Cor. 3:7-18 also illustrates the way that privileged persons have the luxury of temporarily forgoing their privilege. In a society that revered antiquity, Paul is able to point to an ancient and glorious ancestor, but he is secure enough in his own status that he is able to relativize the esteem accorded to that figure. Yet, when the situation has degraded to the point that he felt forced to address the charges against him, he makes an explicit appeal to his ethnic heritage, even though he recognizes as he does so that the boast is the height of foolishness (11:21-22). Taken together, it may be that Paul recognizes the power of his proud heritage but takes it up only in service of the greater good (cf. Phil 3:4-8).

This does not imply that when Paul rejects knowing Jesus *kata sarka* in 5:16-17, he is undermining Jesus' Jewish heritage; Paul is clear on the point that Jesus' Jewishness demonstrates God's faithfulness to Israel (Rom. 9:5; cf. 1:4). Rather, from Paul's perspective, both he and Jesus inhabited privileged identities, but their confidence in God enables them to eschew these social privileges to become effective conduits of divine power. As a coda to a section that began by exploring the paradoxical juxtaposition of weak human vessels with the manifest power of God, in these verses, Paul not only grants that even the most privileged identities will reject privilege in the new age, but he also makes this humility *normative*.

Conclusion

The overall arc of Paul's personal narrative is a fascinating study when examined with an interest in racial differences and the hierarchical ordering of privilege. We have only to consider the remarkable nature of how Paul moved from stylized attitudes about Greeks, gentile sinners, barbarians, and others then prevalent among Jews (Rom. 1:18-32; Gal. 2:15; Col. 3:11), to becoming a "slave" of such people through his missionary endeavors. Paul went from being "blameless" with respect to the law as a Pharisee who outstripped his colleagues in zeal for the traditions (Phil. 3:4-6; Gal. 1:14), to being a broke-down preacher in Corinth who needed to remind people that he shared that proud ethnic heritage. In reflections on ministry in Corinth in 2 Cor. 2:14-6:10 that were perhaps designed to preempt the growing opposition to him that emerges directly in 2 Corinthians 10–12, Paul defends his identity as a leader who can be compared favorably with Moses, as one who is bolder and more confident in his ability to speak as an ambassador for God. Yet even there, this breathtakingly audacious claim is juxtaposed with an acknowledgment of his likeness to a common, humble, disposable, and fragile piece of clay pottery. Even later in 2 Corinthians 10–12 when the defense of his ministry is more direct and full throated, he continues to identify as a fool for Christ, one of the weak and despised of the age, while still maintaining that his authority and standing are equal to any others to whom he has been compared (10:6; 11:5-6; 12-14).

It would be tempting to divide the message of 2 Corinthians into one exhortation to the majority race in the United States and another one to minority groups. One could exhort privileged groups to imitate the way Paul embraced weakness as a prerequisite for authentic, other-focused ministry, reminding them that the way of Jesus is the way that endures for the sake of others. Similarly, one could exhort the oppressed to mimic Paul's boldness and confidence in their confrontation of the evils of racial and ethnic injustice. Yet it is more interesting to note that both of these behaviors resided in the same servant of Christ. In 2 Corinthians, Paul describes his countercultural ministry with a combination of subtlety and boldness, shifts that probably reflect changing circumstances or movement in the nature of his opposition. It may be that the best adaptation of his ethics for race relations in the United States is one that sees privilege and humility as two sides of the same coin, both deployed for the sake of and in service to the ethnic other.

Notes

1. Throughout, I use the term *ethnoracial* to indicate the difficulty in differentiating "ethnicity" and "race," both in modern discourse and in ancient discourse. For more on this topic, see Buell 2001: 450; 2004: 236.

2. For more on body-soul dual in Christian theology, see Green (2008: 1–71). The negative effects of a disembodied dualism in Christian thought is aptly captured in Green's comment on this philosophical tradition: "Angst among Christians in recent decades over how to prioritize ministries of 'evangelism' and 'social witness' is simply wrong-headed . . . since the gospel . . . cannot but concern itself with *human need in all of its aspects.* Only an erroneous body-soul dualism could allow—indeed require—'ministry' to become segregated by its relative concern for 'spiritual' vs. 'material' matters (Green 2008: 70).

3. For examples of studies that deliberately challenge this common construction of Christianity, see Hodge 2007 and Sechrest 2009.

4. Though 2:14—6:10 is ostensibly a defense of apostolic ministry in general and Paul's ministry in particular as corroborated by his more direct comments in 2 Corinthians 10–13, there are several indications that the comments throughout apply to Christian life broadly. J. Lambrecht points out that 2 Cor. 1:3-11 uses much the same language as 4:7-15: Paul suffers and shares in Christ's suffering, suffers for the sake of Corinthians, and sees God deliverance of him from death.

See Lambrecht 1994: 331–32). Further, 2 Cor. 1:6-7 explicitly maintains that the Corinthians endure the same kind of suffering as Paul does (that is, the sufferings of Christ; 1:5). Further, the opposition of "we" and "you" in 4:7-15 disappears in the next section, indicating a broadening of the concern to all Christians. The "we all" in 5:10 is explicit and probably applies back to 4:16-18 (331).

5. While interpreters frequently debate whether 3:11 refers to the fading or the abolition of the old covenant, Georgi's exegesis helpfully points out that the contrast here is a contrast between two *ministries* rather than two covenants. See Georgi 1986: 229–56.

6. This is perhaps more evidence for Paul's "solution to plight" thinking, a phrase popularized in Sanders 1983; cf. Thielman 1989.

7. Note also how Paul uses a participle when referring the passing glory of Moses' face (3:7, 13; cf. 1 Cor. 1:26 NAS) and the fading glory of the old covenant (3:14), but that he uses the finite verb when referring to the removal of the veil over the old covenant (3.13; cf. 1 Cor. 6:13; 13:8, 10; 15:24, 26 NAS). The NAS translators capture the distinction between the participial and finite forms of *katargeō* well by translating the participle with the less negative "fade" in 3:7, 11, 13 but the verb with "removed" in 3:14, a distinction they preserve in the only other appearance of *katargeō* in a participial form in Paul, where the milder translation "fade" also suits the context (cf. 1 Cor. 2:6; 2 Cor. 3:7, 11, 13).

8. On Paul's *qal vahomer* argument see Thrall 1994: 239–40; Harris 2005: 279–90; cf. Ben Witherington (1995: 380), who also notes how this argument of the lesser to the greater appears in Greco-Roman discourse.

9. The temporal relationship between 2 Cor. 1–9 and 10–13 is connected to an interpreter's assessment about the literary integrity of 2 Corinthians. For more on this issue, see the discussions in the following: Furnish 1984: 30–48; Barrett 1973: 11–21; Georgi 1986: 9–18; and Thrall 1994: 3–61. For more discussion about the identity of Paul's opponents, see the good overview in R. Bieringer 1994: 181–221; and the two frequently cited monographs by Georgi (1986) and Sumney (1990).

10. Barrett (1973: 122–23) relates freedom in this verse to the law.

11. *Tharrountes* ("be of good courage") in 5:6, 8 functions similarly as a synonym for confidence, freedom, and boldness.

12. See Savage (1996: 54–99) for a discussion of personal characteristics valued in status-conscious first-century Corinth.

13. So many interpreters: Thrall 1994: 248; Witherington 1995: 279–380; Furnish 1984: 203; Barrett 1973: 116; cf. Harris 2005: 290–91.

14. 2 Cor. 5:1-10 has elicited more comment that just about any other passage in 2 Corinthians. One set of questions focuses on the extent to which Paul adopts or rejects Platonic dualism or other Greco-Roman philosophical categories: see Heckel 1993; 2000: 117–31; Aune 2001; Green 2008: 170–78; Betz 2000: 315–41; Glasson 1990: 145–55. For articles on the relationship of this passage to Paul's discussion of resurrection in 1 Cor. 15:35-58, see Benoit 1970: 107; Gillman 1988: 439–54; Harris 1974: 317–28; Hettlinger 1957: 174–94; Ellis 1960: 211–24; Perriman 1989: 512–21.

15. Georgi: "From the beginning of chapter 10 on, the argument is over how to appear in public" (Georgi 1986: 33).

16. Furnish also mentions the connection of the earthen vessel imagery to the Old Testament metaphor of God as the divine potter and creator of humanity. See Furnish 1984: 253; Harris 1974: 340; Matera 2003: 108.

17. The manuscript evidence is widespread and diverse for both the omission of *kyrion* ("lord") and its inclusion in 4:14, though with Metzger, I favor the longer reading. See Metzer 1994: 510–11. While the committee maintains that the shorter reading is assimilation to Rom. 8:11, I would point to the fact that the inclusion of *kyrion* is the *lectio difficilior* in 4:7-15, where every other occurrence of *Iēsou* ("Jesus") occurs without a title.

18. For a good summary of the scholarly literature on the question, see Fraser 1971: 293–97.

19. See, e.g., Fraser, who after noting the heavy incidence of this usage in 2 Corinthians, merely correlates the usage with Paul's references to *Christos* (as opposed to *ho Christos*), insisting that both usages refer holistically to Jesus' earthly ministry, passion, resurrection, and postresurrection work (Frazer 1971: 299). The exception to this might be Georgi, who reads the usage in light of his hypothesis about allegorizing Hellenistic Jewish missionaries (Georgi 1986: 271–77); cf. Sumney's critique of Georgi's methodology in Sumney 1990: 49–55.

20. Georgi notes that all of these references occur in proximity to traditional pre-Pauline material except in 2 Corinthians, concluding that this is an indication that this usage is intimately connected to the situation in Corinth vis-à-vis his opponents (Georgi 1986: 272).

21. According to Georgi (1986: 274), in 4:7-16, Paul says that the significance of the preacher is tied to the earthly Jesus inasmuch as the minister bears Jesus' body in theirs and manifests a continuation of his suffering and death.

22. See Craig Keener's list of these similarities (Keener 2005: 179).

23. Matera mentions the "broad agreement" on this point (Matera 2003: 120); see also Thrall 1994: 362, 367–71; Harris 1974: 370; Aune 2001: 224.

24. See Thrall for a comprehensive discussion of the interpretive options in this section, beginning with the possible interpretations of the "dwelling from God": the resurrection body; an intermediate state; a present "spiritual garment"; the resurrected body of Christ; a heavenly temple (Thrall 1994: 363–68). Thrall herself, in agreement with "older scholarship," opts to understand the reference to the believer's resurrection body, which is available at the moment of death (367–78); cf. Furnish, who sees a reference to existence in a future eschatological age (Furnish 1984: 294–95), and Harris, who interprets the section with reference to Paul's desire to avoid a disembodied intermediate state (Harris 1974: 317–28).

25. Note that the difference between the permanent and temporary is also an important issue in Paul's interpretation of how the new covenant differs from the old (3:7-18).

26. There is much stronger manuscript support for *endysamenoi* (P^{46}, a, B, C, D^2, Y, etc.; see NAS translation) than for *ekdysamenoi* (D*) in 5:3 (see NRSV translation).

27. For example, Aune 2001; Furnish 1984: 292–99, who interprets the heavenly dwelling of 5:1 as a corporate reference to the eschatological age vs. a reference to individualistic concerns about embodiment.

28. For an exploration of the association of "shame" with nakedness in Jewish literature, see Green 2008: 385–86.

29. For a definition of internalized racism, see Jones (1997).

30. Literally, "boast in the face."

31. Also note that there may be a similar parallelism between *kata sarka* in 10:3 and *kata prosōpon* in 10:7, as is seen here in 5:12 and 5:16. On the question about understanding the syntax of "knowing according to the flesh" (*oidamen kata sarka*) in 5:16, many think that the evidence slightly favors an adverbial construal of *kata sarka* (see Thrall 1994: 418; Fraser 1971: 298). However, it is not inconceivable that Paul is intentionally ambiguous here. If Paul normally places *kata sarka* after a noun when using it adjectivally (e.g., Rom. 1:3) and before the verb when using it adverbially (for example, 2 Cor. 1:17), he could not have been more ambiguous than he was in 5:16, where it appears *before* the noun and *after* the verb (*egnōkamen kata sarka Christon*; cf. 2 Cor. 10:18). Thus it is possible that both senses are alluded to here, and we cannot rule out the idea that *kata sarka* includes the notion of physical descent (normally associated with an adjectival understanding of the phrase) alongside an adverbial interpretation that speaks of a fleshly way of knowing or perceiving. See the discussion below on *kata sarka* in 2 Cor. 11:22; 12:10.

32. For a full discussion of the history of scholarship on the question of 2 Cor. 5:16 and the question of Paul's knowledge of the historical Jesus, see Fraser 1971: 293–313.

33. The author's perspective on the action communicates "verbal aspect." Paul himself uses the perfect tense form for *oida* 58 times and the pluperfect only once, usage that suggests that this word is aspectually vague since authors could not choose from among multiple viable tense forms for this lexeme. Usage in the rest of the New Testament supports this idea since the word appears

in only two tenses: 228 times in the perfect and 31 times in the pluperfect. That Paul uses two forms of "know" in 5:16, *oida* and *ginōskō*, the latter of which appears in tense forms that were not available for the word *oida*, may indicate that Paul switches to a different verb for "knowing" to communicate verbal aspect. For more on interpreting the aspect associated with perfect and present tense forms, see Porter 1995: 20–42; 1993: 75–108, 211–38, 251–59.

34. See Porter for more on the way that the perfect tense communicates an author's focus on the complexity of the state of action in a verb used in this way (Porter 1993: 256–59). Here Paul refers to a complex understanding that emerges from judgments made in accordance with a common set of standards (for example, *kata sarka*) that goes far beyond the simple temporal question of knowing Jesus in the past. Below we explore this set of standards as they are illuminated in 2 Cor. 11:22—12:10, when Paul ironically "boasts" *kata sarka*.

35. Georgi rightly notes that the argument in 5:16-17 is an argument from the greater to the lesser, extending standards used in forming opinions about the most important figure in God's economy to everyone participating in the new order (Georgi 1986: 253). O'Neill, on the other hand, thinks that it is nonsensical to think that Paul would advocate disregarding Christ's miracles, earthly ministry, or his humility as a servant (O'Neill 1987: 101-2).

36. For more on the use of *kata sarka* in 1 Cor 10:18, see Schweizer 1972: 125–35; Sechrest 2009: 132, 142–44.

37. Georgi infers that the opponents accuse Paul of acting *kata sarka* in 10:2 because he acts contrary to their own *kata pneuma* proclivities (Georgi 1986: 236–37). Sumney, however, thinks that the phrase *kata sarka* originates with the opponents, though he does not reckon with the different use of the phrase in Galatians and 1 Corinthians, epistles that likely precede 2 Corinthians chronologically (Gal. 4:23, 29; 1 Cor. 10:18; possibly 1 Cor. 1:26), or in usages like these that appear in Romans (Rom. 1:3; 4:1; 9:3, 5; cf. 8:4-5, 12-13). See Sumney 1990: 156.

38. For more on allegations from Paul's opponents that he was a "flatterer," see Marshall 1987.

39. In 11:18, *kata sarka* appears after the verb with the same ambiguity as it does in 5:16. See the discussion about "knowing according to the flesh" (*oidamen kata sarka*); see Sumney 1990: 129.

40. The word "Hebrew" in other Jewish literature in the Greek-speaking Diaspora seems to be the preferred way of talking about Aramaic, the language commonly spoken among Palestinian Jews in the Second Temple period; see, e.g., Niebuhr 1992: 105–7.

41. Charismatic displays of spiritual power play important roles in Sumney's identification of the opponents as Pneumatics (Sumney 1990: 177–79) and Georgi's proposal about Hellenistic *theios anēr* (Georgi 1986: 254–83).

2

_____

Identity and Human Dignity amid Power and Liminality in 1 Corinthians 7:17-24

Jeremy Punt

INTRODUCTION

April 27, 1994, was the historical moment when South Africa formally changed from a minority-ruled apartheid state into a modern, democratic, new South Africa, installing the iconic Nelson Mandela as the first democratically elected, black president of South Africa.[1] Set against a long, troublesome, and mostly turbulent few decades, which should also be understood within the framework of centuries of colonial rule in one form or another, the country at the southern tip of the African continent comprising a "rainbow people"—to use Desmond Tutu's famous phrase—of indigenous ethnicities such as the Khoisan, southern moving tribes from further north on the continent, and initially Dutch and later British, French, German, and other settlers, evolved into another phase of sociopolitical development.

The former Dutch settlement of 1652 that was reshaped into a British colony (1895) and later became an apartheid state (1948) had its democratic awakening in 1994. It saw the country move into a postliberation, democratic dispensation that has brought about many changes, of which the transfer of power from a white minority to a black majority was the most telling—but not necessarily decisive—moment. Facing many problems of various kinds, the new dispensation in South Africa has thus far not brought about the expected significant improvement in the lives of the majority of its citizens, while at the same time, it has developed more of a global profile; attempts to enhance the country's profile, especially at an economic level, often further complicate an already complex situation. Communities differentiated by social, cultural, political, and economic differences attempt in varying ways and degrees to deal with an increasingly technology-based economy in the information era—contributing to what can be described in many ways as a postcolonial setting. Interestingly, the role of organized religion and Christian groups in particular, often with strong appeals made to the Bible, were important and influential factors both in providing justification for as well as in combating the apartheid regime. While the participation of religious groups and figures in postapartheid South Africa thus far has been of a different nature and complexion,[2] the link between religion and politics has evidently not been severed[3] (Punt 2007; 2009).

The South African context of today serves as the interpretative canvas for 1 Cor. 7:17-24. Rather than a literary or historically focused exegesis,[4] overtly or otherwise oblivious of any real-life, flesh-and-blood context, my reading here takes life in the contemporary South African context, marked as it is by power and liminality as primary interlocutor. It is an explicitly contextual interpretation of the text,[5] and in the next section a rudimentary thumbnail sketch of the South African context follows.

THE NEW SOUTH AFRICA AND ITS CHALLENGES

Apartheid's social engineering with its political disenfranchisement, creation of structural disadvantages, and imposition of socioeconomic control and distortions probably hit South Africa the hardest, at its most vulnerable level, in destroying human dignity through the colonization of the mind (Ngugi 1986) and establishing a coloniality of being (Mignolo 2007).[6] Many communities and individuals still suffer from a serious lack of self-esteem and self-confidence, and have not acquired even very basic life skills, all of which are not unrelated to the surrounding moral landscape. Much of this has naturally filtered through into communities where a breakdown of relationships is characterized by broken families and family structures, rampant teenage pregnancies, high levels of HIV and AIDS infections, pervasive substance abuse, unacceptable levels of corruption in the business and civil sectors, widespread criminal and violent crimes such as murder, rape, and assault, and so on. The strategy of making the land ungovernable as part of the liberation movements' struggle against apartheid grew into a popular groundswell, which has to date proved difficult to turn around in full, even though the erstwhile liberation movements are now in large part represented in political parties and in government. The strong claims about and appeals to human dignity, enshrined in the new South Africa's constitution and bill of human rights, are yet to become part of its social fabric.[7]

Second, the quest for identity in an increasingly multicultural country, continent, and world may appear a fool's errand but is a pronounced pursuit in the South African society. Tensions were evident, for example, in public debates surrounding the ox-slaughtering ceremonies for the 2010 World Cup soccer tournament, with the ceremonial killing of an ox by Xhosa warrior Zakhele Sigcawu on Tuesday May 24, 2010, in securing ancestral blessings for the Soccer City stadium in Johannesburg and the tournament that was to follow ("Ox Killed" 2010). Ongoing discussions of the polygamy of state president Jacob Zuma are at least as vibrant as those about manifestations of white Afrikaner nationalism, whether these discussions are about culture and its assertion or subterfuges for (respectively) legitimating a certain lifestyle or clinging to privileges reminiscent of apartheid times.

Third, South Africa today is challenged to deal with inequalities of its recent and more distant past, including desperate poverty (children dying from hunger, terrible infant mortality rates, etc) and disease (vast numbers of people infected by HIV and AIDS, high incidences of tuberculosis, malaria deaths) amid regular reports of national and local government representatives' and employees' involvement in distortion and/or corruption.[8] South African citizens not only are deprived of their legitimate claim to resources but also must observe public officials' squandering such resources on exorbitant yet fleeting materialist tokens of wealth and prosperity.[9] Authorities have begun to admit that the country suffers a serious problem with violent crime, often dubbed the murder and rape capital of the world, with little respect for human life amid what has become almost nostalgic invocations of an *ubutnu*-based concern for others. It may have become a cliché to refer to crime-ridden South Africa, but its effects on society are, if anything, increasing: violent crime is surging, and white-collar crime is fast becoming another scourge.

Fourth, in South Africa, race and gender remain major dividing lines. Significant problems in the country are related to what is often called a race "fault line" that both defines and divides the people of South Africa at many different levels. Deep-seated ethnic differences and conflicts that brew just under the surface add to a climate susceptible to polarization.[10] Serious gender and sexuality concerns arise amid claims to traditional culture, which proclaims patriarchy as sacrosanct and is strongly heteronormative and largely homophobic. Such factors work hand in hand with oversimplified but popular notions of majority and minority politics; of (black) political versus (white) economic power; of the (re)distribution of arable agricultural lands and mineral prospecting rights; of affirmative action as an initiative of the (black) majority aimed at the (white) minority, with relentless energy.

Attempts to read 1 Cor. 7:17-24 as primarily suggesting that people should make the best of their particular life situations (Thiselton 2006: 110–11), notwithstanding hardships and injustice, secure privilege while placating the marginalized without apparent concern for addressing structural inequities and systemic injustices, and this in a context already perceived to be skewed in favor of the powerful and privileged. With the tension between the South African context characterized by different power constellations and varying manifestations and degrees of liminality, the interpretation of 1 Cor. 7:17-24 not only will be contextual but also will relate to issues of identity and human dignity in particular. A few words on the context and setting of 1 Corinthians are appropriate at this stage.

ANALYSIS OF THE TEXT: OVERALL PRESENTATION OF 1 CORINTHIANS

Shortly after leaving Corinth around 51 CE, Paul apparently established himself in Ephesus in Asia Minor, probably his pastoral and missional basis from 52 to 54 CE and from where he visited churches in Galatia, Antioch, and elsewhere. Receiving disturbing news about the Corinthian followers of Jesus in 53 or early 54 CE, he wrote the first letter to the Corinthian church (1 Cor. 5:9). When shortly thereafter Chloe's people (1 Cor. 7:11) reported to Paul about tension and ructions in the congregation, and Paul received a letter from the Corinthian community (1 Cor. 7:1) with questions about marriage and celibacy, meat offered to idols, gifts of the Spirit, and other matters, he wrote what is today known to us as 1 Corinthians. In 1 Cor. 7:1-40, Paul responds to questions about marriage, and in 1 Cor. 7:17-24 expands on the notion of receiving and living the calling of God amid certain circumstances.[11]

Corinth was an important city in New Testament times because its location on the Corinthian isthmus made it a strategic city for military as well as trade and economic reasons.[12] After Corinth became involved in the political issues of Sparta and Rome, the city was destroyed in 146 BCE by the Romans, but reestablished in 44 BCE as Roman colony *Colonia Laus Julia Corinthiensis*, in honor of Julius Caesar, who was murdered in the same year. Although the rebuilt city was initially inhabited by retired Roman soldiers, Roman freedmen, and Roman slaves, traders and businesspeople from elsewhere soon made Corinth their home. With its cosmopolitan, international makeup and firm Roman control, with access to crucial trade routes, and with sufficient natural resources for manufacturing and a blooming business culture, Corinth was a world-class city like few others in the first century CE. Competition, patronage, and what today would be called a consumerist culture and a focus on success in various ways were important elements of life in the city.

The primary sociohistorical setting that Paul's first letter to the Corinthians addressed has remained a matter of dispute, with the traditional position holding that he challenged the realized eschatological framework that prevailed in the Corinthian church and that gave rise to a worldly contentment. An important consensus is forming that the base of the tensions in the community in Corinth was less theological (narrowly conceived) and more sociological—in fact, that it was about problems arising from socioeconomic divisions (Martin 1995). Paul's challenge to an ideology of privilege in 1 Corinthians also countered the tensions between the more numerous but lower-status "charter members" and the more recent converts, fewer in numbers but whose wealth, power, and status had unsettled the standards and expectations within the community (Elliott 1994: 204–14; Meeks 1983: 117–18; Theissen 1983: 106–10). Paul's first Corinthian letter most likely addresses problems that were brought about by social stratification in the communities.

ANALYSIS OF THE TEXT: COMMENTARY ON SELECTED THEMES

First Corinthians engages the social reality of the early Jesus-follower community in Corinth on a wide front, addressing in chapter 7 some specific and primarily sociocultural and economic structures and configurations. Paul focuses on marriage but in the middle of the chapter also addresses two other important aspects related to the social makeup of the community: one is the ubiquitous system of slavery, and the other, connecting with Paul's broader sociocultural point of reference, is Jew-gentile relationships. The links and connections informing constructions of the social situation make for a rather complex argument, as exemplified in the past range of interpretations of 1 Cor. 7:17-24.[13]

First Corinthians 7:17-24 has in the past often received negative press, understood through the lens of a specific translation and interpretation of 1 Cor. 7:20 that encourages and emphasizes the maintenance of the sociocultural status quo. At times, this line of interpretation has been described even as Paul's theory of the *status quo* (Schweitzer 1968: 187–94).[14] However, rather than insisting that his readers stay in a certain state or social position, Paul's focus in this passage is probably more on the implications of God's call and the believer's service to Christ within particular contexts or situations. "The key point is . . . that Christians can fully serve Christ as Lord *in whatever situation they find themselves*" (Thiselton 2006: 111, emphasis in the original). While the latter readings provide an important corrective to the notion that Paul merely seeks to justify the status quo, the criteria to determine the "key point" may be too strongly biased toward a theological perspective, oblivious to determinants of social location and driving an unwarranted disjuncture between theological obedience and social responsibility.

Another range of interpretive positions on 1 Cor. 7:17-24 claims more social engagement for Paul's words. In the recent past, the text has received at least in some quarters positive acclamation, viewing it as Paul's encouragement for slaves to avail themselves of freedom should it come their way[15]—a realistic possibility in first-century slavery, in contrast to its later colonialist variant. Earlier readings of 1 Cor. 7:17-24 that ascribed a socially conservative position to Paul have been challenged by scholars who argue that Paul tried to overcome the basic socioeconomic power relations that governed people's lives under the Roman Empire (Horsley 1998: 100). The charge of sociopolitical quietism leveled against Paul based on this passage is challenged by arguments that the rule in 7:17-24 is not a rule of the status quo but that the focus of remaining in one's calling is a call to peace along the same lines as the appeal that discourages the believer to dispute divorce from an unbelieving spouse (1 Cor. 7:15), and that it is not binding individual followers of Jesus to a particular social status (Elliott 1994: 211–14).

In a contextual reading of 1 Cor. 7:17-24, a passage that exposes the marginalized status of people but could also possibly be read as a theological legitimation for differentiating social structures, and in a context like South Africa, where power and liminality concerns are crucial, the following three concerns require some discussion.

KLĒSIS AS DIVINE ASSIGNMENT OR SOCIAL POSITION?

Emancipatory or socially challenging readings of 1 Corinthians 7 hinge of course on the interpretation of *klēsis* ("calling") and related terminology, and in particular on the insistence that someone's calling is not necessarily the same as the person's standing in society. For Paul, social location was not a matter of indifference, but given that God's calling—to put it theologically—is a calling to holiness, it brings the person into the sphere of God's lordship, and thus liberation. From 1 Corinthians 7, it is clear that Paul perceived the call of God as a divine action, bestowing apostolic authority on him and bringing about a different perspective and ethos for Jesus-followers, which created a community with a different ethos and that was centered on Christ.

The call/calling topos is important in 1 Corinthians, particularly in the first and seventh chapters, with Paul identified in 1 Cor. 1:1 already as the *klētos* ("called") apostle, and the Corinthian community as *klētos* ("called") saints in 1 Cor. 1:2.[16] The result is that the elite would have been prevented from identifying superiority to the powerless as a sign of God's preference, so that while the "educated, powerful and well-born" (1:26) were found in the congregation, their presence would not define it. To the contrary, the presence of the powerless, the nobodies (1 Cor. 1:27-28), was a sign of God's calling, since the bodies of the powerless were holy, even if their labor belonged to others within structures of society. According to Elliott (1994: 214), this did not mean that Paul acquiesced to the imbalances of power and privilege within that society, but rather that the bodies of the poor were holy but not yet free, although their holiness was a guarantee of coming freedom (Rom. 8:9-17). The notion of the calling of God would have strongly influenced a context characterized by ethnic tension and the disparate social status of members of the community (Braxton 2000: 71–105). Calling cannot be read as equivalent to social position also because Paul's point in every specific case is of someone's receiving their calling in a particular setting: called as circumcised or uncircumcised (7:18), and called as slave (7:21).

In Paul's letters, circumcision and uncircumcision refer to *ethnic* distinctions, even if ethnic credentials were not required for inclusion in early Jesus-follower communities.[17] Non-Jews were received into the movement without requiring ethnic credentials, and apart from belief in one creator God, many other fundamental axioms of Judaism such as covenantal nomism were abandoned to accommodate non-Jewish believers (Runesson 2008). However, early Jesus-follower texts regularly invoke racial and ethnic categories,[18] contrary to scholarly opinion.[19] The early followers of Jesus used racial stereotyping "to denounce Christian rivals as barbarians and Jews" (Buell 2001: 473) in the first-century Greco-Roman world, where kinship and ethnicity were expressed with a variety of different terms.[20]

Regardless of their link to birth and descent, terms were used interchangeably to signify a different understanding of race and ethnicity, which were often closely associated with religious practice. Ethnic terms were mutable and did not presuppose "essences."[21] The variety of terms used to express ethnicity allowed for people to claim different ethnicities and to rank their importance. Those terms could also simultaneously tolerate an insistence on ethnic particularity and a universal ideal,[22] and allow Christian conversion to be expressed in ethnic terms (Buell 2011: 469, 473). "Race" and "ethnicity" were terms that were therefore inevitably involved in identity negotiation in communities of Jesus followers.[23]

Slavery was a *social position* that knew multiple forms in the first century CE, as it was neither restricted to nor constituted a social class or status, although slaves' lives were determined by their owners and their whims.[24]

Slavery was generally not a desired state of being,[25] and where it became a necessity, it was tolerable given the prospect of its eventual cessation—which still left the former slave in the position of freed person, and mostly resulted in his or her dependence on the former owner-turned-patron, with limited claim to social position and the privileges available to (especially male) free persons.[26] Slavery as institution was maintained by the threat and use of violence, including punishment, torture, and even execution (Osiek 2005: 206). First-century patronage stands juxtaposed to slavery as an entire network of patron obligations, which regulated perceptions of the world while also regulating the activities of communities and individuals. It was particularly important in securing the dominance of imperial culture and its societal workings,[27] with household ethics and patronage understood as sanctioned by the gods.[28] Paul's constructions in 1 Cor. 3:23 (cf. 3:5-6), where the relationship between the Corinthians and God is seen as mediated by Christ, and in 4:14-15, where Paul as spiritual "father" mediates between the Corinthians "children" and being in Christ, exemplify patronage relations.

For Paul, the pervasive and far-reaching effect of God's calling was to unsettle privilege and bestow (new) value on those in marginalized positions, whose lives were regulated by ethnic connotations or social position such as the distinction between Jews and others, or slavery. The focus on the calling is clear in 1 Cor. 7:20, where the emphasis is to remain in the calling (*en tē[i] klēsei*) in which someone was called (*eklēthē*). However, while it can be agreed that *klēsis* should be understood here as calling and not be equated with social position, the double statement in 1 Cor. 7:17a is not necessarily resolved, as it can be understood as either two equivalent or parallel statements: Paul requires that a person live (*peripateitō*) the life that God has assigned (*emerisen*) him (*ekastō[i]*), adding, as God called (*keklēthen*) him. That the riddle of 1 Cor. 7:17 can be resolved by appeal to 1 Cor. 7:20 and a claim that the two statements thus are not identical, and that the second part relates to God's call that is received in specific social locations (the first part), is a reasonable explanation, but it does not remove all ambiguity and tension from the text.[29] Such ambiguity is in fact exacerbated by Paul's less-than-clear account of the implications of God's calling for the Corinthians to remain in their existing social locations (see Braxton 2000: 48).

PERIPATEIN/MENEIN IN THE ALLOTTED LIFE

In 1 Cor. 7:17, 20 and 24, Paul's appeal to the Corinthians to live or remain as they are therefore appears to have concerned their membership in the *ekklēsia* rather than to serve as a reference to social status in a general sense. A change of status is neither a precondition for the call nor a consequence of the call from God, as much as Paul's appeal to the call of God is not an attempt to argue for the maintenance of the status quo (Braxton 2000: 50–53). The emphasis on living out the calling of God is supported by the literary makeup of 1 Cor. 7:17-24, which suggests careful attention to detail: the general call to serve the Lord (7:17), or to remain in God (7:24) wherever people find themselves in life, forms an *inclusio*.[30] Dealing with the distinction between people based on circumcision (7:18-19)[31] or slavery (7:21-22), these two sections both conclude with the call to remain (*menetō*, 7:20; 7:24) in the calling in which they were called.[32] Ethnic distinctions are not affirmed here or slavery commended, but neither is the calling of God seen as disruptive to these social situations—unlike what Paul appears to suggest elsewhere (Gal. 3:28; Philem. 16-18).

It is difficult to deny the intertextual links between 1 Corinthians 7 and Gal. 3:28,[33] without requiring or assuming some form of literary dependency. It is noteworthy, though, that 1 Cor. 7:1-16 is all about sex and gender matters, in different configurations (marriage, celibacy, widowhood, single state), with the focus in 1 Cor. 7:17-24 shifting to matters concerning the Jew-and-gentile distinction (7:18-19) and to slavery (7:21-23), before returning to the issue of celibacy and marital relationships in 1 Cor. 7:25-40.[34] Notwithstanding the danger of romanticized readings (see Punt 2010a: 140–66), Gal. 3:28 appears to contemplate, even if momentarily and in a cultic setting, the absolving of identities based on gender or sex, ethnic and social status in Christ.[35] However, 1 Cor. 7:17-24 not only assumes but even calls for the maintenance of such social standings, even if insisting on their irrelevance for the call of God. In fact, the concessions characterizing 1 Cor. 7:1-16 and 25-40 serve the immediate purpose of maintaining sex and gender divisions, and structures built on them.

Some scholars insist that Paul addresses all the issues of gender and sex, race and class together in order to avoid any simplistic handling of these matters, since "crosscurrents and complexities prohibit overeasy or overhasty 'solutions' to a pastoral and a moral theology that applies the gospel and liberation to a series of differing and changing contexts in the real world" (Thiselton 2000: 545, agreeing with Bartchy, Cartlidge, and Deming). But this comment does not explain the differences in approach to gender and sex concerns on the one hand and ethnic and social status concerns on the other hand. "The force of the argument [of 1 Cor. 7:17-24] may be to enjoin the Corinthians to remain as they are. Since, in the divine scheme, people have different gifts, acceptable concessions are suggested by Paul" (Braxton 2000: 15). In short, 1 Corinthians 7, specifically verses 17-24, is cast in ambiguity.

One of the short but crucial instructions of Paul is *mallon chrēsai* ("avail yourself of the opportunity"; RSV) in 7:21, and its interpretation has in the past led to a wide variety of suggested options, the repeating of which here space does not allow.[36] Suffice it to note that *mallon chrēsai* cannot be read or understood in isolation, and certainly is not to be disconnected from the first part of the verse (*doulos eklēthēs, mē soi meletō*, "if you were called as a slave, do not worry about it"). A reasonable conclusion is that Paul's use of *mallon chrēsai* is deliberately ambiguous, meant to suggest that concern about social status and position do not match up with giving expression to living according to God's calling. What would the implications have been in the first century, and what are contemporary readers to make of it in the twenty-first century? Such questions are important when on the one hand Paul is perceived not to have been a quietist intent on preserving the status quo but rather consciously and constantly challenging it, but on the other hand Paul appears to have strived to establish his authority in the Corinthian community with its different groups and aspiring leaders?

As I noted above, ambiguity is maintained throughout 1 Corinthians 7 and 7:17-24 in particular (Braxton 2000; following Wire 1990: 72). The notions in 1 Cor. 7:22 are paradoxical, as it holds that being called in Christ while a slave changes such a person into a freed person belonging to the Lord; while, called in Christ as free person changes free status into being a slave of Christ. The status of a freed person in any case hovered between truly and really free, or enslavement, given the indissoluble bond between former owner and freed slave perpetuated through the uneven relationship built on the patronage system of the day. Given the careful literary construction of the text, it can be concluded that the ambiguity in 1 Corinthians 7, including 7:17-24, is deliberate. It invites engagement and interpretation (Braxton 2000: 271–73; cf. Kim 2008: 58). The positive message of remaining with God (1 Cor. 7:24) not only retains ambiguity as "intrinsic feature of the text" but, in connection with 1 Cor. 7:22 on being called "in the Lord" as emphasis on a ministry of justice, at the same time creates the possibility for challenging slavery (Braxton 2000: 220–34). Indeed, "remaining with God" (7:24) is not a passive mode of doing nothing, but can be understood positively; the Corinthians should stay with *God's initiative*—God's power that passes beyond human ideology and power. In this way, Paul can be read as challenging social conservatism and nullifying human constructions of power. "Remain with God" can be read as an injunction to focus on God's initiative (Kim 2008: 58).

The ambiguity of 1 Corinthians 7 is operative on a larger scale as well, as becomes evident when this chapter is read as part of the letter as a whole. In fact, the ambiguity can be traced to the author and his claims to power.

AMBIGUITY AMID CLAIMS TO POWER

A clear and often-cited formulation of the insistence on self-renunciation, the claim to disinvest from what accrues to the self and what reasonably can be claimed, is found in the previous chapter: 1 Cor. 6:7b: *dia ti ouchi mallon adikeisthe? Dia ti ouchi mallon apostereisthe?* ("Why not rather suffer wrong? Why not rather be defrauded?" RSV). While in this context Paul discouraged lawsuits among fellow believers, with both his telltale enthusiasm and sarcasm, castigating the Corinthians for "wronging and defrauding . . . brothers" (*adikeite kai apostereite . . . adelphous*, 1 Cor. 6:8), he also reproaches them for their unwillingness to suffer wrong.[37] In chapter 7, however, apart from promoting a celibate lifestyle where possible, self-renunciation does not seem to be the nature of Paul's appeals in 1 Corinthians 7—regardless of whether eschatology or social inequity formed the theological backdrop for Paul's letter.

As mentioned earlier, in the past the eschatological edge in Corinthians was made into an interpretative grid for reading the letter, suggesting that tensions and questions in the community can be explained through an investigation of the distance between Paul's expectation of an imminent end as opposed to the Corinthian community's realized eschatology. But the theological fault line in the Paul-Corinthians relationship was probably situated in the disparate, unequal social standing of the community members, and Paul's deliberate attempts not only to address the clashing values and social positions of the community members but also to position him in a particular way (see Martin 1990: 142; 1995). Paul's tentative approach to both the wealthy and the poor in the community probably affected his handling of slavery. Slavery in the first century could not be disconnected from the structural, social system and complex set of convictions regarding hierarchical notions of human beings accompanied by ideas about exercising power and related expectations of submission, corporeal availability for sexual purposes, and punishment. This raises at least the question: Why was Paul not—as with his instructions to various versions of married, unmarried, and previously married people—at equally great pains to qualify and nuance his argument when it came to slavery?[38] Although there is much ambiguity in 1 Corinthians 7 on many levels and even freely indicated by Paul in terms of agency, why such ambiguity in 1 Cor. 7:21-23 in particular—again, particularly given the multitude of different marital contexts he entertained?

First-century slavery may not have entailed a life sentence of enslavement, since both informal and formal manumission were common. However, his letters provide no indication that Paul experienced slavery as a sociopolitical concern in the way he did the inclusion of gentiles in a faith or convictional system deriving from and adhering to its Jewish origins—where he was willing to formulate different paradigms of understanding (for example, a different theological notion, with God embodied in crucified, corporeal form) and systems of praxis (for example, beyond sacrificial notions, even beyond legal requirements with potential legalistic, static tendencies).

On the one hand, 1 Cor. 7:17-24, like other Pauline texts, could be understood in terms of his belief about the relativization of all things in Christ (Campbell 2008: 89–93). On the other hand, in this text, Paul is caught up in identity and power issues, and the flickering of emancipatory light happens amid an all too human response. Paul's claims to authority abound in 1 Corinthians 7.[39] He explicitly refers to his perception of speaking on behalf of Christ regarding the position of unmarried people because he is trustworthy through God's grace (*gnōmēn de didōmi ōs eleēmenos hypo kuriou pistos einai*, 7:25). And in 7:40, he explicitly claims to have the Spirit of God (*dokō de kagō pneuma theou echein*) and therefore presents his own insight (*kata tēn emēn gnōmēn*, 7:40). It is noticeably apparent from the beginning of the chapter that Paul assumes a knowledgeable position, responding to questions directed to him by the community (*Peri de ōn egrapsate*, 7:1), and in 1 Cor. 7:17, Paul assumes a position of issuing instructions (*diatassomai*), adding, to *all* the churches (*en tais ekklēsiais pasais*).[40]

Agreeing with the notion that 1 Corinthians 7 is deliberately steeped in ambiguity, but unlike scholars who seek to resolve the ambiguity in Paul's well-meaning intentions (for example, Thiselton 2000) or in Paul's sincere inability to conclude on matters because of genuine incapacity to do so (for example, Braxton 2000: 234), 1 Corinthians 7, with its ambiguity, is also an attempt of Paul to establish his control and authority in a fluid, liminal context.

Conclusion: 1 Corinthians 7:17-24 for South African Christians

The ambiguous and relativizing sentiments of 1 Cor. 7:17-24 can neither be appropriated with simplistic appeals nor be set aside with claims to a different context or ancient perspectives on humans and society. To the contrary, it is the metropolitan, "yuppie" context of first-century Corinth and a text set amid and brimming with liminal perspectives that provides an interesting inter(con)text for the vibrant, fast-evolving new South Africa, with its many dangers and opportunities, excitement and despair, celebrations of life and desperate miseries. It is the new South Africa that illustrates both the aptness as well as the obscurity of a claim such as the following: "One practical upshot of Paul's reply to Corinth is to establish the principle that *neither freedom in the new creation nor obedient response to divine call can be compromised by the constraints of a person's circumstantial situation or status in everyday life*" (Thiselton 2000: 545; emphasis in original). Crucial to a contextual interpretation of 1 Cor. 7:17-24 is how notions such as freedom and obedience as well as social circumstances and divine calling are understood, and the scope and implications of such notions.

Paul's insistence on separating out call from social situation, distinguishing between God, who calls people, and the social locations in which people find themselves, is important in South Africa for past and present reasons. While previously privilege, whether racial, political, economic, or social, was grounded in an appeal to divine providence bestowed on the white rulers, a worrying current danger is a prosperity-oriented faith (in Christian churches or otherwise) that equates God's calling with wealth and privilege. The ambiguity of 1 Cor. 7:17-24 lives on, however, in its appropriation in South Africa today. On the one hand, the primary importance of the calling of God is not about invoking notions of providence, which were historically so harmful in the South African context. Rather, on the one hand, it emphasizes the initiative of God toward people without consideration of their contested identities or liminal position, without requiring of Christ-followers to take leave of their initiatives and designs. But on the other hand, identity and liminality are not theoretical constellations only, but configure people's real, flesh-and-blood lives; indeed, marginality through race, sex, or gender and social status are all too real in South Africa today.[41]

A major concern regarding the moral fiber of contemporary South African society is the question about authority, and moral authority in particular. With many communities of faith dented by predecessors' support for apartheid or the struggle against it, and with realization about lingering racist and even stronger patriarchal and homophobic attitudes, to name a few, moral leadership has become problematic.[42] On the one hand, disavowing a conservative or quietist Paul bent on perpetuating the status quo and affirming a subversive tendency in Paul's challenge to the perceived natural and social orders of the day creates interesting interpretive possibilities. On the other hand, awareness of Paul's usurpation of power and authority, issuing instructions and at times confusing commands, triggers the realization that Paul's socially challenging concerns in an ironic way relies on a show of support for him, buying into his understanding, his evaluation, and his program.

Notes

1. Edited version of a paper read at the SBL annual meeting (Contextual Bible Interpretation), November 2010, Atlanta, Georgia. An earlier version appeared in *Verbum et Ekklesia*, and is published here with the kind permission of the editor.

2. In the words of emeritus-archbishop Desmond Tutu, "Now the church can go back to being church," words he has been reproached for by many as suggesting a withdrawal of organized religion from the public sphere, and even hinting at the privatization of religion.

3. Indicated by ongoing cordial although not necessarily amicable relations between national and local government and church leaders and groups in South Africa, including meetings and forums held between religious leaders and the government, and even calls by the government for church to assist in "moral regeneration."

4. The bibliography refers to a number of detailed studies, variously focused. A few caveats are appropriate, particularly for limited discussion of important exegetical matters that lie outside the purview of this investigation. However, for a more complete overview of previous interpretations of 1 Corinthians 7, the structure of the passage, and how it fits into the larger body of 1 Corinthians, see Braxton 2000: 9–34; Kim 2008: 76–77.

5. Not in any way apologetically: as much as biblical reading, biblical scholarship is always socially located; is done by readers with particular gender, cultural, social, and other identities; and requires the rejection of the Enlightenment tradition's "attempt to erase the identity of the reader by means of the rhetoric of reason and objectivity" and its derivative, the belief that Western biblical critics can justifiably speak on behalf of all other readers (Brett 1998: 305).

6. Discursive colonialism is often more pervasive and enduring if less tangible than historical colonialism: "a colonization of the mind and the soul, a rendering of the whole individual captive to a different worldview" (Vena 2000: 92). Colonialism through apartheid affected various aspects of South African society, but probably nowhere as strongly as on human worth and dignity, the value of human lives.

7. The consistent resurgence of human indignity and accompanying claims during South Africa's apartheid years was met by the government's blatant denial of and restrictions on human dignity.

8. An important example, though certainly not the only one, is the ongoing saga of South Africa's arms deal, a multi-billion Rand venture in which some of the country's highest-ranking politicians and leaders are implicated.

9. Such practices have given rise to neologisms in South Africa, which would be funny if the impact of what they refer to were not so serious: For example, *tenderpreneurs* refers to those who manipulate government tender processes, from the inside and the outside, through corruption, to enrich themselves; the terms *fat cats* riding on the *gravy train* are use in reference to local representatives in different levels of government intent on enriching themselves at the cost of the general population.

10. Leaving aside for the moment the question of the origin of such ethnic differences or claims in this regard, and without discounting the role of colonial authorities over many decades or that of the apartheid government in both constructing and appealing to such differences and violence emanating from it for political expediency, ethnicity is considered important from both emic and etic perspectives in South Africa.

11. 1 Cor. 7:17-24 is not viewed here as a digression, but rather as an integral part of the argument in 1 Corinthians 7 (see Braxton 2000: 55–56), contra Bartchy (1973: 158), Dawes (1990: 681–97); on the structure of 1 Corinthians 7, see also Braxton (2000: 9–34); Kim (2008: 76–77).

12. With two harbors, Lechaeum to the northwest of the Gulf of Corinth and Cenchrae in the Saronic Gulf of the Aegean Sea, Corinth was a true port city and a vital connection point between north-south and east-west trade routes.

13. The different scholarly reactions to this passage underline the complexity, with Wire (1990: 72–97) seeing this passage as Paul's attempt to restrict the emancipatory energies of holy women in Corinth, and the concessions functioning as leverage to ensure women move back into conventional, patriarchal marriage structures and associated roles; Braxton (2000) believes 1 Cor. 7:17-24 to be an example of deliberate ambiguity on Paul's part due to his inability to provide comprehensive and exhaustive final answers regarding celibacy, marriage, divorce, and remarriage.

14. Paul's theory or even theology of the status quo meant, "If, therefore, a slave became a believer he [sic] should not, on this theory, if he were afterwards offered freedom, accept it" (Schweitzer 1968: 194–95).

15. Not only was manumission a possibility for many if not the majority of slaves in the first century CE, but such mediating aspects of slavery also perpetuated the system. Caution is therefore advised for references to manumission that serve as attempts to portray a system with more tolerable conditions for slaves at the time, and more palatable for contemporary readers—in the latter case especially since slavery was employed as theological metaphor by Paul.

16. For further occurrences of *kaleō/klēsis* in this sense of calling from God, see 1 Cor. 1:9, 24, 26, besides 1 Cor. 7:15, 17, 18, 21. (In 10:27, *kaleō* is used with meaning of "invite.") For the notion of a philosopher responding to the divine call in Cynic philosophy, see the Stoic philosopher Epictetus, *Discourses* 3.22.23; cf. Braxton 2000: 43n94.

17. Ethnicity is a cultural construct and a matter of self-ascription and as a constructed notion drafted from the inside, intent on scripting borders for the group complete with the necessary protection (see Braxton 2000: 72–93; Campbell 2008: 3–5).

18. Historical constructions of early Christianity often tend to assume that the notion of Christian identity excluded any racial connotations, perhaps due to the ascendency of scientific racism in the late nineteenth century. Buell (2001: 449–76) investigated authors from the time of early Christianity, including Christian authors such as Diogenes, Clement of Alexandria, Athenagoras, Justin Martyr, and Origen, but also a wider array of ancient authors of a wider temporal spectrum such as Philo of Alexandria, Isocrates, Dionysius of Halicarnassus, and so on. Biblical references to race and ethnicity include Matt. 21:43 (*genos*); John 1:46 (Nazareth); 7:52 (Galileans); 1 Pet. 2:9-10 (*genos, ethnos, laos*); etc.

19. Scholars who insist on the perceived universality of early Christian thought as authoritative ideology, as well those from the margin that emphasize the apparent inclusive nature of early Christianity as embracing the vulnerable, share the modern opinion of race as biological, natural identity *and* the conviction that early Christian thought detached itself from racial or ethnic categories. Together with erasure, silencing, and marginalization, universality can be an ideological strategy in racialized thinking, intent on reinforcing the Euro-American perspective, see Kelley 2000: 213–19.

20. *Genos, ethnos, laos,* and *phylos* can all four be translated interchangeably with terms such as "people," "race," and "ethnicity," although some other uses can also be identified (Buell 2001: 456n20).

21. "Early Christians inhabited a world in which many facets of one's self, including race or ethnicity, were perceived as mutable—sex, status, citizenship, even humanness" so that "boundaries between animals, humans, and gods, those between slave and free, and those between male and female were all seen to be breachable." Rather than understanding race or ethnicity as givens, early Christians used these concepts when speaking of conversion (Buell 2001: 466–67; 467n50).

22. Christian universalism was at times expressed in ethnic terms (see 1 Pet. 2:9-10), demonstrating that it was less about the incorporation of other ethnicities into an agglomeration where such distinctions were unimportant than about other ethnicities co-constituting a new race or ethnicity: it was more about enlisting for a new identity than being included in nonethnic or raceless obliqueness. See Buell 2001: 473.

23. Early Christians found race and ethnicity useful for self-definition against outsiders, as "central organizing concept for Christianness" as well as for authorizing specific forms of Christian conviction and practice as a universal norm, and also against other insiders, in competition with rival groups and in asserting a particular form of Christian identity (Buell 2001: 451).

24. Although some slaves may have had a low status, they could have had a disproportionately high class indication as the slave-agent of a high-status person; claiming to be someone's slave then turned into a claim to prestige rather than an act of humility. See Martin 1990; Osiek 2005: 209.

25. For early ambivalence, see Epictetus, *Discourses* 4.1: "The slave wishes to be set free immediately. . . . 'If I shall be set free, immediately it is all happiness, I care for no man, I speak to all as an equal and, like to them, I go where I choose, I come from any place I choose, and go where I choose.' Then he is set free; and forthwith having no place where he can eat, he looks for some man to flatter, some one with whom he shall sup: then he either works with his body and endures the most dreadful things; and if he can obtain a manger, he falls into a slavery much worse than his former slavery; or even if he is become rich, being a man without any knowledge of what is good, he loves some little girl, and in his happiness laments and desires to be a slave again."

26. In all of these discussions, it is important to distinguish between various social locations, and two are important to keep in mind here: Roman slavery and Greek or Eastern slavery show some differences; and with rural and especially slaves in the mines being exposed to vastly different circumstances from household slaves in the cities. See Briggs 2000: 111–12.

27. The materiality of Roman social practices was the external manifestation of an intangible morality (that is, the patronage practices within the traditional sanctity of the household) that offered a holistic perception of the world in which Roman religion and society were intimately connected.

28. As far as the Roman Empire was concerned, the social order and the divine order were one and the same, and therefore the ethics of Roman society was sacred and nonnegotiable. "The Romans always understood themselves to be the world's rightfully dominant culture, the gods' own people, and they understood the workings of their society, the ethics of household and of patronage, to be sacred" (Hollingshead 1998: 113).

29. The ambiguity of Paul's language emerges early in 1 Corinthians, when in the first four chapters he encourages unity among the Corinthian followers of Jesus by utilizing an apocalyptic framework. Placing another world in opposition to the world of Greco-Roman rhetoric and status, accompanied by upper-class ideology, Paul's world of apocalyptic reality proclaimed in the gospel of Christ, has its own, alternative system of values and status attribution. In one sense, the apocalyptic world picks up on the conventional values of the time, but in another sense counteracts and subverts those values (Martin 1995: 57). People holding positions aimed at defending Paul's liberative stance are fond of citing bishops from the ranks of slaves such as Onesimus of Ephesus, Pius I of Rome, and Callixtus of Rome (see Payne 2009).

30. Not only a matter of appealing structure, the argument is carefully formatted for maximum effect; for a diatribe structure in 1 Cor. 7:21-22, see Deming 1995: 130–37.

31. Paul generally insists that non-Jews remain non-Jews with regard to ritual and cultural behavior (Runesson 2008: 77).

32. While the verses on slavery largely follow the pattern of the verses on circumcision, 1 Cor. 7:23 adds the further warning to the Corinthians not to become slaves of men because they are already slaves of God (*times ēgorasthēte*, "you were bought with a price"; cf. 1 Cor. 6:20).

33. Gal. 3:28 has over many decades evoked much discussion, with some scholars seeing the text and Paul in general as a model for harmonious, multicultural communities (e.g., Barclay 1996: 197–214), but others have argued that Paul's rhetoric relies on ethnicity rather than trying to obliterate it, and that his concept of ethnicity is not static and monolithic but flexible and complex as he differentiates between gentiles and Jews in Christ, and those who are not in Christ. For further discussion of the link between Gal. 3:28 and 1 Cor. 7:17-24, see Braxton 2000: 54–56. On Gal 3:28, see Punt 2010a: 140–66). For another intertext, see 1 Cor. 12:13.

34. Braxton makes the point that either clarity about the meaning of 1 Cor. 7:17-24 or the meaning of the remainder of the chapter could have assisted in clarifying the other, but as it stands 1 Corinthians 7 in its parts and as a whole is shrouded in some ambiguity as far as meaning is concerned (Braxton 2000: 7–67).

35. According to Braxton, Paul's sentiments in Gal. 3:28 are echoed here in 1 Cor. 7:17-24 since he believed that "in light of one's entrance into the eschatological community via God's call and the believer's baptism, certain social identity markers lose their importance or at least become relatively less important with respect to one's identity in Christ" (Braxton 2000: 55).

36. Much literature is available on the topic, and a brief but accessible summary is provided by Thiselton 2000: 553–59; 562–65.

37. Noticing that similar sentiments were expressed in Plato's *Gorgias* 509C, hasty conclusions about the New Testament's supposedly either superior or idiosyncratic moral code should be avoided (see Orr and Walther 1976: 195).

38. Given especially Paul's concern with the avoidance of *porneia* in 1 Corinthians 5–7, his claims about the link between bodies, sex, and on the one hand pollution (1 Cor. 5:16) and on the other hand sanctification (1 Cor. 7:14, 16), and the sexual availability of slaves to their owners.

39. Other indications of power and authority are the references to *anagkē* in 7:26 and also in 7:37 (translated with "distress" or "necessity"), and the frequent references to control of passions and desire (7:2, 4-5, 9, 35, 36, 37). Some scholars argue that Paul deliberately goes beyond the teaching of Jesus in 1 Corinthians 7; for example, Keener's (1991) argument that 1 Cor. 7:11 presents alternatives or exceptions to Jesus' teaching.

40. Contemporary interpreting communities need "to choose the moment" in which to interpret texts, choosing whether to align themselves with an authoritarian role claimed by Paul or that of dependency required of the communities addressed, but also whether the particular attitude accompanying the role is appropriate today (see Polaski 2005: 80–81).

41. The "ideology of the dominant culture" assumes and often claims universality, seeing diversity as a problem and therefore as something to be overcome, which can be accomplished through negating or isolating and bracketing diversity. Because of its assumed or claimed universal status for its own context, the dominant culture bestows privileged authority on its own readings (Vena 2000: 104).

42. A situation further complicated by the current presidency's call for moral rebuilding of the country amid the president's alleged implication in corruption, his extramarital affairs and polygamous lifestyle, and the formation of a National Interfaith Leadership Council, suspiciously closely aligned with the ruling party and presidency while ignoring existing structures such as the South African Council of Churches (not to mention structures of other faith communities), which incidentally was quite prominent in the antiapartheid struggle.

3

An Intercultural Latino Reading of Paul
The Example of 1 Corinthians 9:19-23

Efrain Agosto

INTRODUCTION

On a vacation with my wife in the southeastern part of the United States a couple of summers ago, we stopped at a restaurant and sat in a booth behind a family that was clearly speaking something other than English. I sat with my back to the family, so I could not see them as they spoke. Olga, my wife, however, not only heard them speaking but also saw their faces as they spoke. For some reason, I thought I heard them speaking Spanish. Olga corrected me when I mentioned this. She assured me they were speaking Portuguese, a language not too far from Spanish but nonetheless not one either one of us understands fully, like Spanish.

I was taken aback by my mistake and reflected later that because I did not see the faces of the family, nor was I really within distance to hear exactly what they were saying, but rather only mumblings, I could not really make out the actual language, only accents and occasional Spanish-sounding words. Not having a "visual," I was relying on sounds and linguistic similarities. I was wrong.

I also reflected later, and even discussed this with a New Testament introductory class, that so it goes with interpretation of texts, especially religious texts like the New Testament. Some readers, especially those who come from religious backgrounds in which they are accustomed to hearing their sacred texts read out loud and interpreted by authorized leaders, think they understand because they have "heard" these texts before. Yet they have not really "seen" them to their fullest possible extent, "face-to-face." This "visual gap" is compounded by the cultural blinders that all of us have in reading and understanding ancient texts like the New Testament. Not only are we removed by historical distance (over two thousand years in the case of the earliest Christian literature), but also, no reading is "purely" devoid of our own cultural, historical, religious, economic, and educational biases. Even the most expertly trained reader tries to check his or her cultural baggage at the door to read these ancient texts more carefully; yet we cannot! We must acknowledge that reading texts, especially religious texts from the first century CE, is often an exercise in finding out what we ourselves bring to the table of interpretation, so that we "read ourselves" and our cultures as well as "read" the text and its culture.

U.S. Latino/a interpreters of New Testament texts want all readers to understand how *we* "visualize" the various documents present in the collection we call the New Testament. Not only do Latino and Latina readings provide unique insights into meaning of New Testament texts, but also, because of our cultural, linguistic, religious, and socioeconomic concerns and experiences, we can provide readings that few "see" the same way because of what we "see" up close that sometimes resonates with the struggling, marginalized communities represented in much of the New Testament world.

In this chapter, we will explore how the apostle Paul, especially in a passage from his first letter to the Corinthians, visualizes his ministry to his congregations, and how a Latino/a "intercultural" approach to reading Paul can help "visualize" his letters with distinctive cultural "eyes" in order to enhance meaning and avoid "blinded" or "near-sighted" approaches to reading and understanding. The ancient culture in which Paul was immersed and the culture of this reader—a male, U.S. Latino/Puerto Rican New Testament critic—will engage in an "intercultural" reading that hopefully produces new insights into the encounter with a Pauline text.

Latina/o Resources in Understanding Paul

First, we should acknowledge that the U.S. Latino/a presence in biblical, theological, and religious studies has grown exponentially in the last twenty years. Generations of immigration from Latin America and targeted efforts by various scholarship organizations[1] have yielded, especially more recently, a wonderful crop of Latino/a scholars in religious and theological studies, including a good cohort in biblical studies. However, this growth has produced few Latino/a biblical scholars that have focused on Pauline studies. Jean-Pierre Ruiz asserts this point in a recent essay and goes on to cite Latino/a attention to Johannine materials (for example, Fernando Segovia and his students from Vanderbilt University, Francisco Lozada, and Leticia Guardiola-Saenz). Another example of such focused attention is the themes of hermeneutics and interpretation in general. Segovia, in particular, has devoted much attention in his own work to these themes, as we shall see below (Ruiz 2009: 47–68).[2] There are a few of us who have done scholarly work in Paul (Agosto 2005; Martinez 2003).[3] However, perhaps because of Paul's often extreme polemical and defensive approaches to opposition within his assemblies, his apparent disdain for the role of women in the overall Pauline mission, and the seemingly limited, overt sociopolitical concerns and even conservatism, according to most readings of Rom. 13:1-7, for example, Paul has not been considered a "friend" to Latino/a scholars of religion, theology, and the New Testament.[4] Thus many stay away.

However, my own research in Pauline studies has been fueled by studies produced by scholars associated with the Paul and Politics section of the Society of Biblical Literature. They have provided critical rereading of Pauline texts in the light of the fact of "empire." Briefly put, Paul did not proclaim his gospel, establish his assemblies, or write his letters to them in a vacuum. In fact, he used the terms of the Roman Empire to describe his movement, such as "gospel" (*euangelion*—"good news"—usually associated with some triumph or celebration of the empire or the emperor), "assembly" (*ekklēsia*—the Greek word for the old "town meetings" in Greek city-states that were pretty much eradicated under the empire, but Paul saw himself reconstituting those groups under the banner of the "Lord"—*kyrios*—Jesus Christ; the term "lord" itself was reserved for the emperor), and "faith" (*pistis* or *fides* in Latin, which Paul understood as a dynamic relationship of trust between God and the believer, but was understood as "loyalty" to the empire by the Roman overseers). These are just a few of the terms of power and domination that the Roman Empire celebrated and that Paul and other early Christians co-opted as positive dynamics of his and their gospel communities.[5]

Such acknowledgment of the domination system under which earliest Christianity, including the Pauline mission, functioned and how the various entities that constituted this emerging first-century movement responded to its surrounding political realities energizes the study of New Testament in general and Paul in particular for those of us whose communities have also faced a measure of imperial domination, albeit in perhaps more subtle ways, as residents of the "American empire." However, our forebears from Latin America and the Caribbean, some more recent than others, have experienced the hegemony of U.S. global and economic domination on their own homeland in more direct and oftentimes devastating ways. To know that perhaps the apostle Paul and his communities may have had some "anti-imperial" tendencies in certain aspects of his message and ministry has driven some of us to study his work more closely.

In fact, a recent volume on the hermeneutics of liberation theology included an essay on Paul and liberation themes. The essay's author, Theodore Jennings, argues that it is the more-recent development on studying Paul's interactions with the Roman Empire as "anti-imperial" in many ways that has merited the inclusion of Paul in a book on liberation hermeneutics. I would agree (Jennings 2009).

However, before looking further at some more-specific anti-imperial aspects of Paul, especially as noted in his first letter to the Corinthians, I think we need to take a step back. I would like to explore, however briefly, some avenues of Latino/a cultural and methodological approaches to biblical criticism that, while not specifically focused on Paul, have helped me think more expansively about critical and cultural hermeneutical approaches to the New Testament. These can help us "see" Paul through Latino/a eyes; that is, read Paul *latinamente*, in a way that reflects the concerns and approaches of Latinos and Latinas in the United States. Fernando Segovia, for one, has written important methodological works that can help us in reading Paul. Once I discuss his work on Latino/a biblical criticism, I will explore a specific passage from Paul—1 Cor. 9:19-27—that will illustrate the sociopolitical implications of understanding Paul anew, in light of the reality of empire, yesterday and today, as well as the critical concerns of Latinos and Latinas today.

FERNANDO SEGOVIA: CULTURAL AND INTERCULTURAL STUDIES

Fernando Segovia's widely read works on critical hermeneutical theory include a variety of essays on Latino/a biblical criticism, such that we can explore *latinidad* (the state of being Latino or Latina in the United States) as part of the enterprise of intercultural biblical interpretation. In a recent essay titled "Toward Latino/a American Biblical Criticism: Latin(o/a)ness as Problematic," Segovia posits that being a Latino/a biblical critic entails two foci: "membership" in the Latino/a community, whether "by 'flesh and blood,' signified or attributed," and "second, the element of conscientization, of praxis and agenda, from within such a community," that is, a commitment to action on behalf of justice for that community (Segovia 2009: 203). This does not mean that being Latina or Latino in the United States is in any way a monolithic reality, given all the various dimensions of race, ethnicity, gender, class, nationality, and language that may encompass any one of us (Segovia 2009: 203–7). However, several common elements speak to the need for incorporating the notion of "Latino/a studies" in any biblical critical approaches that acknowledge the Latino/a exemplum as an important cultural contribution.

In fact, a "conscientized" Latina or Latino biblical critic must be situated "between two standing scholarly frameworks, biblical studies and Latino/a studies" (Segovia 2009: 207). Thus Latino/a biblical critics not only "dance between two cultures" (or more) but also dance between two academic disciplines (or more) (Segovia 2009: 211).

In his earlier work, Segovia had detailed this hermeneutical "dance" as a critical engagement between two texts—the biblical and the Latino/a cultural/ historical reality—which are "other" to each other. Yet, it is in recognizing this "otherness" that good and productive biblical interpretation takes place. Segovia has also called these encounters a function of cultural studies, or indeed, "intercultural studies" (Segovia 1995: 57–73). He has consistently critiqued the myth of objectivity in traditional historical critical biblical studies and suggested that authentic biblical interpretation takes into consideration not just the cultural and historical situation of the original text but also the cultural and historical situation—the social location—of the reader. In the case of the Latino/ a reader, he or she becomes an exemplum for an interpretative approach that is a conversation between the ancient text and the flesh-and-blood reader of today. By taking into account the context of the Latino/a reader, or any flesh-and-blood reader, for that matter, "fully and explicitly into the theory and practice of biblical criticism," an interpreter thereby allows "fully for contextualization, for culture and experience, not only with regard to texts but also with regard to readers of texts" (Segovia 1995: 57).

In other words, Segovia sees historical-critical methods as one set of tools in biblical interpretation, but these are not sufficient in and of themselves. In particular, a Latino or Latina reader, like other readers of texts, represents "not so much . . . a unique and independent individual but rather . . . a member of distinct and identifiable social configurations, . . . a reader from and within a social location" (Segovia 1995: 58). Latino/a culture in the United States is a bilingual, bicultural reality. Latinas and Latinos have an experience of being "the other" in whatever situation they are thrust in this society. Many of us, as Mexican Americans, Puerto Ricans, or Cubans, for example, are never fully comfortable, either in this North American world or the world of the "South" in which we or our parents were raised. Segovia discusses this phenomenon and the interpretative lenses that emerge from it as "a Hispanic-American hermeneutics of otherness and engagement, whose fundamental purpose is to read the biblical text as an other" (Segovia 1995: 58). Accustomed to being in a bilingual-bicultural place, the Latino/a reader of the biblical text relates well to "reading and interpreting from a variety of different and complex social locations" (Segovia 1995: 59). The cultural complexity, distance, and "otherness" of the biblical text resonates in many ways with what Segovia calls the "diasporic" situation of a U.S. Latino or Latina. Thus "meaning emerges, therefore, as the result of an encounter between a socially and historically conditioned text and a socially and historically conditioned reader" (Segovia 2000: 42). The Latino/a reader, in other words, navigates a complicated existence as a bilingual, bicultural person, one who straddles two or more worlds—the U.S. context and the Latin American world of his parents or grandparents, or even his or her own if he or she is a more recent immigrant. As a result, he or she is well situated to engage the complexity of biblical interpretation, including reading Paul *latinamente*—from a Latino/a cultural place. Thus, for example, in the passage from Paul's letters we will study more carefully below, 1 Cor. 9:19-23, Paul clearly sees himself as a multicultural individual in the Roman imperial order who is ready to cross cultural and religious divides in order to get his message across. What some interpreters see as a rather pragmatic, self-serving approach by Paul (he seeks to be "all things to all people") resonates well with the bilingual/bicultural reality of U.S. Latinos and Latinas. We too can use our complex, multilayered *latinidad* in service to community survival in the marginalizing, "minoritizing" U.S. context.

Thus we need to incorporate the historical and cultural situation of the current reader, including the Latino/a reader, squarely in the midst of the whole enterprise of biblical interpretation, and not just rely on the use of historical-critical tools. Fernando Segovia writes, "Just as historical criticism called for a radical contextualization of the text (a focus that must by no means be abandoned but rather properly expanded and grounded), so does this type of reader-response criticism call for a radical contextualization of the reader of the text" (Segovia 1994: 168). How does one go about "contextualizing" the Latino/a reader and his or her sociocultural location firmly within the context of the engagement with the distant text, the "other," known as the Bible, including the New Testament?

First of all, one must describe the overall context of the U.S. Latino/a community as a way of understanding our approach to texts. In doing so, we realize that it is not a monolithic community, given all the national and ethnic groups represented in Latin American and Caribbean presence in the United States. Nonetheless, these communities represent a large diasporic community from mostly poor and oppressed social and economic areas from Latin America and the Caribbean. Thus many Latin American communities in the United States represent "postcolonial" communities, that is, the U.S. Latino or Latina comes from nations forged in colonialism from Spain, Europe, and the United States. We now live the reality of an existence still affected by that colonial period of the nineteenth and early twentieth century, although now most of us must be considered "children of the colonized" (Segovia 2000: 119–42).

Second, in addition to being diasporic and postcolonial communities, Latino/a communities in the United States, as noted above, especially those who have been here for two or three generations, represent a bicultural and bilingual reality—situated between two worlds, that of the United States and that of our homeland or our parents' homeland, which still remains very much a great influence for Mexican Americans, Puerto Ricans, Cubans, and other Latin American peoples, even those who were not born in or have not even visited their parents or grandparents' home country. For all of these various generations, the situation is best described "as having both two places and no place on which to stand" (Segovia 1995: 60; 2000: 119–42).

Moreover, by being present in the United States for several generations and for generations to come, Latino/a reality is becoming more and more a mixed, multicultural, or intercultural reality, also known as a *mestizaje* or *mulatez*.[6] "The emerging Hispanic-American reality in the United States may in the end give rise to an even greater degree of biological and cultural mixture than ever before" (Segovia 1995: 63). At the same time, we are growing farther and farther away from our original roots, and thus becoming "others" to the homeland of our parents and even to our homeland here in the United States. We become defined by others as well, both by those who see us as aliens and those who no longer see us as part of their own. For example, the Puerto Rican born in New York City, like this author, has become the "nuyorican." New Yorkers call us that, but so do our relatives left behind by our parents in Puerto Rico. Segovia paints a somewhat dour picture of such status, or lack thereof: "Such 'otherness,' bestowed upon us and defined for us, overwhelms and overrides us, depriving us not only of a present, past, and future but also of self-definition, and self-direction" (Segovia 1995: 64). Nonetheless, it is in the search for identity that results from such status that Latinos/as find much affinity with the struggles of first-century Christians. Segovia asserts that often such a dire situation, rather than lead to "passivity and submission," can be the impulse for finding a voice, including a "theology of otherness and mixture, the hermeneutics of otherness and engagement, and the interpretive strategy of intercultural criticism" (Segovia 1995: 64–65).

Thus "otherness" becomes a source of identity in the Latino/a context and a resource for finding one's power and voice, including its hermeneutical voice in reading texts. The Latino or Latina "voice" accepts its status as being part of two worlds at the same time, although each world considers the Latino/a presence as an "other." Yet, having an identity as an "other" is a source of power because Latinos and Latinas "do know how to proceed at a moment's notice, from one world to the other" (Segovia 1995: 65). One can see how such skill facilitates biblical hermeneutics, from the present-day world of otherness to the ancient world of the biblical text as "other." The Latino or Latina interpreter also knows that all worlds, including the ancient world depicted in our New Testament texts, are constructions from a social and religious place. Since we have to construct our world in light of an identity of otherness, we understand the plight of the first Christians as meaning-makers and world-constructors in light of their experience of the "Christ event." Certainly, the apostle Paul saw his role as a meaning-maker for his faith communities from the multicultural perspective of Hellenistic Judaism. Again, 1 Cor. 9:19-23 will be one reference point for this idea in the latter part of this essay.

Finally, this diasporic, increasingly multicultural Latino/a community tends to read texts such as the New Testament, including Paul, with upfront agendas. Once we understand that acknowledging a reader's context is part of the hermeneutical process, and the engagement of an ancient text is an encounter between two distant but related contexts, it must be understood that such interaction is not neutral. Rather, "an unavoidable filtering of the one world or entity by and through the other" occurs between reader and text (Segovia 1995: 65). Thus construction rather than reconstruction takes place because both "texts" are influenced by each other in the encounter to produce a new "text," the text of interpretation. Interpretation in this model, an intercultural model, is not a one-way encounter, that is, a detached, ideal reader engaging a text to find ancient meaning without acknowledging his or her strategy, agenda, or social location. Rather, "the hermeneutics of otherness and engagement," influenced by the Latino/a experience of otherness and engagement in an alien, multicultural context, "argues that the historical and cultural remoteness of the text as an other is in itself not a reconstruction but a construction of the past on the part of the reader" (Segovia 1995: 71). Moreover, the reader, especially the Latina or Latino reader, who is not neutral in her or his interpretative efforts, carries an agenda, whether conscious or not. In the case of the Latino/a reader, a construction that facilitates liberation from oppressed situations is of utmost importance.

Such an agenda of liberation on the part of Latino/a readers of biblical texts includes historical research into the life and times of a text, *and* the encounter between readers and texts as engaged others. Again, Latino/a experience in the United States, with the encounter of multiple cultures and realities, points toward a hermeneutics of otherness and engagement, and a hermeneutics of liberation. Such engagement is not without resistance, especially by those who experience the United States as "monocultural." As Segovia argues, the bicultural reality of Latinas and Latinos in the United States "shows us that such a fundamental sense of reality as construction is very difficult to attain within a monocultural matrix" (Segovia 1995: 72). U.S. Latinas and Latinos, as well as other children of diasporic experiences, learn the need for "a commitment to critical dialogue and exchange with the other, subjecting our respective views of the world to critical exposure and analysis" (Segovia 1995: 72). Such critique and analysis is what needs to happen in the encounter between reader and text, as well as between a reader and other readers of the same text. Interpreters of a text, both past and present, become another conversation partner in the construction of new "texts." These new texts, hopefully, are texts of liberation, as we encounter the biblical text, our social location, as Latinos/as or otherwise, and the history of interpretation of said text.

Thus the key to a Latino/a hermeneutics of the New Testament, or any ancient biblical text, lies in the process of engagement. We engage texts as constructs of their own reality, in whatever time period and with whatever ideological strategy they employ. We will construct a new reality of that ancient reading, using the tools of history, the social sciences, and engaging the readings of others, including an investigation of *their* social location, ideological agendas, cultures, and otherness. Segovia calls this process a "humanization," that is, an acknowledgment of human reality as it stands under a variety of categories and emphases. This humanization of textual encounters stands against the "dehumanization" of texts that fails to recognize the variety of forces and diversities of the human condition, and it stands against the mere "rehumanization" of texts such that some universal, all-encompassing categories are invoked to the exclusion of the reality of otherness, whether cultural or otherwise.

Given these important signposts—(1) being a diaspora community, (2) a bilingual, bicultural, increasingly multicultural community, and (3) being a community that confronts texts to create a new, liberating reality, all of which move us toward an intercultural hermeneutic spurred by the Latino/a experience of reading and experiencing the variety of life-texts—we now turn in the rest of this essay to see how such methodological considerations of otherness, cross-cultural engagement, and the construction of a liberating space, can help us read the apostle Paul. Specifically, we analyze a passage from his first letter to the Corinthians, in which Paul is most explicit about his "cross-cultural" approaches to ministry.

A U.S. Latino Reading of Paul:
1 Corinthians 9:19-23—a Layered Analysis

There are several layers to a reading of 1 Cor. 9:19-23. First is its immediate, one might say, "surface" context. The immediate context of 1 Cor. 9:19-23 is the middle of an argument in which Paul defends so-called weaker believers in the Corinthian assembly. First Corinthians 8 indicates that several, so-called strong Christians challenge the faith of their "weaker" brothers and sisters because they do not eat food offered to idols in the temple districts of Corinth. The "stronger" believers think they possess "knowledge" (*gnōsis*) that convinces them that the gods worshiped in these temples are powerless. Therefore, eating food offered to those gods is harmless. Paul refuses to grant "the strong" their absolute "authority" (*exousia*) to practice what they believe, because if it harms the spirituality of their "weaker" brothers and sisters, then they should avoid it or at least keep it quiet and personal, rather than public and visible (see especially 8:9-13 and 10:23-33).[7]

However, one might legitimately ask, "Why should my liberty [*eleutheria*] be subject to the judgment of someone else's conscience?" (10:29). Paul's answer lies in 1 Cor. 9:1-27, in which he offers himself as an example of giving up personal freedom for the common good. Several of the areas of his life and ministry cited here, leading up to the passage on which I want to concentrate for this essay, include the right to marry, the right to financial support from his congregations, and the right to use his apostolic authority for all these matters. Because his discussion of financial support is extended here (9:6-18), and he discusses it elsewhere in his correspondence with the Corinthians (e.g., 2 Cor. 11:7-11), the reader deduces that Paul has a problem in this area of finances in the eyes of some local leaders of the Corinthian assembly. One argument goes that Paul refuses financial support from the Corinthians because they misinterpret such support as establishing a patron-client relationship between Paul and the Corinthians, a relationship Paul will not accept (Marshall 1987).

Thus this is the second, more sociopolitical layer of this passage—Paul's self-defense against attacks from the community about his leadership and authority. The circumstance of defending others attacked for their lack of freedom becomes an occasion for another moment of self-defense for his apostolic authority (a previous apostolic defense in this letter being in particular 1 Cor. 1:10—4:21). Here in 1 Corinthians 9, he writes that he will forgo certain privileges as an apostle to defend the well-being of the common good. He will not take money for his support from the Corinthian community so as not to undermine the authenticity of his gospel message:

But I have not used any of these rights. And I am not writing this in the hope that you will do such things for me, for I would rather die than allow anyone to deprive me of this boast. For when I preach the gospel, I cannot boast, since I am compelled to preach. Woe to me if I do not preach the gospel! If I preach voluntarily, I have a reward; if not voluntarily, I am simply discharging the trust committed to me. What then is my reward? Just this: that in preaching the gospel I may offer it free of charge, and so not make full use of my rights as a preacher of the gospel. (1 Cor. 9:15-18)

This self-defense about matters of compensation in the context of defending the rights of the weak to demand the strong to give up certain of their rights for the good of all sets up a further rationale for the Pauline mission—he will be "all things to all people" in order to win a few over to the cause of the gospel (9:22). Again, he sets aside rights to serve the common good.

So these are two layers of the passage: (1) the immediate literary context of what is said—the overt rhetoric of the passage—and (2) the political context of what Paul really wants to say about his own ministry and agenda. However, a fair question arises: How does one become "all things to all people" and still retain a measure of integrity? That is the third layer of our conversation with this text and the one where some reflection on the Latino/a reality of today might help unpack the "hidden transcripts"[8] of Paul's claims here.

1 Corinthians 9:19-23 and "Border-Crossing"

In order to "see" more fully, like when I heard Portuguese-language speakers and mistook them for Spanish speakers because I could not see them directly, and mindful of Segovia's challenge to engage the context of the flesh-and-blood reader to "see" the ancient writer better, I would like to explore the concept of "border-crossing" in Latino/a cultural studies and how it relates to this passage, where Paul insists he needs to be "all things to all people" in order for his mission and message to be "seen and heard." First, a reading of 1 Cor. 9:19-23 puts the passage in the context of what we read above in 8–10: Rather than the language of *exousia*—"authority" or "right"—Paul invokes the language of "freedom"—*eleutheros*—to further emphasize his power in the matter. He freely and strategically gives up power and in a sense, he writes, becomes a "slave" to all to "win" them over—body and mind—to the gospel (9:19). What follows is a series of cultural, social, and religious groups, those no doubt present within his assemblies, for whom he is willing to adapt his own cultural, social, and even religious practices in order to reach them for the gospel. Included are Jews and "those under the law," "those outside the law," and the "weak," who at first glance may be read to mean the "spiritually" weak, but more likely are the same, economically "weak" of the previous section (ch. 8—those with little or no access to "meat offered to idols"). They are "weak" only according to some, perhaps the most elite in Corinth. Yet Paul identifies with the former, indeed, quite specifically and emphatically, especially since he does not mention the "strong" at all in this list. Rather, after listing these groups with which he would identify in concrete ways, to a limit (i.e., he already is a Jew and probably practices the dietary and other rituals expected of a Jew, although he won't impose it on "those outside the law," 9:21), Paul declares himself a border-crosser: "I have become all things to all people, that I might by all means save some" (9:22b).

According to Gloria Anzaldua, borders are not just dividing lines or safe/unsafe spaces. Rather, they are also spaces for power to be asserted, negotiated, and resisted (Anzaldua 1987: 25; Mata 2010: 247–66). By being willing to "negotiate" the engagement of Jews, non-Jews, the socially "weak," and the socially powerful in his assemblies in order to create a new space for service and liberation with God (to be "saved," "rescued," "delivered," variable meanings of the Greek word *sōtēria*—"salvation"), Paul crosses various borders in his ministry (in addition to the geographic ones) to establish his communities and secure them. Thus an image that is important for understanding Latino/a reality today—"border"—becomes a metaphor for Paul's pragmatic missionary approach, especially in this passage of 1 Cor. 9:19-23. He gives up certain rights and security in order to carry out this mission; he crosses borders. To complete the argument of the rest of 1 Corinthians 8–10, Paul is asking, "Why shouldn't the 'strong' do so as well?"

This puts Paul and his gospel communities on the margins of Roman imperial society and makes the Pauline mission an "alternative society," to cite language from Richard Horsley's essay on 1 Corinthians in his *Paul and Empire* (Horsley 1997: 242–52). Anzaldua, describing border-crossers as the *atravesados* (literally, "the crossed"), asserts that such people and communities are viewed by those in power as "the squint-eyed, the perverse, the queer, the troublesome, the mongrel, the mulato, the half-breed, and the half-dead, in short, those who cross over, pass over, or go through the confines of the normal" (Anzaldua 1987: 4). At the beginning of 1 Corinthians, Paul describes most of the constituents of the community there as not "wise by human standards, not . . . powerful, not . . . of noble birth" (1:26). Yet Paul asserts these are the chosen ones of God: "God chose what is foolish in the world to shame the wise, . . . what is weak in the world to shame the strong; . . . what is low and despised in the world, the things that are not, to reduce to nothing things that are" (1:27-28).

Thus it is clear that when "the weak" challenge the irresponsibility of "the strong" in 1 Corinthians 8–10, Paul is there to defend these so-called weak ones and "cross borders" in order to demonstrate their proper interpretation of the meaning and practice of the gospel message, including with regard to such everyday matters as eating and drinking. Paul asserts that, like Latino and Latina immigrants, who most times have *la facultad* ("mental facility") to help them see beyond the surface to the deeper meanings of life on the margins of existence, because they have to in order to survive, the "weak" in 1 Corinthians 1 and 9, have seen the "truth of the gospel" (Gal 2:5, 14). Anzaldua describes *la facultad* as "an instant sensing, a quick perception arrived at without conscious reasoning. It is an acute awareness mediated by the part of the psyche that does not speak, that communicates in images and symbols which are the faces of feelings" (Anzaldua 1987: 38). In 1 Corinthians 8–10, the "strong" assert that they have the "knowledge" (*gnōsis*) necessary to exercise their faith more wisely than the "weak." Yet they are wrong. When Paul describes all the groups he border-crosses in order to reach with the gospel message, the "strong" are not among them. Earlier in the letter, he describes persons who think they have the gospel message in even better order than Paul himself "arrogant," "puffed-up" ones (1 Cor. 4:18; 5:2). And again, they make mistakes in a variety of ethical-moral issues on which Paul, and others, challenge them (see 1 Cor. 5:1—6:20). They have not used their *facultad* to cross over into the new, safer grounds of the gospel truth, according to Paul.

In short, being in dialogue with the concerns of colonized and postcolonial communities of the "American empire" today, particularly Latino/a immigrants and their border-crossing, puts us in touch with what might have been some of the dynamics the apostle Paul and his communities were facing in their day over two thousand years ago as the early Jesus movement crossed over into more and more of imperial Roman society. Two distinct cultures, removed by time and space, encounter each other as "the other," mediated by an ancient text and a flesh-and-blood (Latino) reader. In the encounter, new meaning is constructed in ways that promote a gospel, an agenda, of liberation.

SUMMARY AND CONCLUSION

What have we learned about reading Paul interculturally, especially *latinamente?* To do such a reading, we have explored (1) the U.S. Latino/a context; (2) Latino/a biblical hermeneutics in general; and (3) a reading of 1 Cor. 9:19-23.

We have seen, in the first place, that the encounter between the imperial society of Pauline communities and the postcolonial societies of today, including the U.S. Latino/a cultural and sociopolitical reality, while very different in terms of time, space, geography, language, and culture, does have some resonance, in particular, around the navigation of power, politics, authority, freedom, and leadership. Putting the societies in conversation, that is—like Segovia, among others, reminds us—securing an encounter between these "others," lies at the core of a Latino/a, intercultural reading of Paul.

Second, "crossing borders" is a fundamental reality of the U.S. Latino/a community throughout its history, whether Spanish conquistadores crossing the borders of our indigenous ancestors in the Southwest and the Caribbean or U.S. policies of "manifest destiny" crossing borders into Mexican lands and creating new borders with other people's lands (Texas, "New" Mexico, "Colorado"—the "Redlands," etc.). In 1898, of course, the United States crossed the "wet" borders of the Caribbean Sea to take over Puerto Rico and Cuba as spoils of the Spanish-American War. Crossing borders the other way, of course, has been a Latino/a and U.S. reality ever since those initial border-crossings by Spanish and U.S. forces, but especially in the twentieth and early twenty-first centuries, with much resistance from those who want to "close" "our" borders. Border-crossing is a theme prevalent in the Bible, including Israel's exodus from Egypt and exile to Babylonia, for example, and Jesus' border-crossings from Galilee to Jerusalem.[9] And then, as we have seen in this essay, Paul uses "border-crossing" as a motif of the nature of his ministry in 1 Cor. 9:19-23. The community of U.S. Latino/as and their experience of crossing borders and the various communities of the Bible, including the early followers of Jesus in the New Testament, become "conversation partners" in cross-cultural biblical interpretation.

Thus the U.S. Latino/a reader of Paul encounters the "other"—the apostle Paul and his first-century communities—and reads him in light of some parallel experiences of empire, colonization, and border-crossing. Like Paul sought "salvation" (*sōtēria*—"deliverance"—for his communities) and "justification" (*dikaiosynē*—"just, joint living") in anticipation of the Parousia (the return of the *kyrios* ["Lord"] Jesus), so U.S. Latinos and Latinas seek liberation, justice, and solidarity in their newfound lands. In this way, we read Paul cross-culturally, interculturally, and *latinamente*.

Notes

1. The Hispanic Theological Initiative at Princeton Seminary is a prime example of these important efforts (www.ptsem.edu/hti).

2. See Ruiz (2009: 48–50) for references to several Latino/a biblical scholars and their work over the last several years.

3. Although writing in Spanish, Martinez works from a U.S. Latino/a context, which he references in this and other publications on Paul and the New Testament that he has produced (Martinez 2003).

4. For example, Ruiz discusses the "friendship" between Latino/a New Testament scholars and Johannine literature (Ruiz 2009: 47–50). Such "friendship" does not characterize most Latino/a biblical critics and Paul. For an analysis that challenges or nuances most of these negative takes on Paul, see Elliott 1994.

5. See Georgi (1997: 148–57) for a discussion of the "terms of empire" appropriated by Paul in support of his communities and his message. For other approaches to Paul and empire, see Horsley (1997; 2000; 2004).

6. For discussion of these terms, one of which relates to Spanish and indigenous "mixture," especially in Central and South America (*mestizaje*) and one of which relates to racial, "color" mixture (African, Spanish, and indigenous), especially in the Caribbean (*mulatez*), and their connection to biblical interpretation, see González 1996.

7. I have outlined the issues of these three chapters (8–10) of 1 Corinthians more extensively in a Spanish-language commentary written for Latino/a faith communities (Agosto 2008).

8. The notion oftentimes hidden between asymmetrical relationships of power is understated or unstated truths about where true power lies—in forms of resistance (Scott 1990). Here, in 1 Corinthians 8–10, Paul wants to uncover that the so-called weak in Corinth resist eating practices of the well-to-do as a way to subvert their power, and Paul supports them. See also Horsley 2004; Elliott 2004: 97–122.

9. However, Jesus is not the only border-crosser in the Gospels. See Guardiola-Saenz (1997: 69–81).

PART II

Ritual, Culture, and Food

4

2 Corinthians 7:1 against the Backdrop of African Purification Rites

J. Ayodeji Adewuya

INTRODUCTION

This essay is an attempt to show how the reading of 2 Cor. 7:1 from an African cultural context not only enhances the understanding of the text but also complements its scholarly interpretation.[1] It is an example of what Justin Ukpong describes as "inculturation biblical hermeneutic" (Ukpong 1996: 190), an approach by which interpreters consciously and explicitly seek to interpret the biblical text from sociocultural perspectives of different people. It is a method that includes giving due consideration to the religious and secular culture as well as the social and historical experiences of the readers. "Ordinary" African readers of the Bible do not dwell on a passage as somebody else's text to be read and analyzed; rather, they see the text as intended to provide them with a framework to look at their own lives. As such, they immediately appropriate a particular text and situate themselves inside of it, trying to understand what it expects of them. Thus discussing a text really means discussing the life of the people without making any great distinction between method and content. Reality and the biblical text merge, each shedding light on the other and competing for attention. Hence, as John Pobee states, "Culture then is a hermeneutic for reading Scripture" (Pobee 1997: 166). Specifically, then, one must ask how the experience of an African could facilitate the understanding of 2 Cor. 7:1. Paul calls the Corinthians both as individuals and as a community to make their holiness complete by cleansing themselves from every type of pollution because of the fear of God. Three elements of Paul's exhortation are important for the discussion here. These are the motif of cleansing, the idea of pollution, and the fear of God.

HOLINESS: CLEANSING FROM POLLUTION

In 2 Cor. 7:1, Paul, as a summary exhortation of the preceding verses (6:14-18), enjoins the Corinthians *katharisōmen heautou* ("cleanse yourselves"). Paul, including himself, summons the Corinthian church to stop unacceptable relationships with iniquity, the powers of darkness, Belial, unbelievers, and idols. Paul's exhortation to holiness and a call for separation in 2 Cor. 6:14 are now formulated in terms of cleansing from defilement of both flesh and spirit, a circumlocution of the total person (Adewuya 2011: 122).

Paul's call to cleansing will no doubt ring a bell for traditional Africans, as they are not only familiar with purification rites but also understand the underlying reasons for such acts. Various kinds of purification rites in Africa are tied to various events and for various reasons (Ray 1976: 90–100). Not all purification rites are done for religious purposes. Nevertheless, many religious purification rites are specifically concerned with each society's relationship with the deity. In such cases, there are basically three major grounds for purification: taboos, the holiness of God, and relationship with the deity. Among Africans, as Awolalu notes, "purification is a positive approach to the cleaning and removal of sin and pollution. It involves an outward act that is consequently believed to have a spiritual inner cleansing. The cleansing may be of the body, or of a thing or of a territory or community" (Awolalu 1976: 284). If one is aware or is made aware by a diviner that he or she has committed an offense that has resulted in the disruption of his or her peace, he or she will have to undergo a ritual cleansing. This may include ritual shaving of the hair followed by ritual bathing in a flowing stream. The "washing off" of stains is undertaken by the sinner under the guidance of a priest on an appointed date, time, and place. The sinner provides what the priest directs him or her to bring for the "washing." The whole event is symbolic and dramatic. Sin is here portrayed as a stain and a filthy rag, which can be washed off and cast off respectively. The disappearance of sin brings new life, just as the rejuvenated person takes on a clean, white cloth and casts off the old one.

The significance of purification among many African societies is evident in the words that are used. Among the Zulus, purification is called either *ukuhlambulula* or *ukusefa*, both of which mean "to make thin" or "to make a person free, loose, and unbound" and derive from the word *ukuhlamba*, which means "to wash" (Sundlker 1961: 210). In Zulu traditional life, purification rites are understood as the process through which a person is made free and refined of dross and imperfection. From the practice of ritual, in the figure of impurity, a concept of guilt develops and, as such, purification becomes atonement. It is also evident that in the sphere of purification, ritual and ethical reflection often merge without a break. The common Swahili word for cleansing is *utakaso*, a word translated as "cleansing" or "sanctification," which is used both for moral and ritual cleansing. For example, it is used for rituals such as cleansing of evil spirits and the removal of a curse. It applies to the cleansing of the widow/ widower after the death of the spouse. In short, the word refers to the total removal of evil. It is used in contrast to *kusafisha*, which refers to the cleaning of a house or washing of clothes. The wide range of meaning of *utakaso* fits well with the multifaceted nature of holiness articulated by Paul in 2 Cor. 6:14—7:1. In addition to the foregoing, for traditional Africans, purification is a social process. To belong to a group requires one to conform to its standard of purity—the outsider, the uninitiated, and the rebel are considered unclean. Therefore, the emotionally charged activities that accompany purification or cleansing constitute a ritual demonstration.

All this is helpful in understanding the exhortation in 2 Cor. 7:1. Paul uses the word *katharizein* ("cleanse or purify"), a word that rarely occurs in the Pauline corpus, and which is frequently used to translate the Hebrew word *taher*. It is used in the Priestly materials with reference to making persons, things, or places ceremonially fit for participation or use within the cultus.[2] In Psalm 51 (2, 7, 10), for example, the adjective and verb are both used in the prayer for ethical purity in the entire person. In its general usage, the word group denotes physical, religious, and moral cleanness or purity in such senses as clean, free from stains or shame, and free from adulteration (Adewuya 2011: 158). Purification in the Old Testament usually has to do not simply with dedication to holy use but also with removal of ceremonial uncleanness (or ritual impurity), which occurred in several ways. Isaiah 52:11, a passage to which Paul alludes in 2 Cor. 6:17, mentions purification in anticipation of the return from the exile. This need for purification, along with the usual purification for holy service, was probably in mind as the priests and Levites purified themselves (Ezra 6:20) and then the people and the rebuilt city gates (Neh. 12:30) after the exile (cf. 12:45; 13:22). Thus the notion of separation to a dimension beyond the external is implicit in the idea of purification.

When Paul demands cleansing of *sarkos kai pneumatos* ("flesh and spirit"), he is referring both to the physical body[3] and to the "seat of emotion and will" (Burton 1988: 486). Every aspect of the believer's life is to be rendered free from any pollutant or contaminant that would disrupt his or her relationship with God. Furthermore, "making holiness perfect," as Paul exhorts, is not a second process done alongside of making oneself personally clean, but results from making oneself personally clean. When believers have cleansed themselves from every defilement, they will thereby have made holiness perfect.

MOLYSMOS ("Pollution") and the African Concept of Taboos/Pollution

An important word in 2 Cor. 7:1 that is germane to the purpose of this essay is *molysmos* ("filthiness or pollution"). Paul's choice of the word *molysmos* (NT *hapax legomenon*) is striking. In its simple sense, it means pollution. What is pollution in African traditional life, and how does its understanding enhance our understanding of Paul's argument in 2 Cor. 7:1? These are the questions to which we shall now turn. When an "ordinary" African reader comes in contact with pollution or contamination in this verse, the concepts of sins and taboos readily come to mind. They are very important concepts among traditional Africans. This is because in relation to human behaviors and attitudes, they constitute on the one hand what could be referred to as moral demands and on the other what results from the default of such demands. Diedrich Westermann rightly notes, "The many taboos which a man has to observe are not to be regarded as things mechanical which do not touch the heart, but that the avoidance is a sacred law respected by the community. In breaking it, you offend the divine power" (Westermann 1949: 65). Africans tenaciously hold the belief that moral values are based on the recognition of the divine will and that sin in the community must be expelled if perfect peace is to be enjoyed. Also, Awolalu is correct in his pointed observation,

> Society, as conceived by Africans, is a creation of God and it is a moral society. In African communities, there are sanctions recognized as the approved standard of social and religious conduct on the part of the individuals in the society and of the community as a whole. A breach of, or failure to adhere to the sanction is sin, and this incurs the displeasure of Deity and His functionaries. Sin, is, therefore, doing that which is contrary to the will and directions of Deity. It includes any immoral behaviour ritual mistakes, any offences against God or man, breach of covenant, breaking of taboos and doing anything regarded as abomination and polluting. We cannot speak of sin in isolation. It has got to be related to God and to man. (Awolalu 1979: 13–14)

There is awareness that the behavior of the individual determines what happens to all. As such, one may say that sin is not a private matter. It may bring honor and prestige; at the same time, it may bring shame, ignominy, and even destruction.

Taboos generally have to do with forbidden conduct. They are recognized as actions that go against the good and well being of other individuals, the community, and even against the gods. Thus, if there are going to be harmonious person-to-person, person-to-community, and divine-person relationships, these actions must be forbidden. Among the Yoruba, this is referred to as *eewo* ("things forbidden"). On the whole, in African religion, taboo embraces everything that could be considered as sin (Jacob 1977: 240). Invariably, there are many forms of taboos in consonance with the multifaceted activities of African society. It must also be indicated that taboos differ from one society to another in Africa. In fact, what is a taboo in one African community may be permitted in another one. What is important, however, is that taboos are to be kept with all sincerity. To break a taboo is to bring disorder not only on oneself but on the whole community as well, which may entail severe penalties. Taboos are also important to the African in the sense that they inculcate spiritual and moral values as the hallmarks of African religion. Their observance goes a long way in promoting the needed sense of mutual responsibility and communality on which the African culture and religion are solidly built. Thus, in Yoruba beliefs, *eewo* are essentially religious rules associated with spiritual beings.

The breach of prohibitions is an abomination. Generally, abominations are serious offenses, which are believed to threaten the cosmic and social order. They threaten the natural order. A case in point is incest. Incest is a taboo in Africa. Among the Nuer, for example, *rual* ("incest") is regarded as the greatest sin. It is believed that if two people involved in incest "are very closely related, death may follow possibly within a few days" (Evans-Pritchard 1956: 18).

Among the Yoruba, if a person commits incest, those involved in the immoral act are exposed to ridicule and are required to offer propitiatory sacrifice to assuage the anger of the ancestral spirits. The breach of *eewo* generally incurs for the offender a state of pollution and the threat of supernatural sanctions. The state of pollution and the threat of supernatural sanctions can only be removed through purification rites.

The discussion about holiness in African traditional life is cognizant of the concept of ritual dirt and ensuing purification. We will look at the Yoruba of southwestern Nigeria as an example. For the Yoruba, *ìríra* ("abomination, pollution or filthiness") is essentially a religious phenomenon, while Mary Douglas's explanation of "dirt" leads one to believe that is merely a sociocultural phenomenon (Douglas 1966: 64–65). If one were to tell the Yoruba that a certain writer says that *ìríra* is "dirt," and the "reflection on dirt involves reflection on the relation of order to disorder, being and non-being, form to formlessness, life to death," they would probably say that he or she must be speaking metaphorically. Ironically, Mary Douglas's explanation of "dirt" is closer to dirt than to the Yoruba understanding of *irira*.

The idea of pollution, she explains, is best understood in terms of the English word "dirt," defined as "matter out of place." Dirt implies a set of ordered relations and a contravention of that order. Primitive worldviews are holistic, man-centered, and personal. Hence, pollution avoidance is a process of tidying up, ensuring that the order in the external physical events conforms to the structure of ideas about the universe. In this sense, writes Mary Douglas, "If we keep the bathroom cleaning materials away from the kitchen cleaning materials, and send the men to the downstairs lavatories and women upstairs, we are essentially doing the same thing as the Bushmen wife when she arrives at a new camp. . . . Both we and the Bushmen justify our pollution avoidance by fear of danger. They fear if a man sits on the female side (of the room) his male virility will be weakened. We fear pathogenicity transmitted through micro-organisms" (Douglas 1966: 64-65).

Mary Douglas's work is significant. However, her denial of the religious dimension of pollution and purification in the so-called primitive societies is unfortunate. As for pollution in primitive culture, she argues, "The anthropologist does not believe that the often lethal punishments for incest and adultery are externally imposed on them by their severe god in the interest of maintaining social structure." It is important that when studying beliefs about pollution and purification in African societies, one should be less concerned with what he or she believes and focus on what the societies themselves believe. The fact is that a "Bushman" woman as defined by Mary Douglas certainly knows the difference between the dirt she throws away behind her house, and the pollution she feels as a result of breaking a taboo. Dirt in one context is a mere material substance, while the same object in another context is a spiritual reality. It is therefore apt to suggest that "mythico-symbolic patterns of thought," as Emefie Ikenga Metuh describes them, are not restricted to any particular human cultures—they exist in all cultures but in varying degrees.

Based on the foregoing, I would want to suggest, in agreement with Kristensen, that pollution in Yoruba religion is both spiritual and material in nature (Kristensen 1960: 455). Therefore, "dirt" is both "like and unlike" ordinary dirt. It is better described as "ritual dirt," or "religious dirt," which means far more than mere filth. As mentioned above, the Yoruba people see ritual dirt as an essentially religious phenomenon even though their worldview shares much of the characteristics of "primitive worldviews" as described by Mary Douglas. In the same vein, speaking of the Igbo tribe of Nigeria, Metuh argues that the understanding of ritual dirt is to "be sought primarily in its meaning as a mythico-symbolic pattern of expression, rather than in the type of society in which it occurs" (Metuh 1985: 74). He explains that in the Igbo religious worldview, just as we have seen among the Yoruba, Igbo ideas about ritual dirt and purification are a religious phenomenon. "Their ideas about pollution and prohibitions have wide-ranging psychological and sociocultural functions, but they are not to be reduced to a mere psycho-sociological or cultural phenomenon" (Metuh 1985: 74). Such an understanding of pollution necessarily leads to the conclusion that various purification rites among the Yoruba and Igbo are essentially religious in nature: they promote access to the gods in order to perform acceptable worship.

One may ask how the preceding discussion advances the purpose of this essay. It does so by looking at Paul's word for pollution or defilement in 2 Cor. 7:1. As noted earlier, Paul's choice of the word *molysmos* ("pollution") is important. It signifies the full range of cleansing that he evidently has in mind. In 1 Esdras 8:80, it is used to denote the pollution created by the inhabitants of the land with their idolatry. In 2 Macc. 5:27, Judas Maccabaeus retreats to the desert to escape the idolatry and pollution of the temple imposed by Antiochus Epiphanes. It denotes both cultic and ethical defilement in both contexts (see also Isa. 65:4). The word also appears in a judgment oracle against the false prophets for the defilement they have brought to Jerusalem, which was worse than that of Sodom and Gomorrah (Jer. 23:15 [LXX]). The close association of *molysmos* with idolatry suggests that Paul might be thinking especially of defilement that comes from dining in the local temples, membership in the pagan cults, ritual prostitution, active engagement in pagan worship, and the like. This brings the argument in the paragraph back full circle to Paul's opening injunction to stop entering into unequal partnerships with unbelievers (6:14).

THE FEAR OF GOD

What is the motivation for holiness? Paul suggests it is the fear of God (*en phobō theou*). The NIV translation of *en phobō theou* as "out of reverence for God" is on target. This sense is present in Wisdom literature.[4] It strengthens the argument that holiness is predicated on relationship with God. Believers, in 2 Cor. 7:1, are made holy by the cleansing of every defilement, while living a life of reverence for God, that is, submission to his lordship. This brings us to a brief examination at the African traditional view of God and its importance for understanding the need for holiness and ritual purification.

An unspoken awareness of the sinless perfection of God pervades traditional Africa. First, such awareness is evident in the various names used for God in different parts of Africa. The Yoruba people speak of God as *Oba pipe ti ko labawon*, that is, "the perfect King who is without blemish," or *Oba mimo*, that is, "the holy King." Second, the awareness of God's holiness is demonstrated by the strict rules that must be followed during rituals having to do with God. To get into and maintain relationship with God, a person must necessarily enter into a covenant with the divinity (Idowu 1962: 145). Such a covenant is usually based on a number of demands and sanctions. This is accompanied by strong belief that fulfilling or not fulfilling the demand of covenant relationship produces consequences that affect not only the individual but also the whole community. On the whole, it may be said that as far as African religion is concerned, morality arose because of one's consciousness of belonging to the divine being. Consequently, moral values are seen as the offspring of religion. If it is agreed that morality embodies the will of God, then it is what religion (which is the practical demonstration of God's relationship with humankind) approves as being moral that society must also approve, and what religion condemns must also stand condemned by the society. In other words, as Adewale points out, "The ethics of Yoruba (indeed all Africans) from one to another is religious" (Adewale 1988: 70). It is thus clear that, above all things, the basis of holiness is one's relationship with God. As noted by J. Estlin Carpenter, "The historical beginning of all morality is to be found in religion; or that in the earliest period of human history, religion and morality were necessary correlates of each other" (Carpenter 1913: 196). So also Robertson Smith, who cautiously affirms, "In ancient society all morality, as morality was then understood, was consecrated and enforced by religious motives and sanctions" (Smith 1914: 267). Africa is not an exception. As rightly noted and stated by E. G. Parrinder,

> The morality of East Africa is entwined with religion, for the people undoubtedly have a sense of sin. Their life is not overshadowed with a constant feeling of sinfulness, however; the African's happy disposition is well known. If a man breaks a taboo, he expects the supernatural penalty to follow, and his friends will desert him, or even punish him further. . . . If lightning strikes a man or a house, he is judged at once to be an evil doer, without question, for he must have offended the gods. (Parrinder 1949: 199)[5]

Speaking of the ethnic groups of the lower Niger, A. G. Leonard, concludes that religion is intermingled with the whole social system of the people. He writes, "The religion of these natives . . . is their existence, and their existence is their religion. It supplies the principle on which their law is dispensed and morality adjudicated. The entire organization of their common life is so interwoven with it that they cannot get away from it. Like the Hindus, they eat religiously, drink religiously, and sin religiously" (Leonard 1906: 429). The point here is clear. For Africans, morality is not independent of religion.[6] The African view of the holiness of God and its implications just described are in line with Paul's use of *hagiosyne* ("holiness or sanctification") in relation to God. Paul uses *hagiosyne* to express the essential character of God as apartness from all evil, and his just dealings in his relationship with humanity. Believers might possess the likeness of this character in greater or lesser degrees in proportion to their conformity to the will of God. As a result of their cleansing themselves in body and spirit, it will become increasingly possible to describe believers by the term *hagiosyne*—"holiness." When Paul urges the Corinthians to bring holiness to completion, he is not suggesting the possibility of holiness as ethical purity that is somehow not wholly pure. To the contrary, he is exhorting the believers to pursue an ethical purity that is limited but not tainted, an ethical purity that reflects only a portion of the holiness of God and must come to reflect ever more of God's holiness. Holiness may expand—indeed, it must—as the believer comes to be more in the likeness of Christ through a greater awareness of what constitutes defilement of flesh and spirit and subsequently cleanses one of that defilement. One may rightly conclude with Porter that *hagiosyne* as used in 2 Cor. 7:1 is not "merely a static condition, a holiness obtained by observance of cultic practices . . . the context is not one of resting content with an unholy life . . . but one of acting out one's status in Christ" (Porter 1993: 400). Africans uphold the strong belief that God and the divinities have set the standard of holiness. This definitely implies that a person's moral actions stem from religion and cannot be separated from it. One cannot but concur with Egudu that "since good attitude or behavior towards fellow men is one of the very necessary conditions for religion, it has to follow naturally and logically too that there cannot be any morally good attitude or act which does not to that extent share in the nature of religion" (Parrinder 1949: 199; Egudu 1972: 47).

Summary

As I pointed out at the beginning of this essay, the validation of the biblical text's claim to universal validity demands its appropriation by readers with different orientations in different contexts. This endeavor requires fresh ways of expressing the uniqueness and validity of the biblical text and its message while at the same time giving due recognition to other religious ethos as a positive expression of the common religious thought, which in this case is the subject of holiness. As Caraman succinctly states, "The human universal religion is by a circuitous route derived from early and later Christian confidence in the universal comprehensibility of the Christian message and the universal applicability of Christian piety. The divine Word can be expressed in differing human words because that divine Word is somehow behind every human being capable of uttering words" (Caraman 1978: 96). In reflecting on the concept of holiness in Africa as presented above, African purification rites and symbols provide great potential in the explication of 2 Cor. 7:1 and an opportunity of communicating the subject of holiness in an African setting. Second, in African religion, holiness is the nature of God, derives from him, is demanded by him, and is based on a covenant relationship with him. As such, purification rites are required in order to remain in closeness with God. This is the idea in 2 Cor. 7:1. Cleansing in this passage has to do with a proper use of the body as it is regarded as a temple, a dwelling place of the Holy Spirit and through which God is to be glorified (1 Cor. 6:15-20). There is to be no phase of the Corinthians' lives that is to be ignored in their efforts to make themselves clean. This is the essence of purification among traditional Africans. Maintaining a covenant relationship with the deity requires the total removal of pollution.

Notes

1. Lategan (1997: 254) notes that in the interface between the ordinary reader and the scholar in the process of interpretation, the biblical text is dependent on the appropriation of readers with different orientations in different contexts in order to validate its claim to universal validity.

2. Lev. 4:12; 6:11; 11:36-37; 12:8; 13:13, 17, 37; Num. 9:13; 18:11, 13.

3. Bultmann (1951: 200) calls attention to 1 Cor 6:16; 2 Cor. 4:10-11; 12:7; Gal 4:13; 6:17 as illustrations of Paul's occasional interchangeable and neutral use of *soma* and *sarx*, under the influence of the LXX's rendering of *bā-śāb* by either term with no difference in meaning.

4. See, e.g., Ps. 2:11; 5:7; Prov. 1:7, 29; 8:13.

5. It is to be noted that in subsequent editions of the same book (Parrinder 1914), for reasons best known to himself, Parrinder expunged this statement.

6. In Ellis's discussion about the sense of sin and morality among the Twi-speaking people of the Gold Coast (now Ghana), he wrongly asserts that "religion is not in any way allied with moral ideals" and that the two only come together "when man attains a higher degree of civilization." See Ellis (1966: 10–11). He claims, "Among the people of the Gold Coast sin is limited to insults offered to the gods, and neglect of the gods. Murder, theft, and all offences against the person or against property, are matters in which the gods have no immediate concern and in which they have no interest. The most atrocious crimes, committed as between man and

man, the gods can view with equanimity." Ellis's view is not a true representation of the sense of sin among these people. See also Henry (1985: 131), who argues strongly for a morality of good and evil that is intrinsically independent of God.

5

The Issue of Eidōlothyta

An Inter(con)textual Interpretation of 1 Corinthians 8:1—11:1 and Chinese Ancestor Veneration

Menghun Goh

INTRODUCTION

Chinese Christianity tends to condemn Chinese ancestor veneration as idol worship. The attack is considerable given that the ritual, with more than ten thousand years of history, is inextricably related to Chinese worldview, spirituality, and social identity (Lakos 2010: 12–13). The denouncement can be tantamount to rejecting Chinese heritage (Tan 2005). The situation becomes more complicated when Chinese Christians are taught to accept Western traditional theology as *the* orthodox belief. As Chinese people internalize Western worldviews embedded in these doctrines and end up with Western-oriented problems, we distrust our contextual interpretation of the Bible. However, no Chinese would call their ancestors idols, so how has the ritual come to be construed as idolatrous? Why are Chinese statues and images deprecated as idols while their Christian counterparts are admired as icons? For Paul, what are the features of the idol that make it idolatrous?

To address these questions, I analyze 1 Cor. 8:1—11:1 from three *intermingling* poles of meaning production: contextual, textual, and theological or hermeneutical (Grenholm and Patte 2000). As our textual analysis is tied to our existential concerns, we should be aware of our contextual and theological orientation, lest we fail to see beyond our horizons. This awareness is heightened when we interpret 1 Cor. 8:1—11:1 and Chinese ancestor veneration in light of each other. An inter(con)textual interpretation of these two contexts focusing on the concepts of "idol" and "idolatry" will reveal how each context constructs them differently.[1] I argue that a typology of cross-like events is not only crucial to Paul's view of knowledge and freedom (*exousia*) but also fundamental to his critique of food offered to idols and idolatry. As my Chinese context in Malaysia will highlight, Paul's critique is practical in addressing the power of the idol that forms one's *habitus*, which Pierre Bourdieu defines as "systems of durable transposable *dispositions*" that continually form our embodied worldviews (Bourdieu 1977: 72). Jean-Luc Marion's phenomenological analysis of the idol and the icon can further show how Paul's other-oriented notion of love and a God-oriented and Christ-mediated confession challenge the constructions of identity and power structures that depend on closed systems of knowledge (Marion 1991: 1–52; 2011: 152–68).

History of Interpretations in 1 Corinthians 8:1—11:1

In a recent article, Wendell Willis identifies seven areas of consensus in the critical study of 1 Cor. 8:1—11:1. He notes that most scholars do not articulate their concepts of "idol" and "idolatry" or pay attention to the power of idol in *habitus* (Willis 2007: 103–12). In his list of consensus—(1) "The Unity of 1 Corinthians 8–10";[2] (2) "The Function of 1 Corinthians 9";[3] (3) "Quotations from Corinthians";[4] (4) "The Reality and Possible Identity of Suggested 'Parties' in Corinth Related to the Topic of Eating Sacrificial Food";[5] (5) "The Possible Occasions of Eating Under Discussion";[6] (6) "The Nature of Pagan Religious Meals in the Greco-Roman World";[7] and (7) "The Norms and Warrants Expressed by Paul in Response to the Situation in Corinth"[8]—only (6) touches on the notion of idol in terms of its socioreligious aspect in "pagan religious meals." However, if the term *eidōlothyton* ("idol food") "is a Jewish Christian term, possibly coined by Paul himself"[9] (Witherington 1995: 189), and if "all extant sources in early Christianity which discuss the issue oppose idol meat" (Brunt 1985: 120),[10] then *for Paul*, what makes idol food idolatrous?[11] We cannot assume that an idol is necessarily idolatrous. We need to examine Paul's notion of idolatry, whether it is related to the religious features of the eating space[12] or the cultic practices associated with the food that make idol food idolatrous.[13]

To argue that idol food is idolatrous because it is tied to "pagan gods" or demons is tautological. From the Mesopotamian "mouth-washing" ritual[14] (Walker and Dick 1999) to the idol anxiety in Greco-Roman literature (Newton 1998: 114–74), we find that people deliberately oppose idol worship. Whether for Paul it is the religious features of the eating space,[15] the food itself, or the cultic practices associated with food preparation that make idol food idolatrous,[16] we need to tease out Paul's notion of idolatry. It is problematic to argue that an idol is idolatrous simply because it is an idol, especially if an icon can also become an idol. It is also problematic to posit that Paul permits the eating of idol food because an idol is nonexistent *and* as long as such behavior does not cause other believers to stumble (for example, Conzelmann 1975: 137). Not only does it overlook the power of the idol in forming one's *habitus*, but it also assumes a metaphysical and dualistic viewpoint of existence (Odell-Scott 1991: 147). It may even suggest that Paul disregards his Jewishness, which is unlikely (Tomson 1990; Gooch 1993; Cheung 1999), not to mention that Paul's notion of law was not monolithic (Patte 1983; Tomson 1990; Rudolph 2011; cf. Räisänen 1983). The argument for Paul's radical break from his Jewishness not only implies the superiority of Christianity but also depicts Paul as a deceitful opportunist. But, if Paul has become *all* things to *all* people (10:22) and pleases *all* people in *all* ways (10:33), then how does he honor everyone's singularity without erasing the differences? Here let us first examine Paul's notion of idolatry in 1 Cor. 8:1—11:1.

The two scholars who pay most attention to this concept are Derek Newton and Richard Phua. In light of his nine-year experiences of living and working among the Torajanese people in Indonesia, Newton finds that newly converted Christians have a wide range of perspectives on the issues of idol food and idolatry (Newton 1998: 40–78). This variety of notions is the result of different worldviews of the Torajanese and Christian missionaries. Newton argues that Corinthian believers might also have held various notions of idolatry, as the Torajanese do. He substantiates this claim in his historical and archaeological investigation of Roman Corinth (Newton 1998: 79–174). As a result of such a dynamic concept of idolatry, Newton argues that Paul (the outsider) misunderstands and miscommunicates with the Corinthians (Newton 1998: 384). Since there is no clear definition of idolatry, Paul thus has to prioritize communal coherence over individual viewpoints (Newton 1998: 387).

While I appreciate Newton's emphasis on the diverse notions of idol and idolatry, I find it difficult to posit that Paul would miscommunicate with the Corinthian believers so badly, especially given his cross-cultural experiences of evangelism (see Fotopoulos 2003: 31). However, different from John Fotopoulos, I doubt that we can neatly decide an idol as a "false god" of physical representation with divine power for Paul, while for the Corinthians it is an unreality (Newton 1998: 281). But, as Newton points out, the wide range of meanings in key terms like *idol*, *god*, *conscience*, and *demons*[17] means that we must be critical of what we prioritize and bracket out. In many ways, the meanings of terms like *ritual, ancestor veneration,* and *sacrificial food* are also not static in Chinese cultures.

With this attention to discursiveness, we turn to Phua's thesis. Using the work of Moshe Halbertal and Avishai Margalit, Phua argues that Paul views idolatry as "an act that is contrary to the biblical ancestral tradition, a rebellious act that involves partnership with *daimonia* [demons[18]] and breaks partnership with the Lord, an unloving act that can possibly cause a 'weaker' fellow believer to fall, an act that reflects spiritual indiscipline that invites God's wrath and the possible loss of eschatological salvation" (Phua 2005: 205). This definition resembles that of Halbertal and Margalit—that is, idolatry is not just a worship of other gods (or alien cults) but also a misrepresentation of God (Yahweh) (Halbertal and Margalit 1992). In highlighting the marital and political metaphors that depict idolatry as unfaithfulness and betrayal to God and Israel's ancestral tradition, these scholars underscore the visual and cognitive errors in the method and intention of worship (see Weeks 2007: 10–21; MacDonald 2007: 22–39). Thus idolatry can happen in various ways when people fail to worship God with the correct method *and* intention. This notion not only is dialectical (Halbertal and Moshe 1992: 137)[19] but also assumes that differences are oppositional.

The fluidity of idolatry is not always present in Phua's work, however. While Phua helpfully points out that not *all* Jews categorically oppose idolatry (Phua 2005: 91–125; contra Cheung 1999), he assumes a monolithic view of Paul's notion of law, indicated as follows: "The 'Law' is no longer to be the basis for ethical behavior, but rather the advancement of the gospel of Jesus Christ" (Phua 2005: 205). Moreover, when he juxtaposes Christ's "law" against God's "law" (i.e., the Torah) (Phua 2005: 206), he contradicts his own definition of idolatry. If the Torah is integral to "biblical ancestral tradition," Paul would be guilty of idolatry. But are God's law and Christ's law necessarily incompatible? A hermeneutic of typology would say no, as we will see later.

THE USE OF TYPOLOGY IN 1 CORINTHIANS 8:1—11:1

Focusing on Paul's use of typology, or homologation, this essay argues that Paul tackles the issues of idol food and idolatry through the lens of cross-like events, defined by an other-oriented notion of love that cannot be co-opted into any system of knowledge and power.

The reference to typology is found in 1 Cor. 10:6 and 10:11. While most translators render *typoi* as "examples" and *typikōs* as "warning" or "instruction" (NKJV, NAB, NAS, NIV, NRSV), Willis argues that we should translate the terms as "'exemplary' or even 'prefiguring'" (Willis 1985: 140; cf. Yeo 1995: 157–67). Richard Hays further argues that "typology is before all else a trope, an act of imaginative correlation. If one pole of the typological correlation annihilates the other, the metaphorical tension disappears, and the trope collapses (Hays 1989b: 100). This "metaphorical tension" of "imaginative correlation" between the two poles is extremely crucial to maintain (see Gerhart and Russell 1984); otherwise, a typology can become a one-on-one correspondence. The result of such reduction destroys the discursive function of "figure" (Hays 1989b: 101), and it leads to a supersessionist hermeneutic (Hays 1989b: 97–99). As such, "First Corinthians 10 should not be read as unqualified deprecation of the historical Israel" (Hays 1989b: 96).[20] Rather, a typology is "a framework of literary-historical sensibility that creates the hermeneutical conditions necessary for the metaphorical linkage of scriptural text and contemporary situation" (Hays 1989b: 161).

The "metaphorical linkage" is, however, not limited to the "scriptural text and contemporary situation." For a typology to work, the correlation between two poles should also extend into many other poles, as long as they share similar features of a common theme. A typology is thus *always* partial and *always* revealing, challenging one to *continually* look for similar patterns in different people, cultures, religions, and so on (Patte 1983: 134, 320). Hence, in 1 Cor. 10:1-13, we should not expect the "correlation of events" to be an exact match between the Hebrew Bible citations and the believers' situations. Instead, we should pay attention to the *theme* that Paul tries to convey through the typology.

For example, alluding to the gifts and helps of God to "all our fathers" who were under the cloud and passed through the sea (1 Cor. 10:1-4) and the arrogance, idolatry, and evil deeds that "some of them" did (10:6-10), Paul shows that the Corinthian believers could also overestimate themselves, dishonor God, and suffer consequences if they did not stop testing God (10:11-13). To help the Corinthians to see their dire situation, Paul uses such figures as "Moses," "the spiritual rock," "Christ," and so on to signal a *pattern* among the believers when they were not God-centered and Christ-oriented, as "all our fathers" did then. Thus, in 1 Corinthians 8 and 10, Paul stresses the centrality of God and Christ in believers' lives.[21] Likewise, in 1 Corinthians 9, when Paul invokes the figure of "ox" from Deuteronomy 25 and the figure of "running race" in the Roman Empire,[22] he foregrounds the themes of obligation, honor, and self-control in his response to God's calling through Christ, lest after preaching he is disqualified (*adokimos*) (9:27). From the perspective of structural semiotic, the above-mentioned themes are further confirmed in the overall theme of the complete discourse unit of 1 Cor. 8:1—11:1, characterized by the inverted parallelisms of 1 Cor. 8:1-3 and 10:31—11:1.[23] This focus on theme through typology is similar to Chinese correlative thinking, where meanings come from the pattern of association and differentiation.[24]

TYPOLOGY IN RITUALIZATION

In Chinese worldview, there is no sharp dichotomy between the visible and the invisible. Everything, material and immaterial, is made of Qi ("breath or energy"), and the visible and invisible worlds are a continuum where (1) yin-yang (a dynamic complementary system), (2) heaven-earth-humanity (a triadic verticality), (3) five phases (wood, fire, earth, metal, and water), and (4) nine fields or palaces (a horizontal division system) form the essential components of correlative thoughts. As such, gods, ancestors, ghosts, and human beings are not ontologically different (Teiser 1996: 32–36). While they are interconnected, the departed usually "are not worshipped as transcendent powers" (Song 1991: 172). Certain performance of ancestor veneration can be seen as superstitious—such as burning paper goods to aid the underworld journey of the departed, the setting up of the "spirit tablet" at the family shrine for one of the seven souls of the deceased, the ritual bowing and the offering of food and incense before the tablet.[25] But the ritual functions more "as a demand to fulfill the social and family responsibilities *extended* to the deceased person" (Song 1991: 172; emphasis added). The past, present, and the future are existentially interdependent.

Moreover, if the worship of Yahweh was tied to "ancestral tradition"[26] (see Phua 2005) and not viewed as "ancestor worship," then ancestor veneration is not necessarily worshiping the dead. Choan-Seng Song argues, "We must distinguish between ancestor worship as the cult of the dead and ancestor worship as the consciousness of the living presence of the dead in our lives through some ritual" (Song 1991: 171). The ritual is about honoring one's heritage, "preserving family ties," and giving meaning to life after death (Song 1991: 173). As these notions of "living presence" and of ancestors as part of the family underline the continuity of relationships, the ritual should not be about fearing or placating the departed (Song 1991: 172).

The "supernatural" and "superstitious" elements in ancestor veneration cannot be simply bracketed out, however. Even if Xunzi, a fourth-century-BCE Confucian philosopher, focused on the sociopolitical aspect of ritual (*li*) and called those who treated the ritual as supernatural unfortunate (Xunzi

2003a: 89–90), we cannot deny that the ritual has religious aspects. Likewise, even if the sacrificial food in the ritual of ancestor veneration has sociopsychological functions, its tie to honoring and feeding the spirits is irrefutable (Simoons 1991: 28–31; Sterckx 2011). But, as Noah Fehl points out about the change of the notion of ritual among Chinese (Fehl 1971: 221), the concepts of ritual, ancestor veneration, and sacrificial food are rather dynamic.[27]

For example, Xunzi propounds that the ritual comes from "ancient kings" who wanted "to curb it [disorder], to train men's desires [yu] and to provide their satisfaction" (Xunzi 2003b: 93). As such, ritual is "the means by which to rectify" a person's character and emotions [qing] (Xunzi 2003c: 31) and "to apportion material goods" (Knoblock 1994: 50).[28] While ritual can be authoritative, the point is that, as a group-oriented community, Chinese people see family harmony as instrumental to state's stability. At the core of this family order is the value of filial piety in ancestor veneration (Xunzi 2003b: 100–101). Likewise, chapter 19.2-5 of the *Doctrine of the Mean* asserts that perfect filial piety is serving the departed *as if* they were still among us (Legge 1971: 402–3). The *Classic of Filial Piety* further teaches that filial piety is *the* root of all virtue [de]: "It commences with the service of parents; it proceeds to the service of the ruler; it is completed by the establishment of character" (Jing 1899). Concerning the supernatural elements in ancestor veneration, Xunzi writes

> The sacrificial rites originate in the emotions of remembrance and longing, express the highest degree of loyalty, love, and reverence, and embody what is finest in ritual conduct and formal bearing. . . . The sage understands them, the gentlemen [shijunzi] finds comfort in carrying them out, the officials are careful to maintain them, and the common people [baixing] accept them as custom. To the gentleman they are a part of the way [dao] of man; to the common people they are something pertaining to the spirits [guishi]. (Xunzi 2003b: 113)

In the same text, Xunzi further maintains that one should perform ritual in "the middle state" between "form and meaning" and "emotional content and practical use" (Xunzi 2003b: 100). While Xunzi's notion of ritual is hierarchical and gendered, from the details that he gives regarding funeral rites and the mourning period, Xunzi wants people to understand the logic of ritual when performing it (Xunzi 2003b: 99). The ritual is not an end to itself. The ritual of ancestor veneration is a *medium* to cultivate social harmony and filial piety.

This allusion to fundamental values in ancestor veneration is well noted in Daoism and Buddhism. When Ge Hong (c. 283–363 CE), a leading Daoist in the Quest for Transcendence, was accused of turning "back to traditions and abandon[ing] the world," he replied, "I have heard that keeping one's body without harm is what is meant by fulfilling filial piety. Does not the attainment of the way of the immortals [or transcendent], which enables one to enjoy everlasting life . . . far surpass this? Furthermore, if one succeeded in attaining the Dao, his ancestors would be immensely proud of his achievement. In the realm of the immortals, nothing would be lacking (Kunio 2004: 117). This response is a reconfiguration of the theme of filial piety, as Ge Hong states in the *Classic of Filial Piety*, saying that "the beginning of filial piety" is to not harm one's bodies, since we receive them from our parents (Jing 1899).

Buddhism also makes a similar defense when stipulating that monks and nuns renounce their social identity, to receive new names, to shave their head, to adhere to celibacy, and to leave the family to join the *sangha* at a monastery. While these acts betray ancestor veneration and disrupt social order, *Mouzi on the Settling of Doubt* contends that such self-renunciation was actually filial piety![29] Ritual is important to observe, but we need to do things according to the situation, even if it means doing things contrary to ritual, an argument that Mencius, an older contemporary of Xunzi, also highlights.[30] Another example is the defense of Ling Shou. When her father told her to get married, she explained that she was actually being filially pious, since her life as a nun would free her parents from suffering (Tsai 1994: 20–21).

The values in ritual and in ancestor veneration are not only reconfigured in different ways to express filial piety but also modified accordingly. Likewise, the sacrificial food in ancestor veneration also signifies different things to different people, not unlike what Newton posits about the notion of idolatry among the Corinthian believers. Indeed, if "ritualization is *fundamentally* a way of doing things to trigger the perception that these practices are distinct and the associations that they engender are special" (Bell 1992: 220; emphasis added), then we should not be surprised that rituals "have many [messages and purposes], and frequently some of these messages and purposes can modify or even contradict each other" (Bell 1997: 22). For example, Hal Taussig argues that the meal gathering in early *ekklēsia* was a "laboratory" for early believers to test out the boundary of the social norms (Taussig 2009: 20). The contradictions are the results of trials and errors in ritualization, which not only preserve heritage but also provide conditions for assurance and change (Bell 1992: 222). This notion of imaginative construction and maintenance in ritualization is like

Bourdieu's embodied *habitus* that forms and sustains the way we perceive and comport ourselves in the world.

AN EMBODIED RITUALIZATION IN A NONDUALISTIC WORLD

For Bourdieu, *habitus* are "systems of durable transposable *dispositions*, structured structures predisposed to function as structuring structures" (Bourdieu 1977: 72).[31] Produced by the material conditions in societies, *habitus* continually (re)inscribes its marks on our habitual bodies to the extent that we "wittingly or unwittingly . . . [become] a producer and reproducer of objective meaning" (Bourdieu 1977: 78), as if "there is a quasi-perfect correspondence between the objective order and the subjective principles of organization . . . [where] the natural and social world appears as self-evident" (Bourdieu 1977: 164). Bourdieu calls this self-evident correspondence *doxa*, "the universe of the undiscussed" (Bourdieu 1977: 168), where things are taken for granted for what they are.

Given this notion of *habitus* in forming one's *doxa*, it is not surprising that those accustomed (*synētheia*) to the idol would still treat the food as having the power of the idol (1 Cor. 8:7). They were too *used to* it without realizing its *doxa*. This power of the idol becomes more forceful when "an ontological dualism in the Cartesian sense is not found in the ancient world" (Martin 1995: 15), where the visible and the invisible worlds form a "single continuum" (Wink 1984: 15; cf. Gatumu 2008). It is no wonder that one's conscience (*syneidēsis*) or the "*convicting* consciousness" (Horsley 1978: 582; emphasis added) would be destroyed in such *doxa* (see Thiselton 2000: 643). Halbertal and Margalit are correct when they point out that "Idolatry . . . belongs to the area called 'sensibility.' This term describes a type of connection between intellectual conceptions . . . and perceptual and emotional experiences. . . . 'Sensibility' refers to the esthetics of ideas and concepts, where 'esthetics' is understood in its original meaning of 'feeling'" (Halbertal and Margalit 1992: 4). To address the issues of idol and idolatry *effectively*, we must take religious sensibility or conviction into account. But when scholars render *ouden eidōlon en kosmō* in 8:4 as "an idol has no real existence" (RSV),[32] they overlook the *meaning effect* of the idol. While the UBS handbook also translates it as an idol "has no real existence," the authors warn that "care should be taken not to translate this part of verse 4 in such a way as to conflict with verse 5, where Paul admits that other spiritual powers exist" (Ellingworth and Hatton 1994: 185).

However, BDAG (591–92) tells us that *ouden* has both substantive and nonliteral meanings. It can also mean "worthless, meaningless, and invalid," as the Chinese translation takes it. This notion of *ouden* is sidelined in English Bibles.[33] They seem to presuppose a metaphysical and Cartesian worldview, unlike a nondualistic Chinese worldview, where everything is made of *Qi*. To make sense of *ouden eidōlon en kosmō* in 8:4 with 8:5 as well as 10:19-21, Gordon Fee, for example, argues that "Paul does not allow reality to the 'gods' of idolatry. What he does rather is to anticipate the argument of v. 7 [8:7], that such 'gods' have subjective reality for their worshippers; that is, they do not objectively exist, but they do 'exist' for those who have given them reality by believing in them" (Fee 1987: 370). This constructed division of "objective reality" and "subjective reality" is common among biblical scholars (Orr and Walther 1976: 233; Hays 1989: 139; Collins 1999: 319). While David Garland also follows this line of interpretation, he highlights "the intention of the worshippers" (Garland 2003: 480). Hans Conzelmann, on the other hand, argues that Paul sees idols as real beings, and maintains that an idol is real *insofar as* we *make* it into "something" (Conzelmann 1975: 173). But the main issue is not whether something is ontologically "real" or not. It is about the effect of "what *feels* to be real" (Patte 1990a: 111–264; Cargal 1990), which is another possible mode of existence.

Indeed, if an *eidōlon* is related to seeing (Büchsel 1982: 375–76) and if an "idol never deserves to be denounced as illusory since by definition it is seen—*eidōlon*" (Marion 1991: 9), then the notion of an idol hinges on *how* we see things and *how* they appear to us. While knowledge (*oida*) is primarily tied to seeing (Marion 1991: 9), most objects only become objects for us when we turn our attention to them. But, in our everyday life, what we aim at is often not present before our eyes; we see these things in the sense of foreseeing them because of our *habitus*.

In the words of Jean-Luc Marion, objects "are simply the result . . . of expectation that gives access to an object without itself" (Marion 2011: 156). We can associate this notion of seeing the foreseen with the power of *habitus* in idolatry. As *habitus* shapes our comportment and perception, we forget that "what we see most often does not appear" (Marion 2011: 153): our aim precedes our seeing of the object. The object no longer appears before us. At first, the idol lets us see the invisible; but as time goes on, it disguises the invisible by fixing our gaze on the visible (Marion 1991: 12). Consequently, idol "allows no invisible" (Marion 1991: 13).

Icon, however, as Orthodox iconography teaches us (Ouspenksy and Lossky 1982), challenges our vision, as it does not conform to our aim or gaze. It keeps rendering the invisible visible without fixing the invisible. As such, "the invisible always remains invisible" (Marion 1991: 17), exceeding and transforming our gaze. In a similar way, this is what typology does. It reveals the pattern without letting our gaze rest on it. Marion is right when he posits that icon and idol "indicate a manner for beings . . . [and they] can pass from one rank to the other" (Marion 1991: 8). As opposed to our fixated gaze on the idol, the icon appears before us, captivates our gaze, unsettles and saturates our aim. In short, the icon is of the after-seeing; the idol is of the foreseen (Marion 2011: 162). In terms of Chinese ancestor veneration, the ritual is iconic when it works as a *medium* connecting Chinese people to their heritage and value of filial piety. This feature of the icon works in Paul's typology when it empowers believers to *continually* open up their horizons to see the works of God in different situations.

A TYPOLOGICAL AND INTER(CON)TEXTUAL INTERPRETATION OF 1 COR. 8:1—11:1

Biblical scholars tend to overlook the meaning *effect* of the idol (8:7). To assert that an idol is metaphysically nonexistent not only disregards the power of the idol but also presupposes a Cartesian worldview. Given the nondualistic worldview in the ancient world (Martin 1995: 1–25), it is unlikely that Paul held such a view. Even if Paul did, to effectively address the embodied *habitus* in the issues of idol food and idolatry would take more than a mere conveyance of knowledge. So, when Paul reminds the Corinthians of their previous way of being misled *toward* mute (*aphōna*) idols (12:2), we see him highlighting the (unspoken) power of the idol.

If idols are *aphōna*, then how could communication happen? But communication did happen; people did worship idols. How did idols convey meaning (*aphōna*)? By *doxa* and interpellation.[34] That is, once we fall into the power of the idol, we already foresee the objects without seeing them. It is only when things break down that we start to see them.[35] Hence, when Paul in 1 Cor. 12:3 stresses the contradiction in cursing and confessing Jesus as Lord, he wants the Corinthians to see the logic and typology of cross-like events. While most scholars interpret 1 Cor. 12:3 in terms of cultic ecstasy (Conzelmann 1975: 206; Collins 1999: 447–48; Fee 1987: 581), Daniel Patte proposes that Jesus was indeed the Lord and cursed (Patte 1983: 306). That is, if Jesus as the *Lord* is cursed, then Jesus exposes the idolatry of the system that curses and crucifies him. This idolatrous system, however, still remains valid for many; otherwise, people would not have crucified him (2:8) (Patte 1983: 281–90). The tricky thing about the idol is that it will never appear as an idol, at least not until its contradiction is pointed out. It is only when one is in the Spirit of God or in the *Holy* Spirit (12:2) that one sees through the façade of the idol. Thus Paul asks the believers to "*keep* testing [*dokimazete*] all things, and hold on to the good thing" (1 Thess. 5:21). Without an otherness orientation that challenges the mirror image of our gaze, our gaze can be fossilized.

In light of this power of the idol, Paul therefore uses typology to address the issues of idol food and idolatry. For example, in the complete discourse unit of 1 Cor. 8:1—11:1, we note that the overarching theme comes to the fore when a self-oriented, active, and confident stance in 8:1-2 is inverted into a God-centered, Christ-mediated, and other-oriented stance in 10:31—11:1 (cf. 8:6). This inversion shows Paul's attempt to transform the believers' faith by gradually exposing the contradiction in their conviction (Patte 1990a: 129–72).

Thus, even if we *all* possess (*echomen*) knowledge (8:1), Paul tries to show that knowledge is God-oriented, as everything comes from God (1:6, 30; 3:11; 4:7). Not only does Paul stress the limit of knowledge (8:2; cf. 13:8-9), but he also ties knowledge to love: "But if anyone loves God, this person is known by him" (8:3). This change of active voice to passive is significant. The Corinthians might have thought they could fully grasp knowledge, as implied in the perfect tense of *egnōkenai* in 8:2a (cf. Gal. 4:9). But, as Anthony Thiselton argues, the aorist tense of *egnō* and *gnōnai* in 8:2b can stress the "process of coming to know" (Thiselton 2000: 624). Indeed, 8:3 does not say that one knows God if one loves God. Paul defers the result of loving. It is not within one's determination.[36] Love does not seek return. In love, one surrenders oneself to God, as it entails a faith that one is *already* known by God and that God responds to love.

The dative of *hymin* in 8:6 further marks the confession as personal and heteronomous, as the sense of intimacy in the dative (in respect to us) also signals a sense of distance in terms of the suspension of the grasp of love (see Irigaray 1996: 103–13). That is, while *for our benefit* (*hymin*) God is the source of knowledge (cf. 1:5; 4:7), knowledge is not within our grasp. Rather, love is the medium to God. If Christ the mediator died for people so that they may live (8:11; 10:16-17), how could some Corinthians use God's gift of knowledge through Christ to destroy lives! If Jesus Christ is the *kyrios* or the "powerful one" (8:6) (Odell-Scott 1991: 152), then they should acknowledge the authority of their *kyrios*.

The theme of 1 Cor. 8:1—11:1 is also pronounced in the confession (8:6), especially if Paul "intentionally utilizes his understanding of the one God in order to underscore his overall argument" (Nicholson 2010: 4). When Paul writes that "for us [*hymin*] there is one God the father, out of [*ek*] whom are all things and we are oriented toward [*eis*][37] him, and there is one Lord Jesus Christ, through [*dia*] whom are all things and we are from [*dia*] him" (8:6), he highlights the "father" and the "lord" figures in believers' relationship with God and Jesus. This relationship is contrasted with the many "gods" and many "lords" (8:5). Whether the "gods" were the "traditional deities" in Greco-Roman religions and the "lords" in the "deities of the mystery cults" (Fee 1987: 373), the concept of deity in Greco-Roman society "is a loose term, allowing much flexibility while stressing power and accomplishment. Being a god did not denote responsibility, instead it conferred on the person a special status and the responsibility was imported to the worshippers" (Fay 2008: 79). This notion that "a god did not denote responsibility" contrasts sharply with the Lord who died for the sake of the weak (8:11). If the cross is the core of the gospel (1:17) and the power of God to those who are saved (1:8), and if the kingdom of God is in this power (4:20), then the believers should also have this characteristic of the cross. Furthermore, if Suzanne Nicholson is correct about the "subordination" of Jesus to God in 1 Corinthians to stress that God and Jesus must be understood in light of each other (Nicholson 2010: 47–104), then the believers should also take up such a relationship, instead of being self-centered. They must see through the lens of Christ in their handling of the idol food.

Indeed, if individuals in the ancient Mediterranean world "owe [to their groups] loyalty, respect, and obedience of a kind which commits their individual honor without limit and without compromise" (Malina 1993: 45), then the believers should imitate Paul as he imitates Christ (11:1; cf. 4:16) in terms of letting Christ live through them.[38] The metaphor of the one bread in 10:17 is a case in point (cf. the same spiritual food and the same spiritual drink in 10:3-4). In an honor-and-shame-oriented community, the believers should become Christlike. In rejecting the cross, not only did they deny their own experiences in the power of the cross, but they also repudiated the power of God through the crucified Christ! Hence, Paul in 1 Corinthians 9 stresses the power of the cross in his calling (cf. 15:1; 10:6). Like an ox, Paul feels that he has nothing to boast about (1 Cor. 9:9); he was just doing his duty (9:16) so that he might be a partner of the gospel (10:23). For Paul, the reward is in being an ox, to do what an ox is supposed to do (9:16)! The promise of an imperishable wreath of honor is embedded in one's calling (9:24; cf. Rom. 6:4). Just like those preparing for the Roman running contest, Paul enslaves his body so that *he* (*autos*) may not be disqualified (9:27). In other words, even if the ox has worked hard in the past, it still needs to work hard. Like an ox listening to his master, Paul is subject to the law of Christ (9:21).[39]

In the language of Marion, Paul lets the cross event provoke and transform him, instead of letting his past accomplishments become an invisible mirror to satisfy his gaze (Marion 1991: 7–52). Paul realizes that the cross-like event is a pattern that he needs to *watch* out for. So when he uses the word *typos* in 10:6 and 10:11, he *sees* the narratives in the Torah as a typology that can help the Corinthians to *keep* seeing the pattern (note *blepete* in 8:9; 10:12, 18). In using *dokein* ("to seem/think") and the perfect infinitive in 8:2 (*egnōkenai*), Paul in 10:12 urges the Corinthians not to be arrogant, thinking that they have already stood firm (*hestanai*).

When Paul writes that God is faithful (*pistos*) and will help them out in their trials (10:13), he also addresses the weak, just as he did in the confession (8:6), stressing that the believers should live their lives through Christ (the mediating figure) toward God (the father or the source figure). The *dia* language in 8:6 shows that since we exist *through* Christ, Christ should be our mediator. It is when believers, *through* Christ, see God as our source and orientation that an idol becomes worthless and invalid (*ouden*). Idolatry happens when people try to make something meaningless into something meaningful. But, if God the Father alone is meaningful and valid (8:4, 6), then meaningfulness comes from being orienting toward God through Christ. It is in this sense that Paul urges those who are still accustomed to the idol to have "this" kind of knowledge (*hē gnōsis*). If the definite article *hē* in 8:7 refers to the knowledge in 8:1, as many argue,[40] Paul would be naive to think that knowledge alone could adequately address the issues of "convicting consciousness" (Horsley 1978: 582). But, as knowledge becomes power (*exousia*) (8:9), one needs to see *through* Christ to recognize the contradiction in such power. When Paul removes food from the signification of power (8:8),[41] he then forces the Corinthians to rethink their notions of knowledge, idol, and idolatry. He wants them to see beyond the idol food so that the gaze and the discussion do not rest on the visible. His telling of his cross-like experiences, despite his *seal* of apostleship (9:2), further shows that to become *all* things to *all* people (9:22; cf. 1:18) is about recognizing cross-like events in others, learning from them, magnifying them so that others will see them, and being cross-like to them as well (Patte 1983: 320–23).[42] Without this other-oriented imitation through cross-like experiences, even an icon can become an idol.

Conclusion

Instead of asking whether Paul allows the eating of idol food, we have examined Paul's notion of idolatry. But, as Newton and Phua argue for different notions of idolatry concerning idol food among Hellenistic Jews, this essay stresses that Paul was more concerned whether the believers oriented themselves toward God through Christ in their dealing with idolatry. In light of the power of the idol in *habitus* and ritualization in a nondualistic worldview, Paul could not give a universal answer to the issues of idol food and idolatry. To do so is problematic. It can turn such an instruction into an idol, in particular when we lose sight of the fundamental values that undergird the teaching and absolutize it into certain forms. To address the power of idolatry that lies in the area of "sensibility" (Halbertal and Margalit 1992: 4), Paul emphasizes the work of God through Christ in typology. Considering others and pleasing *all* people in *all* manners challenges the believers not to rely on their knowledge but also to continually look for cross-like events in the work of God.

For Chinese Christians, we also need to see such cross-like events in ancestor veneration so that we do not simply accept or reject our heritage. From what we have noted about *habitus*, there are no quick, easy answers to whether we can eat the offering food, in particular if the idol and the icon "indicate a manner for being" and if idol food is not necessarily idolatrous. The idol food can be a sign of heritage, a means of ritual, or/both a signification of interaction with the invisible world. But what we have learned in this inter(con)textual interpretation is that the validity of context in one's interpretation does not exclude textual and hermeneutical analysis (see Derrida 1998: 158; 1988: 136).

Contextual interpretation seeks to stress the ethics of interpretation. It is when we are aware of the discursive process of interpretation that we realize that we *all* make choices in our interpretation! So even though everyone reads the same text, the text *becomes* different for different people. This awareness not only calls us to be *accountable* and *responsible* for our interpretation (Patte 1995) but also reminds us to be open to other interpretations so that we may see their rationale and not co-opt or criticize them outright. As contextual interpretation helps us see new aspects of the text and context, and thus, read it *anew*, it can then promote dialogue.

Notes

1. Such a juxtaposition considers the ubiquity of religious artifacts and rituals in both Roman Corinth and the Chinese Malaysian community. See Engles 1990: 92–120 and Bookidis 2005: 141–64.

2. For scholars who posit the integrity of 1 Cor. 8:1—11:1 through historical and sociorhetorical analyses, see Brunt 1981: 20; Mitchell 1992: 126–49; Witherington 1995: 186–91; Cheung 1999: 82–85; Rudolph 2011: 90. For scholars who contend that 10:1-22 does not fit the

style, theme, and the setting of idol food mentioned in 8:1-13 and 10:23—11:1, see Schmithals 1970: 92; Cope 1990: 114–23; Yeo 1995: 75–83.

3. Most scholars treat it as an exemplum; see Willis 1981: 108; Mitchell 1992: 130; Horrell 1997: 92; Fotopoulos 2003: 223–27. Those who argue that that it is more an apologia of apostolic authority, see Fee 1980: 191–92; Yeo 1995: 76. Cf. Phua 2005: 172–200; Cheung 1999: 138; and Rudolph 2011: 107.

4. Although they differ in details, most scholars see 8:1 and 8:4 as Corinthian slogans.

5. Most scholars assign different social identity to the "weak" group and the postulated "strong" group. For an overview, see Phua 2005: 1–28; Fotopoulos 2003: 4–48. Those who find the divisions hypothetical or rhetorical, see Conzelmann 1975: 147; Fee 1980: 176; Hurd 1983: 124–25, 147–48; Gooch 1993: 62–68.

6. For a recent discussion on this issue using archaeological evidence, see Fotopoulos 2003: 49–178, 252. For the change of sociohistorical circumstance in Roman Corinth, see Winter 2001: 287–301. For a summary of different views on how believers interact with each other, see Newton 1998: 387–90. For the role of apostolic decree in Acts 15 in Paul's prohibition, see Barrett 1965: 150; Hurd 1983: 253–70; Witherington 1995: 190–91.

7. On the little accessibility of meat by nonelites, see Theissen 1982: 121–44. Contra Theissen, Meggitt 1994: 137–41). For the political implication of such food in the Roman imperial cult, see Winter 2001: 269–86.

8. When formulating ethical or theological teaching on the issue of idol food, many biblical scholars stress the difference between law and gospel and argue that Paul was not forming a legalistic exhortation. See Fee 1980: 195–97; Brunt 1981: 27–28; Fisk 1989: 70; Horrell 1997: 105–9; Phua 2005: 205–8).

9. Witherington makes a distinction between *eidōlothuton* and *hierothuton*, in which the former is consumed in a pagan temple and the latter is not (Witherington 1993: 240). Contra Cheung 1999: 39–81, 320; Newton 1998: 179–83. Gooch argues that the term refers to idol food instead of just idol meat; see Gooch 1993: 53–56.

10. Gooch argues for a different reason for such a discrepancy (Gooch 1993: 121–27).

11. See Tomson 1990; Gooch 1993; Cheung 1992; Newton 1998; Fotopoulos 2003; Phua 2005. For an overview of the relationship between food and religion, see Norman 2003: 171–76.

12. See Fotopoulos 2003: 49–178; cf. Gooch 1993: 15–26; contra Willis 1985: 259.

13. See Gooch 1993: 55; Fotopoulos 2003: 176, 258; Rudolph 2011: 93.

14. For example, people were so concerned with idols that they made that they would even ritually and symbolically have their hands cut off and the tools used to craft the statue thrown into the river to signify that the "enlivened statue" was not human made. See Walls 2005; Gittlen 2002; van der Toorn 1997.

15. See Fotopoulos 2003: 49–178; cf. Gooch 1993: 15–26; contra Willis 1985: 259.

16. See Gooch 1993: 55; Fotopoulos 2003: 176, 258; Rudolph 2011: 93.

17. For example, see Newton 1998: 278–90, 292n76, 295–96, 349.

18. "The word demons could refer to good spirits in secular Greek, but almost never in the New Testament (Acts 17:18 is an exception)" (Ellingworth and Hatton 1994: 230). Cf. Newton 1998: 349.

19. As "different concepts of God create . . . different concepts of idolatry" (Halbertal and Margalit 1992: 1), it is "a mistake to articulate an account of what is the *essential* content of idolatry" (Halbertal and Margalit 1992: 241).

20. "The point of Paul's metaphor depends on seeing Israel and church as pilgrim people who stand in different times, different chapters of the same story, but in identical relation to the same gracious and righteous God" (Hays 1989b: 99).

21. From the beginning of 1 Corinthians, Paul stresses the centrality of God through Christ Jesus in their calling. It was in God that the Corinthian believers were enriched in *every* way with *every logos* and *every* knowledge (1:5). It was God who chose and made the fool in the world wise, the weak strong, etc. (1:27-28). People could do great things in preaching the gospel, but it was God who made them grow (3:5). People should realize that everything belongs to God (1:30; cf.

3:21-23; 4:7) and thus do everything on the foundation of Christ (3:11). In an honor-and-shame cultural value, this relationship of God and Christ with the believers is significant. Whatever the believers do, they will affect the honor of God and Christ. So, when Paul heard that the believers form their own groups in the *ekklēsia*, probably around fifty people (Murphy-O'Connor 2009: 182–93), he was devastated (1:13). Not only did they shame each other, they also dishonored God and Christ! Worse, they even "participate[d] in demon-worship" (10:21) (Campbell 1965: 25; cf. Fotopoulos 2003: 176)!

22. Concerning Roman athletic imagery, where the "cult of beauty dominated athletics in antiquity," Harrison argues that Paul "undermines the aesthetic and social canons of athleticism in antiquity: the strong, the beautiful, and the honorable" by honoring the crucified body of Christ. While people would not care for the weak body members, Paul, in imitating God and Christ, cares for them (12:22–24) (Harrison 2008: 103–4). This self-sacrificial lifestyle of Paul is noteworthy, if Paul indeed came from an aristocratic background (Hock 2008: 7–18).

23. This identification of a discourse unit is crucial to underscoring Paul's conviction or self-evident truth (Patte 1990b: 9–22).

24. For different views of correlative thinking, see Fung 2010.

25. For details, see Comber 1956 and Yang 1961: 28–57.

26. Whether the "ancestral graves" in ancient Israel indicate ancestor cult, "the care, feeding, and commemoration of the dead . . . verifies the centrality of kinship and family in religious and social life. These rites, however, neither presupposed nor necessitated the belief in the supernatural beneficent power of the dead as expressed in ancestor veneration or worship or in the deification of the dead" (Schmidt 1996: 275).

27. Given the space limit of this essay, I will focus on the work of Xunzi, who creatively synthesizes the notions of ritual, or *li*, of different schools of thoughts before him. For details, see Fehl 1971; Sato 2003.

28. This self-cultivation through ritual presupposes three bases (*ben*) of rites: (1) heaven and earth as the "basis of life," (2) ancestors as the "basis of family [*lei*]," and (3) rulers and teachers as the "basis of order" (Xunzi 2003c: 95).

29. For the rationale given in this text on discerning situation in observing ritual or propriety, see Kunio 2004: 115.

30. *Mencius, Li Lou I* 7.17. For the full text, see http://ctext.org/mengzi/li-lou-i.

31. This idea of *habitus* can be traced to Merleau-Ponty and Husserl. See Crossley 2008: 228–39; Merleau-Ponty 2005: 77–102, 112–70; 1969: 130–55; Husserl 2002: 151–80.

32. Whether we take *ouden eidolon* "as attributive ('no idol [exists]') or as predicative ('an idol is a nothing . . .')" (Thiselton 2000: 630), these translations presuppose an onto-theological framework.

33. NRSV: "No idol in the world really exists"; KJV and NKJV: "An idol *is* nothing in the world"; NAS: "There is no such thing as an idol in the world"; NIV: "An idol is nothing at all in the world"; NJB: "None of the false gods exists in reality"; NAB: "There is no idol in the world." The Chinese Union renders that the idol in the world does not have much significance or impact (*ou xiang zai shi shang suan bu de shen me*).

34. Speaking of ideology, Althusser argues that "the existence of ideology and the hailing or interpellation of individuals as subjects are one and the same thing" (Althusser 1984: 49).

35. The notions of *vorhanden* and *zuhanden* in Heidegger's famous example of the hammer should come to mind (Heidegger 1962: 95–102).

36. "The knowledge that the faction claims to possess and assumes is 'substantive' and 'certain,' is reversed and relativized by Paul in his reply" (Odell-Scott 1991: 144).

37. "The preposition can be used in numerous ways; Paul most frequently uses εἰς [*eis*] to indicate purpose, although when speaking of God he usually specifies the purpose of God's glorification" (Nicholson 2010: 54).

38. For different notions of imitation, see Castelli 1991; Ehrensperger 2004; and Kim 2011a.

39. Rudolph argues that the phrase "under the law" refers to the Pharisaic law instead of the Torah and that Paul was referring to the open table fellowship when he spoke about becoming "all things to all men" (Rudolph 2011: 173–212).

40. For examples, see Fee 1987: 379; Collins 1999: 324; and Conzelmann 1975: 146; contra Newton 1998: 290.

41. For a discussion on whether 8:8 is partially or wholly a Corinthian slogan, see Thiselton 2000: 647–49.

42. Or as Kim argues, the body of Christ is the "'living' as the *Christic* body rather than maintaining the group as an organism." That is, to be the body of Christ is to live like Christ and to participate in his cross-like experiences (cf. 10:31—11:1)! See Kim 2008: 68.

6

A Conversation with the Story of the Lord's Supper in 1 Corinthians 11:17-34

Engaging the Scripture Text and the Filipino Christians' Context

Ma. Marilou S. Ibita

INTRODUCTION

Daily liturgical celebration of the Eucharist continues to be well attended by lowland Filipinos.[1] However, it is also a common to see many poor people, some of them sitting at the entrance of the church all day, begging for food or money. While they are sometimes given food or money by the Mass-goers, one wonders how Christians today, especially lowland Filipino Christians, who are economically and socially stratified and who celebrate the Eucharist together, can more effectively respond to this concrete form of injustice: hunger. A survey on hunger in the Philippines on December 3–7, 2011, reveals that about 4.5 million families experienced involuntary hunger from September until October of the same year (Social Weather Stations 2011). This is a snapshot of the life context in which I seek to read the story of the Lord's Supper in Corinth (1 Cor. 11:17-34). I will explore how a more conscious reading of the Lord's Supper story, augmented by sensitivity to the Filipino meal culture (*pagsasalu-salo*, act and symbolic meaning of eating together), particularly the value of *hating-kapatid* (sibling-like partaking of food), can potentially challenge lowland Filipino Christians' to a reconsideration of how our culture and faith celebration, embodied in the Eucharist, can enhance our motivation to respond to the issue of hunger.

Filipino Table-fellowship and Social Relationships

Though it does not exhaust the meaning of *pagsasalu-salo* ("table-fellowship") and the relationships of table-fellows in the Filipino setting, it has been observed that one can guess the degree of relationship among partakers of meals in the lowland Filipino setting by the way people treat each other. Carmen Santiago published a study on the language of food sharing in the middle-class town of Bulacan that reflects this view and can help enlighten our understanding this custom (Santiago, 1976).[2] While the study is somewhat dated, the practice is still mostly the same even today. The study focused mainly on middle-class families, but Filipino graciousness as host and gratefulness as guest are not limited to this economic level or to those who can afford to prepare and serve special, expensive, and exquisite meals. Among poor Filipinos, there is sincere and gracious hospitality expressed in the form of table-fellowship despite material limitations.

Table-fellowship among Filipinos mirrors different levels of personal hierarchy and their influence in table-fellowship. The Filipino map of personal hierarchy is part of the interpersonal relations that govern the way Filipinos deal with fellow human beings. The goal of this is *pakikipagkapwa* ("humanness at its highest level, shared inner identity"). In *pakikipagkapwa*, one arrives at the level where the *kapwa* ("other") is *sarili na rin* ("oneself"). The concept of the shared inner self is the basis of the concept of *kapwa* (Enriquez 1994: 3; De Guia 2005) and not just smooth interpersonal relationships (Lynch 1968). For this reason, it is more concerned with the recognition of shared identity (an inner self that is shared with others) and is the only Filipino concept that embraces both the categories of outsiders and insiders (Enriquez 1994: 3).

In what follows, I rely on Santiago's work (Santiago 1976), in which she shows that the interpersonal relationships noticeable in table fellowship can be classified into two categories: *ibang tao* ("other," outsider category) and *hindi ibang tao* ("not other," i.e., insider category). The *ibang tao* category has three levels: *pakikitungo* ("level of amenities"), *pakikibagay* ("level of conforming"), and *pakikisama* ("level of adjusting"). The *hindi ibang tao* category consists of two levels: *pakikipagpalagayang-loob* ("level of mutual trust") and *pakikiisa* ("level of fusion, unity, and full trust"). These levels build on each other. The progression of relationship between table mates is evident in the quality of relationships expressed in the meals, the kind of food prepared, and even the utensils used. The relationship among partakers usually moves from *pakikitungo* (which depicts the widest interpersonal distance among table-fellows) to *pakikiisa* (which shows the closest manifestation of unity and full trust among partakers). What is most relevant in our discussion is the level of *pakikiisa* ("level of fusion, unity, and full trust"), the level where the deepest or closest sense of shared inner identity in interpersonal relationship is recognized. The participants include people who are very familiar with each other, namely, extended family members and very close friends. There is no social distance or distinction, and there is mutual identification and oneness. In the Filipino meal setting, this means that one can share everyday kind of food, no matter how much one has, and meal participants can dispense with utensils and use their bare hands in eating. The one previously regarded as "not-one-of-us" gradually moves from being a guest to becoming a host, and then, finally, even becoming a co-servant at table when the deepest level of solidarity in the relationship has been achieved.

Going beyond Santiago's discussion, I also want to focus on a specific value that is even more helpful in reading the Lord's Supper in Corinth from the context of Filipino table-fellowship. Within the complex development of interpersonal relationship from *ibang-tao* to *hindi-ibang-tao* distinctively shown in table-fellowship, a particular value, called *hating-kapatid*, can be discerned in the insider category. It is evident in the level of both *pakikipagpalagayang-loob* and *pakikiisa*, which is particular among siblings. *Hating* (from the word *hati*, "to divide")-*kapatid* ("sibling, brother, or sister") can be literally translated as "sibling-like division" (Apillera 2007:194). It is a "kind or quality of partitioning or sharing of goods expected among brothers and sisters" (Gonzales and Mañalac 1990: 43). *Hating-kapatid* is apparent and mutually expected in the relationship of blood siblings as well as by people who have come to regard each other as siblings or intimate friends.

Hating-kapatid connotes equal sharing. This is expressed in different ways. The most basic is to divide the food in equal portion. This concept is borne in mind when there is ample and even abundant food. However, it is mostly appealed to when there is not enough food to go around and an equal sharing, no matter how meager, is advocated to make sure everyone receives an equal portion.[3] In the same way, this is invoked in instances of unjust division, when participants in the *pakikiisa* level forget being a *kapwa* ("the other as oneself") to their table-fellows and take more for themselves without thinking about the need of others (*lamang*). *Hating-kapatid* is also true in cases when someone cannot make it to a meal on time. Those who are present must think of the absent one in dividing the food and set aside this person's share (*tira*) before eating instead of satisfying first his or her needs and gathering what is leftover (*tira-tira*). The one who reminds those involved in the act of division and advocates for this kind of sharing are the parents (or any older person) or the siblings themselves, or in the case of good friends, anyone among them. When this concept is appealed to, everyone is reminded to think not only of herself or of himself. Instead, those who partake of the meal are urged to remember the *kapwa* and the most basic principle of treating each other as oneself and sharing equally. From this basic premise, one can also go beyond what is required and be more generous. Those who think that others are more in need of food can take from their own portion and still share more. The value of *hating-kapatid* at meals at the *pakikiisa* level, then, can be an important prism for lowland Filipino Christians in which to view the story of the Lord's Supper in 1 Cor. 11:17-34.

THE CORINTHIAN LORD'S SUPPER (1 COR. 11:17-34) AND SOCIAL RELATIONSHIPS

The story about the celebration of the *kyriakon deipnon* ("Lord's Supper") is found in 1 Corinthians. It contains Paul's multifaceted approach through epistolary presence to the many problems the Corinthians wrote him about and those reported to him. While the Corinthians did not write Paul about this specific problem at their celebration of the Lord's Supper (1 Cor. 11:17-34), Paul heard disturbing news (v.18) that caused him to deal with it in this passage. Paul has already mentioned a related aspect of the Lord's Supper in view of idol worship in 1 Corinthians 10. However, there are abuses at the Lord's Supper when the Corinthian Christ-believers gather (vv. 17-22, 30) that Paul cannot allow to continue. These abuses thus deserve Paul's immediate attention (v. 18, *prōton men*, "in the first place," "to begin with").

The episode of the faulty celebration of the Lord's Supper in Corinth in 1 Cor. 11:17-34 can be clearly delimited from its surrounding context. In the preceding verses, 2-16, Paul commends the Corinthians for remembering him and maintaining the traditions that he delivered to them. Moreover, the topic concerns women and their veiling during liturgical assemblies. The words of Paul in verse 16 are definitive in closing this topic. In 12:1-11, a new topic, concerning spiritual gifts, is recognizable. This shift is signaled by *peri de* ("concerning," cf. 7:1, 25; 8:1; 16:1, 12), an introductory formula that Paul uses to speak about different topics in the letter (Mitchell 1989). These observations clearly delimit 11:17-34 as a compact episode concerning the Corinthian common meal as one among the many topics in the letter.

In analyzing the Lord's Supper in Corinth, I follow the insights of those who consider it in light of the Greco-Roman symposium, which included both a *deipnon* and a *symposium*. Dennis E. Smith argues that the early Christian meals formed part of a "common banquet tradition": "The occurrence of meals in community settings and the symbolic value they carried were part of what I call the common banquet tradition. Early Christianity was made up of varied groups, however, who adapted the common banquet tradition to their own situations. This proposal fits the form of our data, which witnesses to a variety of ways in which early Christians practiced communal meals. The process eventually led to the collapsing of all these traditions into one orthodox form and liturgy" (Smith 2003: 5).

In addition, Smith argues that the foundational story of the *kyriakon deipnon* celebration in 1 Cor. 11:23c-25 has in itself observable characteristics of a Greco-Roman meal (Smith 2003: 188). He writes, "The meal pictured here has the following features of a normal Greco-Roman banquet: (a) benediction over the food, represented by the bread; (b) the division of the meal into deipnon (mentioned by the text) followed by symposium (implied by the wine blessing); (c) a benediction over the wine marking the transition from deipnon to symposium. It is clear, therefore, that the Greco-Roman banquet form provides a backdrop for this tradition" (Smith 2003: 5).

In view of the foregoing, I understand the *kyriakon deipnon* as one that includes the sequence of bread-satisfying meal-cup (see, for example, Smith 2003: 187–200; Klinghardt 1996: 286–301) and not limited solely to the bread and cup sharing. That the Lord's Supper is patterned after the banquet tradition in the cited story in verse 23-25 that includes a mention of a satisfying meal or dinner is explicit in verse 25, *meta to deipnēsai* ("after supper"). I hold that Paul is trying to ask the Corinthian believers to continue celebrating the *kyriakon deipnon* in a way that includes everyone in sharing all the elements of bread-meal-cup.

Turning to the text of 1 Cor. 11:17-34, one reads that Paul criticizes the way the Corinthians celebrate the *kyriakon deipnon*. From this text, one can surmise that the *ekklēsia* ("assembly") in Corinth has opportunities to gather together (*synerchomai* in vv. 17c, 18b, 20a, 33c, 34c; Schneider 1964: 666–84) as an *ekklēsia* particularly to eat together the *kyriakon deipnon*. This show of unity, however, is not present at the *kyriakon deipnon* of the Corinthian believers. Instead, it is at the occasion of eating together that abuses are made manifest (see Theissen 1982: 147–63):[4] there are divisions (v. 18) and factions (v. 19) at the Corinthian gathering. The main criterion for the division seems to be economic, as Paul's criticism in v. 22 attests. According to verses 21-22, the divide is between *hoi mē echontes* ("those who have nothing") and *hoi echontes* ("those who have"). Those who are described as have-nots most probably belong to those who live at or below subsistence level (see Friesen 2004: 339–47; 2005: 367-8; Longenecker 2009). The more-explicit manifestations of the abuses include that some get hungry (have-nots) and some get drunk (haves, as implied in vv. 21-22). This description of the characters as *hoi mē echontes* and *hoi echontes* (v. 22) differentiates the members of the Corinthian *ekklēsia*. It impinges on their relationship in the *ekklēsia* as *adelphoi* ("brothers and sisters"), resulting in divisions (v. 18) and factions (v. 19). The abusers at the Corinthian Lord's Supper allowed this difference, even highlighted this difference, at the common meal. The abuses of the Greco-Roman meal customs at the believers' *kyriakon deipnon* resulted in the hunger of *hoi mē echontes* and drunkenness of *hoi echontes*. If we follow Paul's point of view, these abuses were also tantamount to despising the *ekklēsia* and shaming of the *hoi mē echontes* (v. 22). Hence, according to Paul, the Corinthians do not celebrate the *kyriakon deipnon*, but what they have is an *idion deipnon* ("one's own supper," v. 21).

Concerning *oikia* in verse 22a and *oikos* in verse 34b, Suzanne Watts Henderson's proposal seems to make better sense of these verses. Her analysis shows that Paul's mention of *oikia* in verse 22a and *oikos* in verse 34b are indicative not only of place but also of a metaphorical expression for the Christian community to welcome in their midst those who are hungry (Watts Henderson 2002: 203–7). Rather than the common understanding that these words refer to the private houses of the believers, she translates verse 22 as "For is it not that you (*pl.*) have houses [precisely] for [the community's] eating and drinking? Or do you show scorn for the church of God [by not having all eat and drink] and shame those who don't have [houses of their own for eating and drinking]?" (Watts Henderson 2002: 205). She also suggests that Paul responds to the problem mentioned in 11:17 through verse 34. The two verses are interpreted as an *inclusio* of the command to eat, that is, to eat together in the house where they gather and allow those who are hungry to eat in their midst (Watts Henderson 2002: 203–8, especially 207).

Given the foregoing, the main problem in 1 Cor 11:17-34 is found in the difference between the tradition of the foundational story of the *kyriakon deipnon* (vv. 23-25) and the way it is currently celebrated at Corinth, as an *idion deipnon*. While the former was a tradition faithfully handed over by Paul to the Corinthians, the latter does not resemble the cited story and is characterized as noncommendable (vv. 17-22). Paul repeatedly expresses his lack of praise in verses 17 and 22. For this reason, Paul refreshes and hopes to reform the Corinthians' memory by means of appealing to the story of Jesus' farewell meal (vv. 23-25) in order to encourage character identification with the Lord Jesus and correct what is wrong in the community so that unity will be fostered and nobody will be hungry at the common meal (vv. 26-34).[5]

Indeed, the narrative in verses 23-25 is Paul's way of inviting the Corinthians to have character identification with the Lord Jesus as they celebrate together. This can happen in three ways. Primarily, I see it as Paul's way of grounding his censure in the foundational story from a recent past. He gives them anew the story that serves as the "historical background" why they eat together the memorial meal of the Lord Jesus.[6] Second, in appealing to the narrative, Paul makes the story of the Lord's Supper come alive. He makes the Lord's words rhetorically function as directly addressed to the Corinthians. In particular, the effect of "direct communication" is underlined by the words of the Lord especially *hyper hymon* ("for you," 1 Cor. 11:24c) and the double command for remembering (*touto poiete eis tēn emēn anamnēsin*, "do this in memory of me," vv. 24d, 25d). Here, the Lord Jesus is the Lord who has command of what is going on. He partakes of the meal with his unnamed table-fellows and relates the bread and cup to his own body and blood before he is handed over and crucified. "The narrative effect," Watts Henderson argues, "is to stress the self-giving, sacrificial action on the part of Jesus, not as an empty gesture but as an act performed precisely for the benefit of others" (2002: 201). Third, in appealing to the foundational story in vv. 23-25, Paul uses the Lord's Supper narrative as a means to remind the Corinthians of the symbolic universe they share with the Lord, with Paul, and with one another. I now turn to a brief discussion of this symbolic universe.

A symbolic universe contains traditional knowledge known through language and symbols, which legitimates the social relations and actions of actors and institutions (Petersen 1985: 57).[7] One can find some expressions of this symbolic universe in 1 Cor. 11:17-34 in the way the characters relate to one another in the *ekklēsia*. In particular, they are connected to one another by being followers of the Lord Jesus and by being *adelphoi* to one another in and through the Lord Jesus. Consequently, they need to relate to each other as such, as *adelphoi*. In Paul's idealization of the Lord Jesus' Supper, he takes the effort once more to teach the Corinthians these concrete expressions as part of their resocialization into their newly shared symbolic universe as Christ-believers (see Petersen 1985: 59–63). Succinctly, resocialization is the process in which the different members of the Corinthian *ekklēsia tou theou* ("assembly of God") who have various background and living in the Roman city of Corinth[8] come to acknowledge their common identity as followers of Christ and as such belonging to one another as *adelphoi*. The need to resocialize is given in the form of Paul's reeducation of the Corinthians in verses 23-34. Fundamentally, it is indicated by his reference to what he handed on to them as tradition, the story of the Lord's farewell meal with his tablemates, presumably his disciples (vv. 23-25). In doing so, Paul helps the Corinthians to continue their resocialization as members of the *ekklēsia*, discussing its implications in verses 26-34.

In line with this resocialization, two most important communal expressions need reiteration and reinforcement. First, the expression of following Jesus' example as the host of the *kyriakon deipnon* teaches and reminds the Corinthians of his self-giving example. It directly challenges the present actions of the Corinthians that result in the situation Paul mentions in verses 17-22. Second, the expression of this symbolic universe seen in the *ekklēsia*'s social relation is based on the foundation that they are all children of God and, therefore, *adelphoi* in and through the Lord Jesus. As such, they are to conduct themselves as brothers and sisters at the communal meal. Recalling that those who are hungry are the have-nots, who live at or below subsistence level, it seems that Paul wants to remind the Corinthian believers that protection from hunger is one of the responsibilities of being siblings to one another[9] (see vv. 21-22, 33-34). Their relationship as *adelphoi* has practical, moral implications. As David G. Horrell opines, "The prominence of this kinship description would seem to imply that Paul both assumes and promotes the relationship between himself and his addressees, and among the addressees themselves, as one between equal siblings, who share a sense of affection, mutual responsibility, and solidarity" (Horrell 2001: 299).[10]

The two expressions of following the example of Jesus at table as well as being and acting as *adelphoi* to one another at the *kyriakon deipnon* relate to an awareness of what the future entails according to their symbolic universe. Thus, in the same pericope, Paul tells the partakers of this supper that they must celebrate the *kyriakon deipnon* in a worthy manner, for they are answerable to the body of the Lord (1 Cor. 11:27), and that they have to examine themselves lest they incur judgment (vv. 28-34c). If they do all these things that Paul says in verses 17-34, their supper will be commendable, truly a *kyriakon deipnon*.

Considering the above interpretation involving the symbolic universe and social relationship in 1 Cor. 11:17-34, it is rather difficult to agree with Gerd Theissen's proposed understanding of the text in light of "love-patriarchalism" (Theissen 1982: 145–74). As Theissen explains, "This love-patriarchalism takes social differences for granted but ameliorated them through an obligation of respect and love, an obligation imposed upon those who are socially stronger. From the weaker are required subordination, fidelity and esteem" (Theissen 1982: 107).[11] For Theissen, in the context of the Lord's Supper, "love-patriarchalism" takes the compromise form that allows *hoi echontes* to eat their *idion deipnon* in their own private homes (Theissen 1982: 163–64). He expounds on his interpretation, saying, "Paul's compromise, which simply acknowledges the class-specific differences within the community while minimizing their manifestations, corresponds to the reality of a socially stratified congregation which must yield a certain pre-eminence to the rich—even contrary to their own intentions. Within such a community the compromise suggested by Paul is realistic and practical. It offers a good example of the ethos of early Christian love-patriarchalism in the Pauline communities and which we encounter in the household codes (*Haustafeln*) of the deutero-Pauline letters" (Theissen 1982: 164).

Given the need to consider the symbolic universe and the other textual clues in this narrative mentioned above, I find this understanding of Paul's exhortation in 1 Cor. 11:17-34, especially verses 33-34 using love-patriarchalism, inadequate.[12] I suggest that Paul's response to the Corinthian situation is better seen in light of Theissen's more-recent proposal in response to the work of Justin Meggitt. Theissen, commending some of the insights put forward by Meggitt, replaces love-patriarchalism with what he calls "social stratification and mutualism" (See Theissen 2001: 83–84). When I consider this proposal in relation to the *kyriakon deipnon*, it seems more reasonable to understand verses 33-34 as Paul's attempt to solve the problem at the common meal by making sure that the poor are given the same meal at the Lord's Supper, in the place where they eat together. This proposal recognizes the economic difference and mutualism among all the members in their celebration of the communal meal, without splitting the satisfying meal from the sharing of the bread and the cup. The economic differences are indicated by Paul's description of the effect of economic disparity that influences the treatment of members at the meal: some were given more of the best (those who are drunk), while others were inadequately considered (those who hunger). At the same time, social stratification and mutualism consider the contribution of the different members in the Corinthian *ekklēsia*. Those who were able to share welcomed everyone and shared the food and drink at the *kyriakon deipnon*. Those characterized as *hoi mē echontes* and as hungry, who should eat like the rest of the *adelphoi* at the *kyriakon deipnon*, symbolically represent that the *ekklēsia* upheld the values embodied in the shared meal exemplified by the self-giving of the Lord Jesus. Therefore, I propose that the story of the Lord's Supper in 1 Cor. 11:17-34 is best understood as Paul's attempt to restore unity at the Lord's Supper in a way that embraces and transcends the sociocultural and economic divide in favor of their common identity as Christ followers, united as *adelphoi*.

FILIPINO TABLE-FELLOWSHIP AND THE LORD'S SUPPER AT CORINTH:
A CONVERSATION

The conversation with the story of the Lord's Supper will particularly deal with the settings in the story and the human characters in this episode. In this section, I will discuss these settings and characters in a way that Lord's Supper story (which features the *kyriakon deipnon* and the *idion deipnon*) and the lowland Filipino's *pagsasalu-salo* ("table-fellowship") to converse or dialogue.

From a Filipino meal perspective, a few features of the Corinthian *idion deipnon* and *kyriakon deipnon* can be related to the Filipino *pagsasalu-salo* (table-fellowship). In some way, *idion deipnon* can be linked to some features of the *pakikitungo* level ("level of amenities"). The divisions and factions in 1 Cor. 11:18, 19 somehow reflect the wide gap between the guest and the host and the special food and drinks offered to the special guest. However, there are also differences between these two meal cultures. In the *pakikitungo* level, good manners are highly observed, and the host waits for the guest even though there is a somewhat "stiff" yet pleasant atmosphere. This does not seem to be the case in Corinth since verse 21a suggests that some of the haves eat ahead in the midst of everyone else and devour the food that they themselves brought (see Winter 2001:144–51; Surburg 2006). The rest of the description of the *idion deipnon* in verses 21-22, however, has no parallel with the *pakikitungo* level.

Moving on, the *kyriakon deipnon* can be compared with *pagsasalu-salo* in the *pakikiisa* level ("level of fusion, unity, and full trust"). The *kyriakon deipnon* is based on the foundational story of the Lord's Supper celebration in Corinth, presented by Paul as the ideal way of celebrating the common meal of Christ-believers. In the same way, *pakikiisa* is also the ideal level of Filipino meal in view of *pakikipag-kapwa* ("shared inner identity"). The shaded parts in table 1 show some points of convergence. The unshaded parts suggest some differences between the *kyriakon deipnon* and *pagsasalu-salo*, and the asterisks (*) indicate potential points of further interconnection between the two meals. The italicized descriptions on the side of the *kyriakon deipnon* indicate that these are implied, not explicit, from the text of 1 Cor. 11:17-34.

Comparison of the *kyriakon deipnon* and *Pagsasalu-salo* (*Pakikiisa* level)	
Paul's Ideal Lord's Supper *kyriakon deipnon* (1 Cor. 11:17-34)	*Pagsasalu-salo* (*Pakikiisa* level)

communal unity is preferred over division or faction	level of no social distance; fusion; mutual identification and oneness; apparent (and mutually expected) in the relationship of blood siblings as well as by people who have come to regard each other as siblings
rooted in the tradition Paul mentions about the Lord's meal on the night he was betrayed (vv. 23-25)	based on deeply rooted Filipino meal culture;*Possible mutual influence of *pakikiisa* and Christian eucharistic practice
the actions of the breaking of the bread and the sharing of the cup show the Lord's own self-giving of his body and blood "for you" (vv. 23-25 especially 24c)	value of *hating-kapatid**can potentially enhance the meaning of *kyriakon deipnon* especially the eucharistic verbs when the value of *hating-kapatid* is invoked at the Lord's Supper celebration
done in remembrance of the Lord Jesus (vv. 24d, 25d); a proclamation of the Lord's death until he comes (v. 26)	value of *hating-kapatid**can serve as a cultural prompt for the call to remember the example of the Lord (v. 24d, 25d)
table-fellows of this supper must do so in a worthy manner because they are answerable for the body of the Lord (v. 27); they are commanded to examine themselves lest they incur judgment (v. 28-34c)	partakers at table in this level are expected to be conscientious of others who are no longer "outsiders"; beckons self-examination of partakers especially when commanded by parents or appealed to by siblings/those who have been recognized as siblings or very close friends
when it is shared properly, it does not seem to result in weakness, illness, and death among them (v. 30)	when abuses are prevented in this level (*walang lamangan*, no one should have more at the cost of others), it can promote physiological health and wellness
table-fellows await each other and welcome one another as brothers and sisters when they come together to eat the *kyriakon deipnon* (vv. 33, 34, cf. v. 22a)	Partakers usually wait for each other;Welcoming one another in a familiar way
equal food and drink distribution	when participated in properly, it promotes sharing of food among partakers; *hating-kapatid* gives space to *pagtitira* ("setting aside food for those

	who are late or absent") and not *tira-tira* ("leftovers")
acceptance of and respect for the assembly of God	can promote acceptance of and respect for the church of God but also of the larger group of *kapwa* who may or may not be Christians
results in respect and inclusion of those who have not	can be appealed to in order that those who have not/those who have not enough can be given an equal share.
praiseworthy celebration of common meal in memory of the Lord (cf. v. 17)	commendable table-fellowship

Table 1

In both sides of the table above—namely, the ideal Lord's Supper celebration and the ideal *pagsasalu-salo*—the sense of unity is underscored and division has no room. This is expected for both natural siblings and those who have come to regard each other as such. Likewise, in both, partakers welcome each other and are considerate of each other's presence. Consequently, they both do not allow possible abuses at table that can result in adverse physiological effects such as weakness, illness, or death. Moreover, both are inclusive and respectful, especially of those who are disadvantaged. In this case, they are those who hunger (and at the Lord's Supper, including those who are weak and ill, v. 30). In both, equal food and drink distribution is a significant feature. Paul criticizes the Corinthian celebration (*idion deipnon*) where some eat ahead and devour food in the midst of their *adelphoi*, with the result that some get drunk while others go hungry in the Corinthian version of the Lord's Supper and, consequently, highlights that these observations should not be present in the *kyriakon deipnon*. In the same way, *pagsasalu-salo* in the *pakikiisa* level takes note of the need for equal food and drink distribution that includes those who are present but extends to those who are late and are absent. It includes making sure that there is food enough for everyone present. It also includes *pagtitira*—that is, setting aside food for those who are late as well as keeping and sending food to those who cannot make it to the *salu-salo* ("table-fellowship"). It precludes giving them only *tira-tira* ("leftovers").

We have seen in 1 Cor. 11:17-34 how Paul tries to help the Corinthians resolve the community conflict. However, if we are to understand the story in relation to the Filipino context, what can the *pakikiisa* level of table-fellowship say to the text in view of meal sharing? As explained earlier, the degree of relationship can be measured in the way Filipinos behave with one another at table. Just like in 1 Cor. 11:17-22, recognition of the abuses at the table-fellowship should be made clear so that particular adjustments and changes can happen. The abuses in Corinth run deep with the Corinthian believers' lack of recognition of their common identity as *adelphoi*, followers of Christ who celebrates his life, death, resurrection, and return. They allowed the socioeconomic and cultural limitations to affect them negatively, resulting in the abuses at table. Paul needed to remind them of their foundational story and its implications for their celebration and their relationship to one another. The abuses at Corinth offended the deepest level of relationship, violating their common identity as *adelphoi*, brothers and sisters. If the Corinthian context dialogues with the Filipino *pagsasalu-salo*, the problems will be addressed by values found at the *pakikiisa* level, which taps into the common identity as human beings (*kapwa*). Seen in terms of *pagsasalu-salo* at the *pakikiisa* level, what is broken in the Corinthian celebration is the fusion, oneness, and lack of social distinction that should pervade the common meal at this level.

From the perspective of *pagsasalu-salo* at the level of unity, one of the most important values that can address the problem present at the noncommendable Corinthian celebration is *hating-kapatid* ("sibling-like partaking of food"). This value can be appealed to in order to resolve the conflict. Those who can remind the participants of the need to have a sibling-like meal sharing are the table-fellows themselves, who are clearly cognizant of being *adelphoi* as well as an authority, like Paul, who is also in the level of *pakikiisa* but may not be directly involved in the conflict. These characters can call on *hating-kapatid* to remind those who committed the abuses to right their wrong. Those who are hungry and aggrieved as well as the authority in the community can correct those in the wrong to make changes by appealing to *hating-kapatid*. More importantly, the abusers, remembering *hating-kapatid*, can change their ways so that unity can be restored and the improper celebration of the common meal corrected. This would mean that those who eat ahead in the midst of their table-fellows and devour food at the common meal, who fail to welcome the hungry *adelphoi* or *kapatid* (vv. 21-22, 34), must welcome the hungry ones in the common meal (v. 33) by sharing equally. Equal food sharing by means of *hating-kapatid* also results in food set aside for those who come late through *pagtitira* ("setting food aside for the absent one"). Evaluation of the conflict resolution can be done not only by the authority who appeals to *hating-kapatid* but also by those directly involved, both those who were aggrieved and those who made the mistake of eating in an inconsiderate way. In Corinth, this evaluation is given in Paul's attempt to help resolve the conflict by giving them the reason for reforming their conduct (vv. 23-32), giving them exact commands and his declaration that he will give directions about the remaining things (vv. 33-34).

On the other hand, what can 1 Cor. 11:17-34 say to the *pagsasalu-salo* in the *pakikiisa* level? The story of the noncommendable Lord's Supper at Corinth and Paul's attempts to reform it can also challenge the Filipino celebration of the Lord's Supper in the present-day eucharistic celebration in connection with the surrounding issue of hunger. First, Filipino Christians need to remember that the context in which the Lord's Supper celebration (and the present-day Eucharist) emerged is a *full* meal. This is clear in the foundational narrative in 1 Cor. 11:23-25 (the farewell meal of Jesus with his unnamed disciples as tablemates) and the whole of verses 17-34 (the Corinthian celebration of Jesus' farewell meal). Second, there is a need to uphold the values shown at the meal of Jesus (vv. 23-25) that include sharing a meal, selfless love, and common identity in a manner that includes all. The way the Corinthians forget that the Lord's Supper is also for the hungry ones can easily be replicated if the present lowland Filipino Christians, despite their devotions to celebrate the Holy Eucharist, also forget their hungry brothers and sisters. Paul sought to address the problem by tapping the Corinthians' common identity as *adelphoi*. The lowland Filipino Christians today are challenged as well to recognize their common identity with their hungry brothers and sisters (*kapatid*) in order to embark on the more-complex solutions to combat hunger today. The values in the culture and the symbolic universe expressed in the shared faith and celebrated at the Lord's Supper help them to be creative in finding ways, just as Paul did.

The conversation between the text of 1 Cor. 11:17-34 and the Filipino *pagsasalu-salo* at the *pakikiisa* level, where *hating-kapatid* is very important, is challenged by the question of inclusivity. Can the efforts to share food with those who hunger be limited to those who are Christ-believers? The context in Corinth is limited to the Christ-believers and Paul's reprimand is primarily addressed to the abuses at the Lord's Supper. However, the question of hunger today is overwhelming and transgresses the boundaries of religion. Nowadays, the values and the symbolic universe embedded in the meal-sharing must overcome these boundaries. The Corinthian Christ-believers' common symbolic universe, which present-day Christians share, must be the starting point to help not only the Christians but also all those who hunger in the world in the twenty-first century. In particular, lowland Filipino Christians are challenged to be inclusive in their manifold efforts at addressing this form of injustice whether the hungry one is Christian or not, because they are *kapwa* too.

In solving the problems at Corinth, Paul appeals to the story of the Lord Jesus just before he was handed over. The Lord celebrates life by sharing a meal with his disciples even at the point of death. Paul points out that in continuing the celebration of the *kyriakon deipnon*, the main actor who commands character identification is the Lord Jesus. That is why partakers of the community meal ought to follow his example at table. The Lord, who exemplarily shared a meal in the story, is remembered faithfully when the *kyriakon deipnon* is shared especially to those who have broken bodies (see vv. 22 and 30). Paul's criticism of the Corinthian celebration that it is not "for the better but for the worse" (v. 17) is manifested in the need of the physical bodies lacking in nourishment that are neglected in Corinth to the point that many are weak and ill and many have died (v. 30). Faithfulness to Christ in sharing the Lord's Supper today must also be translated in sharing meals with those who hunger, those who are weak and ill and are dying because of malnutrition and food insecurity. The question of sharing the consecrated bread and wine today raises many doctrinal and liturgical issues. However, the example of Christ at table, commemorated at each Eucharist and in dialogue with the Filipino *pagsasalu-salo*, needs to be expressed at every eucharistic celebration and *at each time* Christians today share a meal with those who hunger and thirst, regardless of any kind of boundaries.

Now, why is a contextual reading of 1 Cor. 11:17-34 important for lowland Filipino Christians today? I hold that an attempt at a contextual interpretation of the Lord's Supper in Corinth is significant since the most common interpretation of Paul's command to the Corinthians to redress the issue in verses 33-34 has been used to separate liturgical/sacramental life from the challenges of everyday life and to justify and perpetuate this separation. The same is true with some current Filipino translations of the text.[13] This is equally important because the episode in 1 Cor 11:17-34 is never read fully in the liturgical readings of the church (Socias 2004: 407 and 1467-68). It is usually read on Holy Thursday but limited to the foundational story in verses 23-26. Verses 11-26, 33, are read on Monday of the twenty-fourth week in Ordinary Time. The rest of the narrative, especially verse 34, is completely silenced. The whole text is not allowed to question the present liturgical practice, whether it is akin to the Corinthian version, an *idion deipnon*, or to one that is faithful to the *kyriakon deipnon*, where the *adelphoi* eat the meal together and are satisfied because of a sharing that replicates Jesus' table-fellowship in the *ekklēsia tou theou*. Finally, the result of this contextual reading beckons Filipino readers like me to be cognizant, responsible, and creative in three ways: in our hermeneutical task in reading texts like 1 Cor. 11:17-34, in our liturgical and social meal celebration, and in our common response as a church of the poor to the injustice of hunger that plagues not only lowland Filipino Christians but a billion people around the world as well.

CONCLUSION

In this essay, I have attempted a conversation between the lowland Filipino context and its three aspects of hunger, meal culture, particularly *pagsasalu-salo* ("table-fellowship") and the value of *hating-kapatid* ("sibling-like partaking of food"), and the story of the Lord's Supper in Corinth (1 Cor. 11:17-34). I employed a narrative approach and focused on the characterization of the settings (*kyriakon deipnon* and *idion deipnon*; *pagsasalu-salo*, especially at the *pakikiisa* level) and the actors (Paul, the Corinthians as the haves and have-nots, Paul and the Corinthians as *adelphoi*; *kapatid*). I focused on the conversation between the Filipino context and the context of the Lord's Supper in Corinth in light of the importance of meal sharing as *adelphoi* from the perspective of the ideal *kyriakon deipnon* and the ideal Filipino *pagsasalu-salo* at the level of unity. I showed that a keen rereading of the Lord's Supper story, seen from the perspective of the Filipino *pagsasalu-salo* at the *pakikiisa* level, particularly in view of the value of *hating-kapatid*, challenges lowland Filipino Christians to reconsider how our culture and faith celebration expressed through the eucharistic celebration enhances our motivation to respond to the issue of hunger. I also underscored the importance of a contextual reading of the Lord's Supper story in the Filipino context.

The insights gathered in this paper may be affirmed or critiqued when this story of the Lord's Supper in Corinth is *read with* lowland Filipino Christians, especially with those who celebrate the Eucharist *and* those who wait begging for food outside of the church. I hope that this dialogue between the story of the *kyriakon deipnon* in 1 Cor. 11:17-34 and the lowland Filipino Christians influence the continued retelling of the story of the Lord Jesus' Supper and celebrating the Holy Eucharist with a renewed fervor. I also hope that partakers of the Lord's Supper today will be more cognizant of our individual and common responsibilities as table-fellows for all those who suffer the physiological effects of hunger in the Philippines and in the whole world.

Notes

1. For a discussion on lowland Filipino Christians, see de Mesa (1979: foreword): "The lowland Christian groups—Cebuano, Tagalog, Ilokano, Ilongo, Bikolano, Waray-Waray, Pampango and Pangasinan. These form a socio-cultural entity because they share a common cultural history and a common belief in Roman Catholicism which have reduced their cultural differences to a point where they are more than counter-balanced by cultural similarities."

2. While this is still generally the case in rural areas, other factors are slowly effecting some changes in the urban context. These changes are most obvious where eating out in fast food and at restaurants generally is becoming more common in cementing relationships through meals. Similar treatment of this section is also found in Ibita 2005; 2002.

3. *Hating-kapatid* can also be invoked involving other nonfood goods or properties to be shared, but it is usually employed in food and meal contexts. See the short film by Ignacio (2011).

4. Gerd Theissen (1982: 147–63) proposes that sociological issues on the background of 1 Cor. 11:17-34 contribute to the problem of hunger in the Corinthian community. These include the presence of the different groups at the *kyriakon deipnon*, variable beginnings for the meal, uneven amounts of food and drink and dissimilar quality of meals. I will not discuss the archaeological remains here due to the paucity of evidence from Corinth. For the most recent overview and proposals on the question of the spatial setting in the Corinthians Lord's Supper, see Schowalter 2010.

5. The predominant view interpreting 1 Cor. 11:17-34 in line with the importance of correct liturgical or sacramental celebration is difficult to hold together in view of vv. 22, 34a. I agree with Suzanne Watts Henderson (2002: 196) that the interpretations of vv. 22, 34 are usually "maintained, often with a touch of embarrassment, that these verses constitute the necessary escape clause of an at home eating option for the hungering 'haves.'"

6. See Hans-Josef Klauck (1993: 64): "Here the ritual practice of the community is anchored in history and referred back to a fixed point in the recent, not to say most recent, past." Likewise, see Watts Henderson (2002: 200): "historically grounded paradigm for transforming the community's eating and drinking according to the logic of Jesus' own self-sacrifice."

7. Petersen follows Peter Berger and Thomas Luckmann (1967: 92-128). David G. Horrell (1996: 53) prefers to refer to the symbolic "universe" as symbolic "order." According to him, "Pauline Christianity may best be understood as *a symbolic order embodied in communities"* (Horrell 1996: 54).

8. On the complex social composition of the Corinthians, see, for instance, Jerome Murphy-O'Connor (1979: ix–xii); Theissen (1982: 69–119); Horrell (1996: 91–101). For those who favor that the Corinthian Christians include both Jews and a gentile majority, see, for example, Gordon D. Fee (1987: 4); Richard B. Hays (1989a: 6); Horrell (1996: 75 and 91); Craig Steven de Vos (1999: 195).

9. See Aasgard (2004: 46), who explains that in times of economic crisis, siblings (specifically brothers), play a central role in taking care of the family needs.

10. See also Horrell (2005: 113–15), who speaks of "mutual regard" or "other-regarding morality."

11. See also Gerd Theissen 1982: 69–119, 107. Theissen (1982: 107 and 118n87) cites that the idea of love-patriarchalism is "derived essentially" from Ernst Troeltsch (1981: 69–89, particularly 78): "This is the type of Christian patriarchalism founded upon the religious recognition of and the religious overcoming of earthly inequality. . . . Its basic idea of the willing acceptance of given inequalities, and of making them fruitful for the ethical values of personal relationship is given. . . . As stewards of God the great must care for the small, and as servants of God the little ones must submit to those who bear authority; and, since in so doing both meet in the service of God, inner religious equality is affirmed and the ethical possession is enlarged by the exercise of the tender virtues of responsibility for and of trustful surrender to each other. It is undeniable that this ideal is perceived dimly by Paul, and only by means of this ideal does he desire to alter given conditions from within outwards, without touching their external aspects at all."

12. For a criticism of love-patriarchalism at the Lord's Supper, see also Kim (2008: 62): "It is not Paul but the rich who seek to practice this 'love patriarchalism': Paul's own view could be described as non-conformist 'compared to that of the rich.'"

13. See, for example, *Biblia ng Sambayanang Pilipino* (1990), which translates 1 Cor. 11:21-22 as *Sapagkat pag kumakain, nagmamadali and bawat isa sa sarili niyang pagkain, at may nagugutom at may nalalasing. 22 Wala ba kayong sariling bahay upang doon kumain at uminom?* and vv. 33-34a *Kaya, mga kapatid, kung magkakatipon kayo dahil sa hapunan, maghintayan kayo at kung may nagugutom, kumain sa bahay.* See also *Ang Biblia para sa Makabagong Filipina* (2005): 21 *Sapagkat ang bawat isa sa inyo'y nagmamadali sa pagkain ng kanyang baong pagkain, kaya't nagugutom ang iba at ang iba naman'y nalalasing. 22 Wala ba kayong sariling bahay upang doon kumain at uminom? . . . 33 Kaya nga, mga kapatid, kapag nagkakatipon kayo upang kumain, maghintayan kayo. 34 Kung may nagugutom, kumain na muna siya sa bahay.* The underlined word in v. 22, *sariling*, is a possessive personal pronoun (which is not in the Gk text) and the double underlined words in v. 34, *muna* (which can be translated as a temporal indicator, "first" [i.e., those who hunger must first eat a separate meal in their own house], is also not in the Gk text) indicate temporal and spatial separation between the personal house and the house where the community gathers. These additions results in a translation that supports the separation of the bread and wine from the full meal that must be eaten together in memory of the Lord Jesus (*kyriakon deipnon*).

PART III

Community, Women, and Sexuality

7

Pauline Theological Counseling of Love in the Language of the Zhuangzi

A Reading of Love in 1 Corinthians in a Chinese Philosophical Context

K. K. Yeo

INTRODUCTION

Paul's series of rhetorical interactions with the Corinthian Christians (as evident in a rhetorical analysis of 1 and 2 Corinthians) can be read as the apostle conducting "counseling sessions" with the divisive, narcissistic, arrogant, and problematic house churches in Corinth (Yeo 1995; Thiselton 2000: 26, 37, 41–47). Almost no Pauline scholars have attempted to read Paul in this way, perhaps out of fear of being anachronistic.[1] Yet scholars studying the Chinese Daoist philosopher Zhuangzi (c. 369–286 BCE) have no such reservations (Craig 2007; Huh 2004; Jung 1958; Rhee 1995; Skogemann 1986); needless to say, Western philosophers and writers have embarked on cross-cultural readings of the Daoist texts with much courage and curiosity.[2] My intention here is not to make any historical claim about an encounter between Zhuangzi and Paul (c. 2 BCE–64 CE). Rather, my attempt is to read 1 Corinthians through the eyes of the *Zhuangzi* (the philosopher's work goes by his name), noting the kind of intertextual relationship that can exist between the two documents for a reader of both classics.

Here, I interpret the theology of love in 1 Corinthians as Paul's way of counseling the problematic church at Corinth. I begin by reading Paul's theology through the philosophical language of love in the *Zhuangzi*. I then demonstrate that despite cultural and linguistic differences between Paul and Zhuangzi, the *Zhuangzi* elucidates 1 Corinthians for Chinese readers familiar with the language of classical Daoism. For readers unfamiliar with a Daoist worldview, this article enriches their understanding with a cross-cultural reading of 1 Corinthians.

LOVE AND CHRISTOLOGY IN 1 CORINTHIANS
AS PAUL'S THEOLOGICAL RESPONSE

The radical problems found in the churches at Corinth reflect an increase in the type of Christian "love-patriarchalism" (Theissen 1982: 122)[3] that Paul hopes will shift toward internal wholeness and external transformation.[4] In his rhetorical strategy, Paul employs the cruciform love (*agape*) to rebuild the body of Christ at Corinth. Paul's "theological counseling"[5] of the Corinthian Christians encourages them to love one another and to love God for the purpose of transforming the distorted body of the Greco-Roman world (Martin 1995; Kim 2008). Both the *Zhuangzi* and 1 Corinthians emphasize love as selflessness or self-offering generosity. Throughout the epistle, Paul prescribes love as the remedy to three serious problems. First, responding to the problem of dullness of worldly wisdom, Paul in 1 Cor. 2:9 quotes the *Ascension of Isaiah* (or paraphrases Isa. 64:3) in order to prove that God through his Spirit has revealed the crucified Messiah to those who love God. Second, responding to the problem of a "personality cult" in the church, Paul uplifts the apostles' "love in a spirit of gentleness" (4:21) with believers so that they may become the beloved (4:14, 17; cf. 15:58). Third, responding to the problem of the self-claimed "strong" and "knowledgeable" ones who are coercing brothers and sisters with a "weak conscience" to eat food offered to idols, Paul admonishes that "knowledge puffs up, but *love* builds up" (8:1).

It is telling that the conclusion of 1 Corinthians (16:1-24) ends with love: "Let all that you do be done in *love*. . . . Let anyone be accursed who has no *love* for the Lord. . . . My *love* be with all of you in Christ Jesus" (16:14, 22, 24). This ending serves as the reminder that *love* is what they need most. No wonder that, of all the Pauline epistles, 1 Corinthians is the only letter that has an encomium on *love* (13:1—14:1; *agape*).[6] Paul's purpose is to explain love as the most excellent way of life for Christians to live out their faith according to the paradigm of Christ. In other words, Paul is eulogizing Christlike love. One can easily substitute the word *love* with the word *Christ* in 1 Corinthians 13.[7]

The Pauline Christology in 1 Corinthians supplements and clarifies his theology of love. In 1 Cor. 1:1-9 (introduction), a Christology of the cross (crucifixion) and of the body (corporeal unity) stands out as Paul's thesis. Though the word *love* is absent, it is obvious that Christ's self-offering on the cross is the result of love because of his authentic nature. The work of Christ on the cross as love makes possible (1) the reunion of all believers with the Lord (1:9) in the community of the triune God; (2) the restoration of all believers as one body (1:2);[8] and (3) the sanctification of all believers so that they are free eschatologically from the power of sin (1:8).

The Christology in the section where Paul responds to hearsay problems (1:10—6:20) highlights God's love in Christ. First, Paul uses the Christology of unity (as seen in the rhetorical question, "Is Christ divided?" in 1:13) to counsel the Corinthians to "be perfectly united in mind and thought" (and in dealing with schism within the church and among church leaders; 1:10—4:21). Paul also chastises them to have "the mind of Christ (2:16) and not to be "infants" and "worldly" (3:1). He upholds Christology as the only, solid foundation of their faith and ministry (3:11). He also underlines that just as "Christ is of God," so are the Corinthian Christians "of Christ" (3:23). God's love calls them to Christ: having the mind of Christ is to embrace the divine love of unity and to build each other up through this love. Paul advocates the love-paradigm that he has lived up to—his "way of life in Christ Jesus" (4:17); for the good of the Corinthian Christians, he willingly becomes weak and is thereby dishonored (4:10-14). He admonishes them to imitate (4:16) his fatherly love (4:15, 21) for them as his beloved children (4:14, 17).

Second, Paul uses the Christology of the Passover Lamb (5:7) and body (6:15) to speak of God's sanctifying and cleansing presence (6:11) as he responds to the problems of immorality and litigation among Christians (5:1—6:20). The sacrificial-lamb motif of the Passover does not simply infer substitution; it illustrates the divine love that causes God to willingly sacrifice God's self in order to protect his own from judgment or condemnation. Thus for Christians to allow the legal standards of the world to condemn one of their own is insulting to what divine love has done (6:1-8). Also insulting to the divine sacrifice is the desire to be "united with a prostitute" (6:15). Such a connection betrays the unity of "bodies as members of Christ" (6:15).

The Christology in the section where Paul responds to the written issues (7:1—15:59) accentuates divine love that is communitarian and victorious over bondage and death. First, responding to issues of marriage (7:1-40), Paul articulates a view of celibacy and ethics of marriage that rests on his eschatological worldview. He maintains generous consideration for the freedom to whomever one is called, at whatever state of life, whether called to marriage or single status. Second, in order to bring the "strong" and the "weak" together with regard to the eating of food offered to idols (8:1—11:1), Paul affirms monotheistic faith in the one who will redeem all as he has created all (8:6). Thus, "wounding the conscience of the 'weak' means sinning against Christ" (8:12). Edifying love is to be understood as the saving Christ. Third, in the matter of worshiping—"communing"—with idols, Paul argues that the body and blood of Christ are the only ways of communion (10:16). Fourth, in the matter of gender relationships in the worship setting (11:2-15), Paul upholds the Christology of headship to imply the uniqueness of male and female. He affirms the mutual interaction of both as the reflection of the full glory of God, as Christ has re-created the fallenness of humanity after the first creation (11:11). Fifth, in regard to the love feast (11:17-24), Paul offers a four-step prescription for the Corinthians' shameful behavior of "divisions" (*schismata*, 11:18) (Maurer 1964: 959–64) and "differences" (*aireseis*, 11:19) (Schlier 1964: 180–83) between the "haves" and "have-nots" (*mē echontas*). The "assembly" (*ekklēsia*) (Roloff 1990: 410–15) "come together" (*synerchomenōn*) (Balz 1990: 304–5; Schneider 1964: 684) as they "eat/devour" (*prolambanei*) (Winter 1978: 73–82)[9] one another. In response, Paul counsels the Corinthians in the following manner:

1. He affirms that Jesus the Lord (used six times in 11:23-24) is the *host/patron* of the meal, who honors all without distinction.
2. He reminds the Corinthians of the sacrificial love of this host, in contrast to the self-seeking honor and promotion of the "haves" (hosts).
3. He teaches them the significance of the celebration of one body (in the bread and also in the ecclesial community), as a proclamation of "the Lord's death until he comes" (11:26).
4. He counsels them to "wait for each other" (*ekdechesthe*, 11:33) (Glasswell 1990: 407)[10] and admonishes the wealthy patrons of house churches to honor the poor at the table. The host is also the eschatological savior and judge.

Sixth, responding to the confusion of practicing their spiritual gifts (12:1—14:40), Paul uses body-Christology (12:12, 27) to teach order, unity, diversity, and mutuality. Seventh, correcting the question of bodily resurrection of believers (15:1-58), Paul proves from the Scriptures (15:3, 12) and eyewitness accounts (15:4-11) that Christ has been raised. The God of love has raised Christ from the dead for the sake of overcoming the power of sin and death: "God has given us the victory through our Lord Jesus Christ, and thanks be to God! (15:57).

Zhuangzi's Prescription and Paul's Theological Counseling

Paul's christological responses to the various problems found in the Corinthian church can be interpreted through Zhuangzi's understanding of love as he responded to vicissitudes of human life and the chaotic world during the Warring States period (480–221 BCE), when various states and overlords were at wars with one another. A few points on love in Zhuangzi are helpful lenses for the reading of 1 Corinthians.

First, love is selflessness, namely, *wangji* ("self-forgetting or letting go and let it happen").[11] Zhuangzi says that "the perfect person (*zhiren*) has no self (*wuji*), the transcendent person (*shenren*) has no accomplishment (*wugong*), the holy person (*shengren*) has no name (*wuming*)" (*Zhuangzi* ch. 1).[12] Second, to love is not for the purpose of profit, power, or self-advantage. Instead, love means befriending all, including other creatures in the universe such as frogs, birds, fish, and even the robber Chih who sucks on human livers (see *Zhuangzi* ch. 29). Ideally, a leader befriends his followers; Zhuangzi advocates that a ruler's love of the people—a sage-ruler's love—never comes to an end (ch. 15). However, elsewhere, he warns that when rulers are full of desire to love the people, they may end up harming them. Unfortunately, this intentional love is bound to become manipulative, and gradually turn to biased and self-serving love. Third, to love is not to follow the "cultured" or "civilized" ways of life, but to freely wander despite the tyranny of traditional mores and prevailing ideology. To love is to be creative and spontaneous, maximizing self and social freedoms. Thus, "to forget one's physical form" (*wang ji xing*) and "to forget one's heart" (*wang xin*) is different from maintaining one's "constant heart" (*zhang xin*), this last being "the ability always to attune harmoniously to changing circumstances" (Fleming 1999: 384). Fourth, love changes all. In Zhuangzi's language, love transforms (*hua*) all because we are intricately connected with the manifold, organic, and changing cosmos.[13] Paul's understanding of the body as an organic whole can be explained more powerfully by Zhuangzi's understanding of *Dao* as the natural, spontaneous, effortless, emerging, cyclical process of all things (*wanwu*). Fleming writes, "The *Dao* also denotes the unity and intimate interconnectedness of all things" (Fleming 1999: 381).

Because all things are organically related, the way of life is unity, and this process is called *hua*. Zhuangzi writes, "All the ten thousand things and I are one" (ch. 1). And, "If you were to climb up on the Way (*Dao*) and its Virtue (*De*) and go drifting and wandering (*you*), neither praised nor damned, now a dragon, now a snake, shifting (*hua*) with the times, never willing to hold on to one course only. Now up, now down, taking harmony for your measure, drifting and wandering (you) with the ancestor of the ten thousand things, treating things as things, but not letting them treat you as a thing—then how could you get into any trouble?" (ch. 20; Watson 1968: 209).

INTERCONNECTEDNESS WITH GOD/*DAO*, OTHERS, AND ONESELF

Paul's rhetorical theology as a way of counseling the church to love one another and to love God is similar to the *Zhuangzi*'s admonitions on living with *Dao*, others, and oneself. That is, the Pauline theology of love advocates that one align with the *Dao*/Creator, to love in the way of *wuwei* ("effortlessness") to relate to others as *wangji* ("self-forgetting, letting go, letting it happen rather than making it happen"). All of these are performed in *cheng* ("sincerity") and *chenren* ("authenticity").

Paul wants to bring the Corinthian Christians to a higher spiritual awareness via the "crucified Christ" (1:23, 2:2)—a "politics of metaphor" (Kim 2008). Robert E. Allinson describes this phenomenon similarly for Zhuangzi as the "myth of deconstruction and reconstruction" for the sake of self-transformation (Allinson 2003; 1989). For example, in the first chapter of the *Zhuangzi*, there is "the myth of a fish that is deconstructed as a fish and reconstructed as a bird" (Watson 1968: 4).[14] Paul preached only "Christ crucified" to the Corinthian Christians, so that they would deconstruct the surrounding cultures' ideals of power (Romans), religion (Jews), and wisdom/philosophy (Greeks). Through such self-deconstruction, they could then reconstruct holistic life found only in the "weakness" of God, "miracle-less" faith, and "foolish" understanding (1 Corinthians 1–2).[15] The deconstruction of body and self is for the higher purpose of attaining union with the *Dao*/Reality so that one identifies with the crucifixion of Christ and also comes into union with his resurrection: "It is because of him that you are in Christ Jesus, who has become for us wisdom from God—that is, our righteousness, holiness and redemption" (1:30). Chapter 3 of the *Zhuangzi* tells of the similar process of a crippled commander. This leader acknowledges that "When Heaven gave me life, it saw to it that I would be one-footed. . . . I know this was the work of Heaven and not of human beings. The swamp pheasant has to walk ten paces for one peck and a hundred paces for one drink, but it doesn't want to be kept in a cage. Though you treat it like a king, its spirit won't be content" (Watson 1968: 52).

The key to attaining *Dao* or entering into Heaven is through self-forgetfulness. The attempt to make things happen only manipulates and distorts the true Daoist nature of things: "Forget things, forget Heaven, and be called a forgetter of self. The person who has forgotten self may be said to have entered Heaven" (Watson 1968: 133). The word "forget" (*wang*) in the Chinese pictogram is made up of "losing" and "heart" (Cua 1977: 305–28). Our extrapolation reveals a self-centered, narcissistic self as the core problem in the Corinthian churches; Paul admonishes them to be forgetters of the self by recalling Christ's selfless love. The *Zhuangzi* advocates that "the Perfect Person (*chiren*) has no self" (ch. 1). It does follow that members of the perfect community be selfless, and by Paul's account, then, this community is unified in Christ's selflessness.

For example, Paul reproves the Corinthian Christians regarding their eating of food offered to idols. On the one hand, they should not allow their freedom to make fellow believers (especially brothers with a "weak" conscience) stumble (8:9). On the other hand, however, their freedom to eat food should not be limited or subjected to "raising question on the ground of conscience" (10: 25-29) but, rather, be conditioned by thankfulness to the Lord that all are created for his glory (10:26, 30-31). Thus Paul comes up with a "situational ethic"—"Therefore, if food is a cause of their falling, I will never eat meat, so that I may not cause one of them to fall" (8:13); "If I partake with thankfulness, why should I be denounced because of that for which I give thanks? So, whether you eat or drink, or whatever you do, do everything for the glory of God" (10:30-31). Paul uplifts a Christian ethic of greater freedom that will benefit and build up all people (10:23).

PAUL'S AND ZHUANGZI'S RHETORIC OF INEFFABILITY

In 1 Corinthians 1–2, Paul's powerful use of "pneumatic rhetoric" juxtaposed with his harsh critique of humanistic rhetoric appears incongruent. However, this discrepancy actually makes sense in light of what the twenty-sixth chapter of the *Zhuangzi* has to say about words and meaning: "The fish trap exists because of the fish; once you've gotten the fish, you can forget the trap. The rabbit snare exists because of the rabbit; once you've gotten the rabbit, you can forget the snare. Words exist because of meaning; once you've gotten the meaning, you can forget the words. Where can I find a person who has forgotten words so I can have a word with him?" (Wu 1982: 136). Allinson rightly explains that the *Zhuangzi* (true also of Paul) has ultimately deconstructed deconstruction:

> *What is forgotten is the descriptive function of the words.* . . . The
> metaphors, analogies, and poetic discourse of the *Zhuangzi* . . . are
> crucial to the very project of understanding. For understanding is
> only possible through the deconstruction of the literal that enables
> the higher cognitive function, which in turn allows one to "forget"
> language, that is forget its literal, descriptive use. . . . *This* is
> deconstructionism with a *difference.* . . . It is a deconstruction that
> never took place at all in the first place because there never was any
> subject matter to be deconstructed in the first place . . . and no one
> to perform the deconstruction. (Allinson 2003: 495)[16]

Thus, "when the shoe fits, the foot is forgotten. When the belt fits, the belly
is forgotten. When the heart fits, 'right' and 'wrong' are forgotten" (Wu 1982:
136). Likewise, the dialogue between Zhuangzi and his best friend Huizi
(Yan Hui) reveals the limitation of categorical and analytical thinking, and the
truth that "*Dao* (Way) gives shape and form to human beings. . . . Instead
of struggling to improve life, one simply abides in occurrence appearing of
itself—the Way it is" (*Zhuangzi*, ch. 5). Chapter 27 of the *Zhuangzi* speaks of
three kinds of rhetoric that are powerful and persuasive; thus Paul's rhetorical
interactions with the Corinthian Christians can be seen as equally therapeutic:

> *lodging place language (yuyan)* . . . This language . . . is to challenge or
> (at least) to relativize the position treated. The second, *repeated words
> (chongyan)* or (under another reading) *weighted words (zhongyan)*,
> involves words or language that gain a special authority because of
> the person who says them. . . . The third, *goblet or spillover words or
> language (zhiyan)*, receives its names because it resembles a vessel that
> tips when full and rights itself when empty or even just less than full.
> It involves language that moves from perspective to perspective or
> usage to usage in an everchanging fashion that utilizes but transcends
> ordinary kinds of linguistic representation. (Yearley 2005: 509)

Examples of *yuyan* occur in 1 Corinthians when Paul exhorts the
knowledgeable (strong) Christians to empathize with the weak-conscience
ones (8:1-13), and when he urges wealthy, powerful hosts to wait and honor
those believers who are in socially lower classes when it comes to partaking
the Lord's Supper at the homes of the hosts (11:17-34). Examples of *chongyan/
zhongyan* in 1 Corinthians are seen in the following: (1) Paul emphatically
proclaims the crucified Christ (1:23, 2:2); (2) Paul affirms the body of Christ

(10:16, 12:27); (3) Paul assures that Christ is risen (15:12-14); (4) and Paul eulogizes self-offering love (13:1-13). Examples of *zhiyan* in 1 Corinthians are: "I do not know whether I baptized anyone else" (1:16); "the message about the cross is foolishness to those who are perishing, but to us who are being saved it is the power of God" (1:18); "the world did not know God through wisdom" (1:21); "God decided, through the foolishness of our proclamation, to save those who believe" (1:21); "God's foolishness is wiser than human wisdom, and God's weakness is stronger than human strength" (1:25); and "God may be all in all" (15:28). Paul's correspondence reflects the dictum that "for now we see in a mirror dimly, but then we will see face to face. Now I only know in part; then I will know fully, even as I have been fully known" (13:12) by the great, ineffable *Dao*. Thus the healthy Corinthian believers ought to boast only in the Lord rather than in themselves (1:29, 31; 3:21; 13:3; 15:31) because the focus on the self leads to the division of the body of Christ (1:11-13; 11:18). If Zhuangzi and Paul are skeptics, they are not of the sense or ethical sort, but mainly of the epistemological and language variety.[17]

WUJI, WUWEI; SELF(LESSNESS) AND (IN)FINITUDE

There are too many strong-headed Christians at Corinth. Self-involvement gets in the way of communal unity. They assume they know fully, but Paul has a closer-to-Daoist understanding that *Dao*/Truth (the "all-in-all God") cannot be conceptualized, and we know only partially, like a frog (trapped in a well) and cicada (brief and temporary).[18] *Wu* ("nonbeing") is the origin and primordial state of all beings. The twenty-third chapter of the *Zhuangzi* writes: "The Heavenly Gate is 'non-being,' all things come from *wu*." One's self is in the constant process of interacting organically with others' as they all in the forms of *chi* ("vital energy") allow themselves to be part of, thus in tune with, the *Dao*, which is the source of, is, *wu*.[19] "Not only is each of us related to others in an infinitely complex, dialectical, and convoluted way, but we are also related to ourselves in similarly complicated ways" (Fleming 2002: 180). Zhuangzi's teaching of "forgetting" of the self and others and "perspectivalism require that we postulate an infinite (or at least indefinite) number of perspectives that are equally valid in regard to any particular situation; our freedom lies in our ability to shift perspectives" (Fleming 2002: 180). Craig writes: "*Wu wei* means, basically, not meddling or interfering with things, letting oneself and the world be. . . . *Wu wei* means *to allow oneself to be in a relational flow with the Dao*, with one's own *Dao*, with the *Dao* of others, with the *Dao* of all that is" (Craig 2007: 118).

The *Zhuangzi* provides numerous paradigmatic people in sync with the *Dao*, and thus they live out their best selves effortlessly; for instance, the cook Ding carves up oxen with such dexterity and ease (Graham 1981: 63–64), the wheelwright Pian's ineffable skill in shaping wheels is something not teachable (Watson 1968: 152–53), and the old man who swims at the Lu Liang waterfalls goes with the flow of the torrent and currents (Graham 1981: 136). What the Spirit does to members of the body of Christ is precisely this kind of difference in harmony, uniqueness in mutuality, interaction in synergy, so that "there are varieties of gifts, but the same Spirit" (12:4), "there are varieties of services, but the same Lord" (12:5), "there are varieties of activities, but the same God who activates all of them in everyone" (12:6), and "to each is given the manifestation of the Spirit for the common good" (12:7). "Members of the body that seem to be weaker are indispensable . . . whereas our more respectable members do not need [greater respect]. . . . If one member suffers, all suffer together with it; if one member is honored, all rejoice together with it" (12:22-26). And then Paul counsels them in "still a more excellent way—love" (12:31—13:1).

CONCLUSION

This essay has shown a slice of human psyche that is universal and that a self can be better diagnosed and healed cross-culturally. To be preoccupied with either one's own self or culture is to be without love. Though they are from different eras and circumstances, both Zhuangzi and Paul share similar views about the human psyche sick with self-inflation. Their prognosis is conflict or schism, and the prescription is selflessness, that is, love. Despite cultural and linguistic differences between Paul and Zhuangzi, Chinese readers of the Bible understand better both Zhuangzi and Paul as they intertextually read the Pauline theology of love with the *Zhuangzi*'s deliberation on *wuwei* ("effortlessness"), *wangji* ("self-forgetting; letting go"), and *chenren* ("authenticity"). The *Zhuangzi*'s admonitions on living with *Dao*, others, and oneself enrich the reading of Paul's rhetorical theology as a way of counseling the church to love one another and to love God.

Notes

1. Malherbe (1987), however, deals more with Paul's pastoral care.
2. In addition to the voluminous translations of Daoist texts by Westerners, there are more works: Charles 1988; 2003; Dreyfus 1991; May 1996; Parkes 1987; Yearley 2005.

3. Theissen (1982) says that "this love-patriarchalism takes social differences for granted but ameliorates them through an obligation of respect and love, and obligation imposed upon those who are socially stronger. From the weaker are required subordination, fidelity, and esteem." On demystifying therapy, see Spinelli 1994: 19–46.

4. Horrell (1996: 197) has a different view: "Paul's focus is certainly upon life and relationships in the church. . . . Paul shows little if any concern about transforming the world."

5. On the background of the movement of "philosophical counseling," see Lahav 1995: 1–24.

6. Reference works on love includes the following: Moffatt 1929; Furnish 1972; Perkins 1982; Warnach 1951; Spicq 1958–59; Brett 1992; Singer 1984; Whitehead 2009.

7. "If I speak in the tongues of mortals and of angels, but do not have *love/Christ*, I am a noisy gong or a clanging cymbal. And if I have prophetic powers, and understand all mysteries and all knowledge, and if I have all faith, so as to remove mountains, but do not have *love/Christ*, I am nothing. If I give away all my possessions, and if I hand over my body so that I may boast, but do not have *love/Christ*, I gain nothing. *Love/Christ* is patient; *love/Christ* is kind; *love/Christ* is not envious or boastful or arrogant. *Love/Christ* never ends. But as for prophecies, they will come to an end; as for tongues, they will cease; as for knowledge, it will come to an end. And now faith, hope, and *love/Christ* abide, these three; and the greatest of these is *love/Christ*. Pursue *love/Christ* and strive for the spiritual gifts, and especially that you may prophesy" (13:1—14:1; substitution based on the NRSV).

8. "The church of God in Corinth" constitutes "those sanctified in Christ Jesus and called to be holy," and all Christians universally are described as joined in one body. See 1 Cor. 1:2. See Thiselton (2000: 103, 179).

9. Witherington (1995: 249) disagrees and favors "go before" rather than "eat." See also Delling 19644:14–15.

10. Witherington (1995: 252) opts for "welcome," and Winter (1978: 79–80) for "receive," while Horsley (1998: 159) and Fitzmyer (2008: 448) prefer "wait for."

11. In Zhuangzi ch. 2: *wu sang wo* means "I have lost myself."

12. Unless otherwise noted, all translations of classical texts are mine.

13. *Hua, pien, fan*, and *huan* are different words used in the *Zhuangzi* to speak of transformation according to the Way and how we are interconnected with the manifold and changing cosmos. See Skogemann 1986: 81–90.

14. English full text available online: http://www.terebess.hu/english/chuangtzu.html. Allinson (2003: 488) writes: "The deeper, analogical truth that is prefigured here is a one-way transformation, from bound vision to unbound vision. It is not an endless, cyclical transformation of fish into birds and birds back into fish. It is a movement from lower to higher, from that which is bound to that which is free."

15. "For Christ did not send me to baptize, but to preach the gospel—not with words of human wisdom, lest the cross of Christ be emptied of its power" (1 Cor. 1:17). "But we preach Christ crucified: a stumbling block to Jews and foolishness to Gentiles, but to those whom God has called, both Jews and Greeks, Christ the power of God and the wisdom of God" (1 Cor. 1:23-24). "For I resolved to know nothing while I was with you except Jesus Christ and him crucified" (1 Cor. 2:2).

16. See also Allinson (2001; 2002).

17. See a helpful definition by Ivanhoe on four related forms of skepticism: "*Sense skepticism* is . . . the belief that one cannot trust one's senses to provide reliable evidence of the way the world really is. Plato is a sense skeptic but not an epistemological skeptic. *Ethical skepticism* is the belief that there are no moral truths. . . . *Epistemological skeptics* do not deny that there are objective facts about the world, a way it really is, they only deny that we can have reliable knowledge of those facts. Finally, *language skepticism* is the belief that knowledge is somehow inadequate for expressing certain facts about reality, at least in propositional form" (Ivanhoe 1991: 641).

18. See *Zhuangzi*, ch. 1; 1 Cor. 13:12.

19. Fleming (2002: 179) says: "The *Dao* is . . . equivalent to 'non-being,' and *te* ('virtue,' or 'potentiality') is a manifestation of the *Dao* in particular persons and things, then . . . one's 'potentiality' is a manifestation of the 'non-being' of the *Dao*. . . . *Dao*, *te*, and *wu* suggest that a particular person is endowed with a particular emptiness or non-being, without which it would be a static plenum of being, with no elbow room."

8

Reading 1 Corinthians 11:1-16 through Habits and Hijabs in the United States

Janelle Peters

INTRODUCTION

Veiling, in the modern American context, means visibility. To veil is to stand apart from the ordinary and the costume of one's contemporaries. This aspect of the extraordinary implied by veiling was found to some degree in Roman antiquity: men wore veils at sacrifice, and women veiled both to sacrifice and to exhibit their status as citizen women capable of being married. In this essay, I will propose that the veils of Catholic and Islamic modernity as expressed in the United States help us to see the authority (*exousia*) that would have been conveyed by women wearing veils at the worship meals of the Corinthian church. At the same time, a reading of modern veils through the antique discussion of interdependence in 1 Cor. 11:1-16 allows us to see an often-obscured system of mutual interdependence. Female veiling, which plays off the veiling of elite men, functions as a corrective to exclusions experienced by Catholics and Muslims as subcultures and by women as a subclass. The visibility of veiling too often draws our attention to the fashions themselves, a problem I myself often face as a Catholic well-versed in the visual grammar of religious habits. However, Paul's rhetoric returns us to the system of interdependence beneath the *habitus* of habits. Paul uses veiling to blur class distinctions and to promote group cohesion as a subculture through gender identification. Giving woman the *exousia* of the veil at the worship meal rather than man interrupts imperial narratives that see man as priest of his family on the order of Caesar himself. This is why Paul invokes the creation of the world, as his cosmogony competes with Roman cosmogonic religious claims.

VEILING IN THE UNITED STATES

The experience of being part of a subculture connects the Pauline house churches living in the early imperial Roman period and the communities of Catholic nuns and Muslim *hijabis* in the United States. While American Protestant biblical commentators on 1 Corinthians such as Richard Hays very generously include Catholics when highlighting the potential for Corinthian-like idolatry in Christian participation in subcultures like the American Civil Liberties Union and the National Rifle Association, sociologists view American Catholics and Muslims as participants in subcultures of a Protestant or secular society (Hays 1997: 144). Historian Martin Marty in his article "The Catholic Ghetto and All the Other Ghettos" has explained the historical underpinnings of this cultural perception among Catholics (Marty 1982). While television shows such as *The Colbert Report* prove that Catholics can participate in American popular culture, the issue persists. At my recent baptism training for my godson at my parish in Atlanta, I was admonished that, if I neglected to choose values to impart to my godson, television, that arbiter of the dominant culture, would choose for me. On a more national level, the *New York Times* recently discovered it was the subject of a media boycott by one of the most visible and influential members of the American Roman Catholic hierarchy.

Though Clifford Geertz has noted that religious symbols are particular to individual cultures, the veils of Catholic and Muslim women coexist in American culture (Geertz 1973: 3–23). Putting the veils of Catholic and Muslim women in the context of the United States in juxtaposition is, on some levels, quite natural on a structural level. The visual resemblance is analogous to the similarity of male and female habits in religious orders, which is meant to inspire solidarity; the viewer is supposed to identify male and female religious of a particular order with each other instead of identifying male clergy with men of other orders and female religious with women of other orders. Paradoxically, the observer must look closely at the veiled to discern the difference between religions, the difference among ethnic groups and religious orders, and the difference among individual women. Rather than a veil of a religious woman resonating with that of a secular one, the veils of nuns and Muslims resonate with each other to suggest female devoutness instead of the simple femininity of a metaphor for long female hair. As Umberto Eco has noted of dead metaphors, the standard, "dead" veil—a shabbier or more severe version of the headgear worn by every woman—has become reinvigorated (Eco 1983: 255).

On another structural level, Roman Catholic women religious and Muslim *hijabis* share a commonality: they are both a female category that exists outside of official, male-dominated hierarchies. Edward Idris Cardinal Cassidy, president of the Pontifical Council for Promoting Christian Unity from 1989 to 2001, has identified the character of interreligious dialogue with religions other than Judaism in terms of provisional dialogues motivated by personal exigencies (Cassidy 2005: 255). Under the heading of interreligious dialogue, he includes lay movements within the Roman Catholic Church, including the Focolare Movement (Work of Mary). Chiara Lubich founded the Focolare Movement, and its rules require its leader to be a woman. From the cardinal's hierarchical vantage point, the recognition of a Catholic female leader as a valid practitioner of Catholicism is the most commendable aspect of this movement (Cassidy 2005: 237). Both Catholic women religious and Muslim women inhabit structural positions similar to the Focolare, being outside of the official hierarchy of the Roman Catholic Church. The challenge, at this point, is to integrate women in theologically acceptable positions within the hierarchy.

MUSLIM VEILING

Veiling is not an immutable Muslim practice. That females should veil is never directly mandated in the Qur'an. The one verse in the Qur'an that uses the term *hijab* with respect to women and veiling is verse 53 of chapter 33: "And when you ask them [the Prophet's wives] for something, ask them from behind a veil [*hijab*]; that makes for greater purity for your hearts and for theirs." The other seven occurrences of the word *hijab* in the Qur'an refer to physical or metaphorical boundaries. Veiling was a restricted and highly honorific activity, indicating a woman had sufficient status to be protected. In the *hadith* tale of Muhammad's wedding with Safiyah, the distinction between wife and concubine turns on whether or not Muhammad presents Safiyah with the *hijab*: "If he confers on her the *hijab*, she is one of the Mothers of the Believers, and if he does not, she is a concubine" (Clarke 2003: 232). As Amina Wadud has noted, the egalitarian nature of modesty that she reads in the Qur'an is the primary appeal of *hijab*: "Modesty is not a privilege of the economically advantaged only: all believing women deserve the utmost respect and protection of their modesty—however it is observed in various societies" (Wadud 1999: 10).

In the United States, where veiling is not common among women, veils become a spectacle unto themselves. They thus can represent an act of female agency that affirms ethnic origin in the crosswinds of a more revealing secular American culture. In immigrant narratives, according to Samaa Abdurraqib, Muslim women have bodies whose veils mark them as other and "must create a new genre that defies the demands American culture places on conformity"

(Abdurraqib 2006: 56). At the same time, the performativity of wearing the veil as a Muslim veil constructs a subculture based on religion rather than on ethnicity.

CATHOLIC VEILING

Veiling has had a long tradition in the Roman Catholic sisterhood, arising out of non-Christian and secular customs and investing the woman involved with the status of being the bride of Christ. The primary contexts in which Roman Catholic women veil are upon meeting the pope and during activity as a woman religious or nun belonging to an order that veils. Roman Catholic women religious are differentiated between cloistered nuns and sisters who have apostolates in the community. Both are colloquially referred to as a homogenous group as "nuns" by Catholics and non-Catholics alike. Both have dress regulations specific to their congregations. In the United States, women religious whose orders veil belong to the Council of Major Superiors of Women Religious (Lafontaine 2008: 85). Nonetheless, individual orders such as the Carmelites have a great diversity of religious garb in different communities within the spiritual tradition. As I was told by a veiled Carmelite nun in my native archdiocese of Los Angeles, solidarity exists not just in fashion but in Rules and founders (Koch 1959; Ackerman 1995).

Despite the importance of Vatican II to many Catholic women religious and laypeople, some sisters out in the community have not worn habits for a much longer time than the 1960s. The first apostolic order of women religious in the United States was Elizabeth Seton's Sisters of Charity, founded in Baltimore in 1809. Upon entering the community, the sisters wore outfits similar to the widow's garb their founder Elizabeth Seton had worn since her death (Metz 1996: 21). In the 1950s and 1960s, sisters participating in government programs associated with the war on poverty and teaching in public schools were required to wear lay attire (Koehlinger 2007: 59). Women religious who wear distinctive religious garb thus assume a much greater visibility in the American context. The intentional nature of this visual play, what Henri Nouwen called "clowning" based on a real practice among post–Vatican II sisters, is evident in such statements as Sister Anne Flanagan's post on Twitter of a *Jezebel* article claiming that veiled Academy member Mother Dolores Hart was upstaging comedienne Maya Rudolph at the 2012 Oscars (Nouwen 1979).

To conclude, the veil in the modern American context is not being directly related to 1 Cor. 11:1-16 by either Muslim *hijabis* or Catholic habited nuns.

Catholic habits are connected with particular spiritual traditions and usually reflect some historical moment in the order's particular history. As such, Catholic habits can elide not only visually but also in remembered history with Muslim *hijabs* because orders such as the Carmelites adopted habits in historical places in which there were similarly attired Muslims. What has developed over time is not the connection of the habit with the biblical passage but the spectacularity of the habit. Veiling is not construed as martyrdom in the Roman spectacle. Rather, the visibility of the veil is extremely important in post–Vatican II American contexts in which most women no longer cover their heads either outside or within the worship setting. The irregularity of the nuns' garb in the present context resonates with Paul's instruction to Corinth that men should uncover their heads and women should cover their heads. Like the veiling of nuns and *hijabis*, the unusual costuming customs at Corinth could have encouraged solidarity across socioeconomic divisions among the Corinthian Christians. The unique dress regulations of Catholic and Muslim subgroups construct a notion of belonging to a subculture rather than assignment to the gender hierarchies of the dominant culture.

VEILING IN 1 CORINTHIANS

In Roman Corinth, the participants at the worship meal of the Pauline house churches were attending the sacrificial banquets of Roman gods. They would therefore have been thoroughly acculturated to Roman worship practices in which men veiled their heads. Paul's contravention of Roman culture would have had the same jarring effect that contemporary veiling in the United States has. Accordingly, Paul brackets his instruction on veiling with calls to social imitation, not of pagan norms, but of the practices of Paul and the other churches of God (Engberg-Pedersen 1991). Paul reminds the Corinthians of the order of creation by alluding to the Genesis creation narratives and referring to nature, inverting Roman anthropogonies. I will argue that what Paul is trying to accomplish by his veiling instructions is to create a subculture at Corinth so that the house churches identify with Christian values rather than Roman ones. As with modern nuns and *hijabis*, Paul's practical stipulations will have empowered the women because they were agents of effecting the transition to right understanding (Engberg-Pedersen 2000: 72–73).

SOCIAL CUSTOMS OF THE CHURCHES OF GOD

The helpfulness of the category of "subculture" for the Corinthian house churches is that the worldview and associated social practices exist both inside and outside of the communal assemblies. Inside the communal assembly, the Corinthian prophets are supposed to control their speech so that outsiders do not take them for barbarians (14:23). In social settings outside of the Pauline house churches, the Christians can recognize each other; this is how the weak are being led into errant theological understandings by the strong (8:1-13). The strong Christians are not supposed to abstain from idol meat in order to evangelize their pagan friends at the Greco-Roman association meal. If the meat is not announced to have been sacrificed to a god, it is acceptable to eat the meat. They do not need to ask their pagan friends if the meat has been sacrificed to a god in order to provoke a theological discussion. They need only abstain from meat they know to be sacrificed to idols in front of their weak Christian friends. This suggests that at least some of the Corinthians would have been participating in a number of associations together—perhaps indicating some socioeconomic homogeneity—and would have developed a subculture with the house churches as their primary identification (Theissen 1975). However, the strong wanted to be able to participate in Roman religious cult without subscribing to Roman religious understandings. Paul's advice to abstain implies that this inauthentic performance of religious cult is nonetheless detrimental to the health of the subculture and should cease.

If the Corinthian Christians are eating idol meat during their participation in the meals of Greco-Roman associations, they must be following veiling customs as well. Moreover, women must be present at these meals of the association. Paul's critique of the Corinthians' participation in the meals of Greco-Roman associations implies that the Corinthian Christians, as a community, cannot properly confine spheres of religious activity in their mental apparatus for faith. Likewise, Paul cannot be expecting the Corinthian Christians to have forgotten Roman status assumptions of veiling, namely, that one is a nonslave.

VEILING AND CREATION

Hence we must turn to the ways in which Paul's configuration of veiling is in contradiction with the Roman veiling schema in the Roman colony in Corinth, helping to establish a subculture of Christian values. Oster, Gill, and Winter believe Roman men were wearing veils at worship (Oster 1988: 484; Gill 1990: 250). Winter attempts to find a philological difference in the way the Roman male veils were described, observing that the veils seem to be hanging down from the head rather than hanging over it as one would expect from the veiled head of a Roman priest (Winter 2001: 95). The Corinthians' thoroughgoing participation in and acculturation to Roman worship meals and food sacrificed to idols means that Roman customs to honor the Christian deity were probably in full force among the Corinthian worship meals. A remnant of this desire seizing the Corinthian men to perform customs in the Roman style in the Roman colony of Corinth may perhaps be reflected in the humeral veil and the Baroque artistic depiction of the veiled Christ, which Julia Kristeva has connected to the veiled phallus at Pompeii (Kristeva 2011: 89–90). In any event, the contentiousness to which Paul refers at 11:16 was not only a custom of women being contentious and Paul suppressing them, as earlier feminist scholars have suggested (Wire 1990). Paul was denying men a custom that they would have found honorific.

Paul's denial of honor to men has not been thought to accentuate the honor of the women in the Corinthian house churches. While this position is common to those who argue for male veiling necessitating Paul's correction in 1 Corinthians, Winter has contended most thoroughly that the complementary female veiling Paul seeks to retain is supposed to be a traditional exhortation to appearing as an appropriate Roman matron. Winter translates *angeloi* at 11:10 as "messengers," envisioning women who need to appear respectable lest outsiders find fault with the Corinthian assembly (Winter 2001: 133). Paul, according to Winter, wanted to present the Corinthian female worshipers as chaste wives. Winter longs to see someone like Junia Theodora, who was honored with a crown by the Lycian Federation, exalted in greater detail in Paul's first letter to the Corinthians (Winter 2003: 186). He sees a filter-down of roles from Junia to Christian deaconesses like Phoebe (Rom. 16:2; Winter 2003: 204).

In determining the filter-down effect of Roman customs, however, it is important to consider the Roman mythico-religious precepts that underwrote the divine emperor. Paul's notation that women must veil "because of the angels" occurs within a unit of instruction rife with other references to creation. I assert that these references to creation both invoke and redefine the Jewish creation narratives from Genesis in order to neutralize the meaning-making activities of Roman myth in the worship meals of the Pauline house churches. First, I will explain what creation meant to Roman imperial theology. Then, I will suggest that Paul interacts with this theology when he alludes to the Jewish creation accounts in Genesis.

ROMAN CREATION

Creation was an important theological event for the Romans. The myth of the metallurgically named ages—gold, silver, and so forth—played a significant role in Roman imperial theology with the idea of the return to the golden age. Virgil's *Fourth Eclogue* prophesied a golden age, at which point the earth would return to its bounty without human work and without pollution from human impiety. Virgil's *Aeneid* specifically identifies Augustus as the one who fulfills the promise of the golden age (6.789-794; Jewett 2004: 26). Calpurnius Siculus (*Ecl.* 1.33-99) and the Einsiedeln eclogues (*Ecl.* 2.15-38) indicate that golden age propaganda continued well into the time of Nero (Harrison 2011: 103). Paul's doctrine of a new creation surely resonated with this Roman emphasis on creation and reconfigured it.

The Romans' perception of the present state of creation was also used to guide theological and behavioral norms. Ovid's *Metamorphoses* presents a Roman retelling of the Greek myth of the re-creation of humanity by Deucalion and Pyrrha, the sole survivors of the catastrophic flood (348–415). Apollodorus's second-century-BCE version (*Bibl.* 1.7.2; cf. *Scholiast on Hom. Il.* i.126) adds an explicit expression of the desirability of civilization to humans, who request additional humans from the deity. Common to these versions is the notion that the re-creation of a vibrant human society happens instantaneously rather than the slow accretion of numerical strength—and corresponding social diversity—as human reproduction runs its course over the centuries. In Ovid's *Metamorphoses*, an oracle tells Deucalion and Pyrrha to "throw the bones of their mother behind them" as they walk away from the temple. As husband and wife throw the stones behind them, humans emerge from the stones in the form of whichever gender has touched them (1.416-37; Wheeler 1995: 116). Ovid's *Metamorphoses* thus understands both men and women to function sacerdotally in the second creation of humanity. This corresponded with the priesthoods of Augustus and his wife, Livia.

PAULINE CREATION

What Paul needs to do is to promote a new creational ideology to promote the worship meals of the Pauline house churches as distinct from those of the Greco-Roman associations of Corinth. Paul's intentional engagement with the Roman creation tradition might be seen not only in his reference to creation in 1 Cor. 11:1-16 but also in the importance tradition plays in 1 Cor. 11:2 and in the letter as a whole. Paul refers repeatedly to passing on tradition, and 1 Corinthians contains all but one of his citations of traditions attributed to Jesus. As Daniel Boyarin notes, this is all in contrast to Galatians, in which Paul's authority derives from Paul's position as an apostle whose calling receives legitimation from a visionary experience of the spirit (Boyarin 1997: 185).

Roman mythology about the creation of humans, of course, is out of the question, as it does not account for Paul's promulgation of celibacy. In 1 Corinthians 7, Paul wishes that all the Corinthians may share in his marital status as a singleton. Such a desire directly contradicts the Roman social programs and legislation that encouraged marriage. Paul thus rereads the two creation accounts in the book of Genesis so that the second account establishes the interdependence between man and woman and the first account establishes the performance of gender differences. In the second account of creation in Genesis, God creates Eve from Adam's rib because it is not good for the man to be alone (2:18). This account, according to Paul's exegesis, means that woman is not independent of man, but that the two are mutually derived from one another. Paul is here referring to human production and reproduction, not the institution of marriage. Paul's notation that woman must veil "because of the angels" (11:10) attributes gender difference to the first creation of humanity, where God speaks to his angelic cohort (Gen. 1:26) and where marriage was not highlighted. The veils are not marriage veils, a fact emphasized by the metonymical role played by veils that stand in for hair.

Although the individual put on the new cosmological order in baptism, Taussig points out that the communal meal would have been the time when the community was most cognizant of belonging to this new world order. The communal meal provided a "protected environment in which the relationship to the occupying empire could be reflected on in a visceral manner but without the high stakes of life outside the meal" (Taussig 2009: 123). Traditionally, a libation was offered to the emperor as well as various patron deities. By sacrificing to Christ instead of the emperor, and by singing cosmic hymns that put forth an order of creation vastly different from that promulgated by the emperor, the Corinthians were envisioning and participating in a *kosmos* that was "at least implicitly and often explicitly an anti-imperial one" (Taussig 2009: 126). Women's liberty at the communal meal confronted the Hellenistic and early Roman *habitus* (Taussig 2009: 142–43).

That the Corinthian community should be re-creating the order of creation in their worship meals is not to be unexpected. The model used by the Corinthian prophets is akin to Philo's description of the cosmic male-female dance of the Therapeutae and Therapeutrides. This Jewish sect lived on the shores of Lake Mareotis, near Alexandria. Both men and women lived celibate lives in individual cells and spent their time in prayer and contemplative study. In *Vit. cont.* 83–87, Philo reports that the ascetic men and women are physically separated by a wall in regular sabbath meeting (30–33), but they share commensality at the sacred banquet (54–55). The culminating ecstatic Bacchic dance features a gradual blending of male and female choruses; it re-creates "in social practice the image of the purely spiritual masculo-feminine first human of which Philo speaks in his commentary—indeed that this ritual of the Therapeutae is a return to the original Adam" (Boyarin 1993: 11). Cosmic imagery resonates in dancing—the stars ordering the cosmos are known from Greco-Roman sources to be dancers (Euripides, *Ion* 1078–80, *Electra* 464–69; *Epinomis* 982e; *1 Clement* 20.3). In all of this, we observe that the invocation of creation at the Corinthian meals would have been familiar to the Corinthian community from both Jewish and Roman traditions.

INTERDEPENDENCE

It is merely Paul's conclusions about creation that would have challenged Corinthian understandings. Immediately after his creational allusion to veiling because of angels, Paul introduces the principle of interdependence. This principle in effect overturns his initial headship language, already severely compromised by its nonsequential presentation. Paul says plainly and clearly that "in the Lord, woman is not independent of man or man independent of woman" (11:11). This interdependence, however, is often thought to subordinate woman. I will argue that Paul's conception of the interdependence between the sexes effectively overturns preexisting societal hierarchies that he invoked earlier in his argument. Thus, unlike Paul's classless androgyne in Galatians, Paul's vision of creation reinscribes gender differences while simultaneously removing women from secular gender differences.

Interdependence is a recurring theme in 1 Corinthians. As a letter of concord, 1 Corinthians is aimed at promoting harmony among the members of the Pauline house churches in the Roman colony (Mitchell 1992: 65). The central metaphor Paul uses to organize this unified group with great diversity of members is the metaphor of the body. Rather than ostracize the less honorable members of the body, Paul clothes the shameful members with greater honor.

In Paul's language of interdependence in 1 Cor. 11:8-12, we find a distinction between mythic time and real time, but that distinction collapses as the mythic time of woman coming from man is compared directly to the real time of man being born of woman. Paul emphasizes the interdependence of man and woman through the logic of biological reproduction (Kähler 1960: 44; Jervis 1993; Gundry-Volf 1997). This was a fait accompli for both men and women, and it did not mandate that women act in the capacity of wives. Paul here frames his argument primarily in terms of the second creation account in Genesis, where Eve is created from Adam's side. To subvert the second creation narrative and return women to the first creation narrative, where men and women are created at the same time, which is the creation narrative of the better Adam according to Philo and others in the Second Temple Jewish milieu, Paul gives women a head-covering "because of the angels." This head-covering gives women *exousia*, "authority," and prioritizes the fact that the divine precedes the biological. Women at the Corinthian worship assembly have already overcome whatever fleshly ontological constraints they might have had, and they worship with men as fully attuned with God, not with imperial norms.

Paul's subversion of the second creation account has manifold ramifications. Individuals need not marry—whether they had the legal ability or not, which was a real question for slaves and those of low birth—in order to form pairs to procreate, in mimesis of God's creation of humanity (Harrill 1995: 122). In a sense, the primal androgyne was being re-created in the Pauline house churches (Meeks 1974). Finally, the Christian male is separated from the pagan male, whom moralists praised for satisfying his lusts lawfully with prostitutes rather than in illicit affairs (e.g., Horace, *Sat.* 1.2.32–35; Pollmann 2005: 95).

INSTRUCTIONS TO VEIL BASED ON NATURE

The same inversion of expectations that we find in the creation narratives happens in Paul's discussion of so-called natural hairdressing practices. Paul's appeal is a last resort, just before his concluding appeal to the customs of God. He demands of the Corinthians whether or not nature itself confirms his views on gendered veiling. In 11:14, Paul notes that if a man has long hair, it is shameful to him. However, in the next verse, we learn that a woman's hair is her glory (*gynē de ean komā doxa autē estin*). This is because a woman is meant to be covered, and her hair acts as a cover.

The metonymic function of the veil for female hair further corroborates the veil as an honorable accessory. Earlier in his instruction, Paul states in 11:5-6 that long hair is a woman's glory and that without her veil she might as well have the shorn head of a slave or a fallen woman. In the early imperial period, both Ovid and Martial refer to "captured hair" (*captivos crines*), which would have come from captured slaves in the case of German blond, as an accessory for the elite (Ov., *Am.* 1.14.45–46; Mart. 14.26; Bartman 2001). Not to have hair meant not to have legal status. To have hair is to have glory (*doxa*). The veil puts *exousia* on top of *doxa* and stands in, metonymically, for *doxa*.

Paul's assignment of the veil as a metonym for female hair causes him theoretically to dismiss Jewish ritual practices involving long hair for men. The "nature" Paul is invoking clearly is not that of the Jewish religious world, modern or ancient (Walker 1975: 108).[1] Naziritic vows, established for Jewish men and women since the times of ancient Israel, involved growing the hair long, abstaining from wine, and avoiding contact with the dead. Naziritic vows remained popular in Second Temple Judaism among both men and women. In Acts, Paul is said to have shorn his head at Cenchreae after a vow (Acts 18:18), and four men (Acts 21:17-26) are in need of hair-shaving and purification (Chepey 2005: 173-74). While it may be that the long hair of a nazirite represents extraordinary ritual time, extraordinary too is the ritual time within the context of the worship meal.

When Paul says that long hair is degrading, he is referring primarily to Roman cultural norms. This is a savvy rhetorical move for an apostle dealing with a community he characterizes as formerly having worshiped Greco-Roman idols. In the modern era, Emmanuel Levinas has argued that medieval Jewish thinker Maimonides's legacy was to have posited in *Guide for the Perplexed* a cosmic order beyond the world's law without borrowing notions from the world (Sirat 1990: 175-204). What former Pharisaic Jew Paul has done is to create a world order that does not correspond to even his own continuation of Jewish practices, let alone Roman order.

CREATING A SUBCULTURE

Thus far, we have seen that Paul is recoding symbols in order to provide the Corinthians with a modified symbolic universe, a subculture in harmonious contact with the dominant culture but demonstrably different from it. Women in the Pauline house churches need not have the social status of a wife in order to veil. But when women with sufficient status to visit the dinner party of a Greco-Roman association went to dine with others, how would they and their husbands have experienced themselves as being part of a subculture? I suggest that these women would have experienced themselves as more liberated in their secular activities because they would have residual understandings of the veil as tied to the Genesis creation narratives rather than the Roman imperial matrimonial imperative. Moreover, men would have been precluded from assimilating to the emperor in his role as *pontifex maximus*, thus depriving men of civic honor but endowing them with Christian orientation.

Scholarship has tended to overdetermine the elision of veiling and seclusion in antiquity. The veil, it is argued, is an extension of the domestic space. Wearing a veil allows a respectable woman to enter the public sphere because she is essentially traveling in mobile seclusion. It is an apotropaic, or, in the language of Dale Martin, a prophylactic device (Martin 1995: 229-49). Plutarch, for instance, uses the image of the tortoise to describe the ideal woman's relation to the world. He observes, "Pheidias represented the Aphrodite of the Elians as stepping on a tortoise to typify for womanhood staying at home and keeping silent" (Plutarch, *Moralia* 142D). A woman should remain in her house, but, should necessity arise, she may leave her abode by carrying it with her symbolically in the form of a veil (Llewellyn-Jones 2007: 251). Lloyd Llewellyn-Jones lists the polysemy that many of the words for veil have with concepts such as curtains, window shutters, city walls, towers, and battlements (Llewellyn-Jones 2007: 252).

Here is where we run into problems, though: veils and curtains exist simultaneously, and curtains are sometimes chosen in the public sphere. Calpurnia, Pliny's wife, sat behind a curtain to hear Pliny orate (4.19.3). Veiling alone was simply not good enough for her. Similar is *Acts of Paul and Thecla*, where Thecla, an unmarried woman, hears Paul preaching from her window. Even Philo's Therapeutrides separate themselves from the Therapeutae for significant portions of their worship life. Even by the most stringent standards, veils mean that men and women are mixing together just as wine and water are intermingling at the Corinthian worship meal. Moreover, Paul's universal treatment of veils means all veils should fall under the Christian system rather than the patriarchal Roman imperial epistemology.

The Corinthian worship meal can more profitably be compared to the cultural musings such as those of Cornelius Nepos, who finds Roman women differ from their Greek counterparts in being able to participate at the dinner parties.

> Who among the Romans is ashamed to take his wife to a party [*convivium*]? In whose household does the mother [*mater familias*] not hold the place of honor and circulate in full public view? These things are quite otherwise in Greece. The woman is not invited to a party except with relatives, nor does she sit down anywhere in the house except in the inner part which is called the women's quarter [*gynaeconitis*], where no man can approach unless closely connected by family ties. (*Lives*, preface, 6–7)

Corinth is a Roman colony in Greece. Paul wishes the Corinthians to split the difference between Greek customs and Roman ones. Rather than being a polemic against the Roman new woman, then, as Winter has argued, Paul's rhetoric might reflect a moderate position. Women, as the glory of men, are visible. It is not necessary for women to hide themselves for men's glory to be evident, as Morna Hooker suggested (Hooker 1963). Rather, unlike Calpurnia, women must be visible for men to have any glory.

DEVELOPING A SUBCULTURE IN THE PAULINE HOUSE CHURCHES

The presence of veiling subcultures in the United States alerts us to methodological possibilities that might be helpful in illuminating the historical situation of 1 Corinthians. There is a tension in Pauline studies between regarding the Corinthian house churches as a microcosm of the dominant culture, with values largely in line with those of the Roman Empire, and regarding the Corinthian house churches as a subculture, with values slightly different from—but not in opposition to—the dominant culture. No one, of course, regards the Corinthian house churches as a counterculture on the order of the communal vision described in the Apocalypse of John, where every rhetorical tool possible is thrown against imperial imagery. After a consideration of what elements the Corinthians are in fact appropriating from Roman culture, I will suggest that the various theories as to Paul's promotion of a tightly knit church with a homogenous outlook, as Jerome Neyrey has suggested, or a strong impulse toward unity based on mimesis, as Elizabeth Castelli has suggested, are based on compelling evidence that points to Paul's intent to bolster a subculture, with its own ethos (Neyrey 1986; Castelli 1991). This would have distinguished the Corinthians from the overlapping *collegia* to which denizens of Corinth would have belonged, helping them to identify themselves as Christians rather than as members of multiple guilds equal to Christianity (Harland 2003).

Studies that envision Corinthian head-covering in the worship assembly as an extension of Roman mores inevitably downplay the formation of a subculture discernibly different from the dominant culture (Robbins 1996: 86–87). Winter, in particular, argues that the Pauline house churches were dependent on the developments of Roman society for the creation of social norms in the Roman Empire. Women like Junia Theodora residing in Corinth (c. 43 or 57 CE), a powerful woman who was honored by the Lycian Federation, provided the secular precedent for the leadership of women like Phoebe in the Pauline house churches (Winter 2003: 183–86). On the other hand, Winter believes that women were restricted from their activities because of Roman elite anxiety about the rise of the "new woman" as a threat to traditional Roman mores. The new woman was influential not only for her social position but also for her novel self-fashioning. Drawing on the work of Richard Bauman, Winter observes that a dossier of three examples of women pleading their cases quite vocally exist in Valerius Maximus. One of these women, known as either Afrania or Carfania, is the reason that women were prohibited from postulating for others (*pro aliis postulare*). Elite male Roman disapproval of such behavior would have chilled Paul's desire to allow women to be overly ostentatious when outsiders were present.

Winter posits external social pressure on the Pauline house churches to embrace conservative norms. He translates the *dia tous angelous* at 11:10 as "because of the messengers" rather than the more accepted "because of the angels" (Bauman 1992: 50–51). For Winter, the Corinthians are being policed by unexpected incursions from outsiders who are inimical to the egalitarian Christian customs that might otherwise be practiced. Winter's theory thus dispenses with the proposal by Murphy-O'Connor that the angels in the community would have necessitated appropriately attired heads for women and those by Dale Martin and Troy Martin that the erotic, beguiling hair of women was protected from the angelic phallus by the prophylactic of the veil (Martin 1995; Martin 2004; Goodacre 2011). Winter constructs a sociological model that assumes active policing of the Pauline community in Corinth by the outside culture.

Other scholars such as Oster and Gill, though, have persuasively argued that the Corinthian house churches to which Paul wrote 1 Corinthians would have perceived a loss of status in Paul's proscription of male head-covering (Oster 1988; Gill 1990; cf. Finney 2010). Support for this perspective may be found in Paul's assertion that the etiology of disease within the community is the unequal distribution of food at the Corinthian worship meal and the squabbles over who has the better baptizer. The Corinthians expect to have the customary forms of status in their new religious association. Paul's appeal to creation is a reminder that the forms of status that the Corinthians seek no longer have mythological justification. This may mean that his reference to the angels is part of his set of allusions to the Genesis creation narratives in 1 Corinthians 11, since angels were present at the moment of creation (Brun 1913; Parry 1916: 161). This could be extended further to posit that gender differences were ordained by angels at creation (BeDuhn 1999: 308). Alternatively, it may mean that Paul literally envisions angels in the community as guardians of the created order, as we see in the Hodayot (Fitzmyer 1990). Such an interpretation certainly seems to be operating a few generations later at Corinth in *1 Clement*, when the church of Rome calls on the church of Corinth to see that the community possesses angels among them who affirm that the order of worship is to be preferred over other orders.

This brings us to the second idea, namely, that Paul is constructing a subculture with a cohesive identity. One approach deals with the charismatic founder-figure of Paul, who exhorts the Corinthians to be imitators of him (Betz 1994: 254). Castelli has analyzed Paul's call to exclusivity in 1 Corinthians in terms of imitation: "The call to sameness (with Paul) in 11:1 is paradoxically bound up with the call to exclusivity (difference) from the rest of the world. The action of imitation again has no specified content, but refers rather to a gesture which would set Christians apart as Christians" (Castelli 1991: 114). Another approach suggests a subculture that is congealing around a shared symbolic universe. Neyrey has described the strong group cohesion of 1 Corinthians in terms of the anthropological group-grid model of Mary Douglas. In Douglas's theory, a strong grid group has a highly homogenous worldview. Neyrey proposes that Paul creates such a worldview through his regulation of bodily orifices (1990: 111). In any event, there are definitely practices such as the consumption of idol meat that Paul wants to regulate in order to inculcate the right theological understanding. Paul specifically states that the strong are to abstain from idol meat for the sake of the theological understanding of the weak.

What we have, then, is a Corinthian community fully enmeshed in the dominant culture of the Roman colony of Corinth and an apostle who is trying to form the Corinthians into a subculture.[2] Paul takes a strident tone at some points in the letter to emphasize the alterity of the Christian experience in empire. Embracing the social death that was the arena, Paul claims that he is a "spectacle [*theatron*] to the world and angels and human beings" (1 Cor. 4:9). Like Christian abstinence from sacrificed food, Paul's male Corinthians must forego the pagan forms of veiling. The status distinctions that would have prohibited some men and women from veiling are eradicated, encouraging cohesion within the subculture and not within social class.

Conclusion

Veils are spectacular by nature. Just as Paul's eyes are helpful by the borrowed veil of a female Christian in the legends surrounding his execution, the acuity of the theological understanding of the Pauline Christian house churches at Corinth is abetted by gendered veiling (*Pass. Paul.* 14, 17; *Acta Pet. Paul.* 80). Rather than prescribing veiling practices derived from the dominant culture, Paul recommends veiling rituals based on Jewish-Christian myth. In this way, Paul subverts Roman imperial ideology, supporting those less enfranchised by the Roman power structure. The Corinthians who attended worship meals at the Pauline house churches would have carried these subversive understandings with them into other worship settings. This type of distinguishing feature is what creates a subculture, something the fractious Corinthian house churches desperately needed.

From our modern experience of veiled Roman Catholic women religious and Muslim *hijabis*, we can see the performed agency such unusual veiling might signify. The Corinthian women prophets and American veiled women both constitute moments of cultural transition. Dialogue and negotiation are an essential part of any transition. Because the veils serve to dismantle hierarchies rather than erect them, they must be a sociological phenomenon in a subculture to retain their unique character. Veils create solidarity within a subculture—as seen when the Corinthian men renounce status as household priests to allow all women to have the high social status connoted by a veil—and between subcultures—as exemplified by the Los Angeles Carmelites' sense of kinship with Muslims. However, when worn en masse, veils replicate the inequalities of the hierarchies of the dominant culture. Paul's grounding his instruction on veiling in the creation narratives of Genesis is an attempt to bypass the congested arteries of the Roman imperial heart and to prime it for membership in the egalitarian body of Christ.

Notes

1. The modern Jewish ritual interest in male hair and grooming may be seen in the Hasidic movement, whose men have long hair. A boy in the Hasidic movement has his head cut for the first time at the age of three.

2. For definitions of "dominant culture," "subculture," and "counterculture," see Robbins 1996: 86.

What Queer Hermeneutics Can Do for Us in Spain

The Case of 1 Corinthians 6:1-9

Luis Menéndez Antuña

INTRODUCTION

In 2004, PSOE (a socialist, left-wing party in Spain) won the elections with the proposal, among others, of legalizing same-sex marriage. Once in office, they passed a bill on June 30, 2005, that conferred marital status on same-sex couples wishing to become legally married. Thus, since July 3, 2005, anyone, regardless of their partner's gender, is able to get state recognition in terms of marriage.[1] It might come as a surprise that a traditionally Catholic society became the third country in the world to open the marital gates for queers.[2] It is less astonishing that the main Spanish religious institution has belligerently opposed such legislation and has mobilized its members against what it considers "a threat to the foundation of Western Civilization." What was new in this case was that the resistance became a well-organized movement that took to the streets in an unprecedented manner.

Documents issued by the Spanish Catholic hierarchy on this matter date back to "Marriage, family and homosexual unions" (Conferencia Episcopal Española 1994), a document that expressed the main views of the Catholic Church regarding homosexuality. Later, in 2003, the Congregation for the Doctrine of the Faith would summarize the official stance in response to the recommendation issued by the European Parliament to lift the ban of same-sex marriage (Sacred Congregation for the Doctrine of the Faith 2003).[3] The official Catholic documents frame the debate in terms of a deep truth crisis (Sacred Congregation for the Doctrine of the Faith 2003: n. 2) that betrays an understanding of sexuality as a transhistorical and transcultural phenomenon.[4] The documents further establish a difference between the "homosexual condition" and "homosexual behavior," the first being nature-given and thus not subject to moral/ethical judgment. The adage "love the sinner, hate the sin" is reformulated by making a conceptual difference between "inclination"—not necessarily a sin but definitely "objectively disorderly"—and a "behavior" portrayed as "always intrinsically wrong from a moral standpoint" (Sacred Congregation for the Doctrine of the Faith 1986: n. 3).

The Catholic documents argue that civil law cannot regulate against the nature of humanity as revealed in the Christian tradition (Conferencia Episcopal Española 1994: n. 8). According to this view, any political organization needs to foreground its legitimacy on Christian grounds: Truth equals revelation, and faith stands over reason. Homosexual behavior opposes "natural law" (Conferencia Episcopal Española 1994: n. 9) by not fulfilling the rule of complementarity between the sexes, and not being open to procreation.[5] Unity and procreation define natural sexuality. Such an axiomatic definition is scripturally based on Gen. 1:27, which, in turn, explains the "why" of the condemnation of Sodom (Gen. 19:1-11), the exclusion of the homosexuals from the "chosen people" (Lev. 18:22 and 20:13) and the resulting Pauline censure of pagan sexual mores (Rom. 1:18-32; 1 Cor. 6:1-11; 1 Tim. 1:10). After lumping together these diverse biblical references, the church concludes that same-sex couples are intrinsically unable to experience true marital love. To put the argument more clearly, since only male and female fulfill complementary roles, and marriage is the manifestation of such fulfillment, no civil law can overturn this God-given order (Conferencia Episcopal Española 1994: n. 11). Although the basic premises and the conclusion of the argument remain constant, the articulation of biblical textual support varies greatly according to circumstances.[6] For instance, marriage as an institution can only be regulated by the state when conforming to nature or to universal history (Conferencia Episcopal Española 2004: n. 4). Traditional marriage equals the marriage between Christ, faithful husband who fecundates the church, and his wife, begetting numerous offspring (Conferencia Episcopal Española 2004: n. 6). In terms of scriptural references, the "Letter to the Bishops of the Catholic Church on the Pastoral Care of Homosexual Person" is the most important document, and as such, I quote it at length (Sacred Congregation for the Doctrine of the Faith 1986: n. 6):

Providing a basic plan this entire for understanding discussion of homosexuality is the theology of creation we find in Genesis. God, in his infinite wisdom and love, brings into existence all of reality as a reflection of his goodness. He fashions mankind, male and female, in his own image and likeness. Human beings, therefore, are nothing less than the work of God himself; and in the complementarity of the sexes, they are called to reflect the inner unity of the Creator. They do this in a striking way in their cooperation with him in the transmission of life by a mutual donation of the self to the other. In Genesis 3, we find that this truth about persons being an image of God has been obscured by original sin. There inevitably follows a loss of awareness of the covenantal character of the union these persons had with God and with each other. The human body retains its "spousal significance" but this is now clouded by sin. Thus, in Genesis 19:1-11, the deterioration due to sin continues in the story of the men of Sodom. There can be no doubt of the moral judgment made there against homosexual relations. In Leviticus 18:22 and 20:13, in the course of describing the conditions necessary for *belonging to the Chosen* People, the author excludes from the People of God those who behave in a homosexual fashion. Against the background of this exposition of theocratic law, an eschatological perspective is developed by St. Paul when, in 1 Cor 6:9, he proposes the same doctrine and lists those who behave in a homosexual fashion among those who shall not enter the Kingdom of God. In Romans 1:18-32, still building on the moral traditions of his forebears, but in the new context of the confrontation between Christianity and the pagan society of his day, Paul uses homosexual behavior as an example of the blindness which has overcome humankind. Instead of the original harmony between Creator and creatures, the acute distortion of idolatry has led to all kinds of moral excess. Paul is at a loss to find a clearer example of this disharmony than homosexual relations. Finally, 1 Tim. 1, in full continuity with the Biblical position, singles out those who spread wrong doctrine and in v. 10 explicitly names as sinners those who engage in homosexual acts.

The Spanish government, on the other hand, passed a bill advocating an altogether different conception of marriage and family.[7] The law traces its origins to the French civil code (1804) as the founding document for the previous national legislation (1889) that defined marriage as taking place between persons of the opposite sex. New legislation needs to be introduced, the government argues, in order to reflect the social changes that Spain has undergone in the past century. Social and cultural changes demand a shift in a law that has become obsolete. While the Catholic Church bases its argumentation on a supposedly immutable human nature, the government seeks to shape the legal system according to a reality that has become "richer, more plural, and dynamic that the society than gave birth to the 1889 civil code." The bill seeks, ultimately, to put an end to a long history of stigmatization and marginalization.

From the church's point of view, a betrayal of "the traditional values" deriving from "eternal knowledge" undermines the basic foundations of the family structure and, by extension, culture and civilization. Thus the conflict is not only about "marriage," or legal issues for that matter, but about who gets to define the moral standards upon which democracy is to be based. This "from-top-to-bottom" ethics is at odds with a civic vision, espoused by the government, sensitive to cultural change. Civil law, it is argued, must account for changes in moral values, especially when related to histories of oppression. No pregiven natural order ought to hinder the dialogic negotiation of common civil rules.

In sum, church and state hold opposite views on tradition,[8] and on the virtual links between law and society.[9] The clash between the religious hierarchy and the government is not exclusively a conflict over the definition of marriage but represents a condensation of struggles for power.[10] To put it differently, sexuality becomes a metonymy of a culture war. By exploring the use of scriptural texts in the national contextual setting, I aim to (1) analyze the theory of meaning underlying the church's interpretation, (2) to sketch a plausible alternative reading of the texts, and (3) to suggest a hermeneutical approach that brings to the fore some of the blind spots resulting from the way the debate has been framed.

MEANING OF TEXT AND CONTEXT

An intercontextual analysis of the function of scripture in the Spanish religious and political reality shows that religious rhetoric does not single out specific passages, but inconsistently merges them to further ideological clams. As shown in the documents, 1 Cor. 6:1-11 and Rom. 1:26-27 are woven together with other biblical references to support the supremacy of the heterosexual family, its procreative role (Genesis 1–3), and the exclusion of same sex-relationships (Leviticus) that culminates in the Pauline texts. The church crafts a univocal biblical tradition with the purpose of countering secular understandings of the erotic.

Although scholarly interpretation disputes several issues pertaining to Romans and 1 Corinthians, most exegetes agree that both texts embody the apostle's indictment of certain pagan practices. The Catholic Church mines this interpretation of "Christ against culture" in order to buttress "traditional values" and dismiss governmental attempts to match cultural and legal changes. The Christian message, condensed in Paul's theological statements, is characterized as having an essence regardless of its contextual and historical roots, and defined against a pagan culture always in decay. Such indictment of secular cultural values is not, by any means, exclusive of the national context, as contemporary political debates on religion, politics, and sexuality show. In this sense, Spain is simply a privileged example of a more global trend because of its complex history of contentions between church and state. Concerning biblical hermeneutics, the Catholic Church resembles many conservative, but also some progressive, denominations in the United States that justify their position on the issue by resorting to literalism and to what I would call a "plain version of historiography." By literalism, I mean, quite simply, the assumption that Paul, although writing his works constrained by a specific context, is able to transcend his setting and speak normatively to Christians across times and cultures. By "plain version of historiography," I understand a view defending a total correlation between the present and the past, with no hint of a sophisticated methodological reflection on the epistemological conditions that regulate our representations of the other. Further, both strategies privilege "authorial intention" as the ultimate criteria in discerning a supposedly original meaning.

Take for instance the similarities between conservative and liberal denominations. Conservative churches, on the one hand, posits a continuum between sexuality in the past and in the present. As the argument goes, since Paul condemned same-sex relations on religious grounds, contemporary Christians cannot condone such behavior. Here, Paul's words are interpreted literally in that his expressions are understood to have a clear meaning in the past (more on this below). Subsequently, the meaning is to be transferred to the present. To summarize the argument, *arsenokoites* and *malakos*[11] refer to homosexual behavior in the past, so Paul's stance still applies regardless of historical variations. Liberal churches, on the other hand, assume the same past-present continuity in terms of the sexual, but take into consideration supplementary arguments, whether historical, anthropological, religious, cultural, or political. For instance, homosexuality is contextualized in the past as dependent on alien gender configurations that no longer hold. In this version, Paul condemns homosexual practices, but such indictment relies on a gender ideology where the male is naturally superior not only to the female but also to those in the household under his command. In other liberal interpretations, Paul's opposition to homosexuality is no more relevant than his recommendations for widows (1 Cor. 7:39) or for women in the assembly to veil their heads (1 Cor. 11:2-16). Here such instructions are to be read as rooted in a cultural milieu alien to our present and thus can be disentangled from the core of the Christian message.

In the Spanish case, the Catholic Church in conservative fashion interprets Paul as a founding figure of a wider tradition that has the upper hand in contemporary debates. Modern interpreters, regardless of their contexts, have access to the original meaning of the text—determined by Paul's intention—and are supposed to submit to the practical implications derived from such a normative reading. This approach lacks any critical reflection on the preconceptions that readers bring to the texts and, as such, is likely to unconsciously adopt contemporary stances[12] (and to some extent, anachronistic regarding the text) on moral issues. Here, the mixing of authorial intention and literalism equals sound interpretation.[13] In sum, Paul's views are the exclusive authoritative source when dealing with sexuality in the present, and since we can trace back a pervasive condemnation of homosexuality, such behavior ought to be banned.

Relying on "authorial intention" as the exclusive source for constructing meaning obviates long-standing hermeneutical theory that has warned against the dangers of proposing as universal knowledge that has not be properly contextualized. Regarding sexuality and the New Testament, Dale Martin has argued persuasively against a theory of meaning tied to "authorial intention." Meaning, Martin argues, is not univocally linked to the person who utters words; it might be as well linked to the addressee, be it a subject or a community. Further, meaning relates to anterior and posterior utterances and to the contextual reality of the community, both in the present and in the past. Meaning, in the end, is determined by context. Martin's critique is fourfold:

1. Authorial intentions do not really exist anywhere in nature so that we could hold up our interpretations against them for testing purposes.
2. Authorial intentions, when used as a factor of interpreting texts, are themselves products of people interpreting texts.
3. In our everyday practices we actually do not always use notions of authorial intention to settle the meanings of texts.
4. Even if authorial intention is something we may legitimately imagine for purposes of interpreting a text, there is no reason to limit

interpretations of all texts to attempt to ascertain intentions (Martin 2006b: 8)

Authorial intention's monopoly is explained as a residue of the modernist framework (Martin 2006b: 14–15), widely questioned both from within and outside the field.[14] A theory of undetermined meaning is, however, the springboard for a critique of church interpretations of sexual identities,[15] and serves as a basis for contextual interpretations that refuse to take meaning as determined exclusively by the ancient context. In this venue, contextuality underscores the ideological underpinnings of every interpretation, pays attention to the ways in which subjects and communities construct meaning in interaction with the biblical texts, and throws into relief the theological, ethical, and political consequences of every textual reading. Meanings shape communities, but more importantly, those communities are formed by the meaning they construct in interaction with the text.

INTERPRETATION OF 1 CORINTHIANS 6:1-9

According to Paul in Romans, men and women fail to live according to the standards God made evident to them (Rom. 1:19) and have thus deviated from righteous practices (Rom. 1:21). In Rom. 1:24, God appears as delivering "them" "in the lusts of their hearts to impurity" and giving them over to "degrading passions" (Rom. 1:26). In 1 Cor. 6:1-9, the context is more specific in that Paul encourages his addressees to solve inner conflicts by not resorting to civil institutions (1 Cor. 6:1) and condemns the use of public courts to solve community issues (1 Cor. 6:6). Both texts pursue the configuration of a minoritized morality vis-à-vis a dominant culture. The lists of sins include vices performed by the "outer world": exchange the natural use of sex, unrighteousness, wickedness, greed, evil, envy, murder, deceit, malice, slander, arrogance, boastful, unloving, unmerciful (Rom. 1:29-31) or covetous, drunkards, swindlers, revilers, adulterers, effeminate (1 Cor. 6:9-10).

The Catholic Church in light of contemporary national events reinterprets Paul's rhetoric of Christian superiority over the Roman morality. The church aligns itself with Paul's position as it identifies the government with the decaying culture. Despite relying on historical-critical strategies of interpretation in order to retrieve the original meaning of the texts, the official documents' ideological agenda lumps together texts belonging to different traditions and creates a "gay biblical canon" (Haggerty 2000).[16] Texts are read in a literalist fashion in order to craft an identity in terms of the "traditional family," "procreative values," and "heterosexual marriage." The construction of a contemporary theological discourse around the sexual and the erotic is created by linking together diverse traditions but also by omitting any reference to biblical texts that would endanger the coherence of the church discourse. To put it differently, methods flirt with historicism, and results do not.[17]

Scholarly work, however, tends to contextualize Romans 1 and 1 Corinthians 6 by retrieving indigenous systems of gender and eroticism and exploring the problematic nature of seeking identification with the past. For instance, for Victor Paul Furnish, Rom. 1:26-27 presupposes "that same-sex intercourse compromises what patriarchal societies regard as the properly dominant role of males over females" (Furnish 1994: 31).[18] Situating the biblical passages within the context of past gender ideologies leads to an understanding of the Pauline position as alien to contemporary conceptions of the erotic: idolatry would be the issue, not sexuality.[19] "Vice lists" should not be read in terms of "sexuality," a term that usually refers to "inner dispositions" or desires coming from a psychological core. Further, natural and unnatural would not refer to the divine order of creation but to consuetudinary societal norms.[20] Other scholars further point out that Paul's statements are imbued with the rhetoric of excess and moderation (Jewett 2000: 229–30; Martin 2006a). All of these interpretations seek to bypass the hermeneutical consequences of "literalism" and the "plain version of historiography" by pointing at the inadequacy of imposing our current sexual regime onto the past. When interpreters read, for instance, "male prostitutes" and "homosexual offenders" in 1 Cor. 6:9-10 as translations of *arsenoikoites* and *malakos*, they are likely to understand those terms in light of contemporary configurations of sexuality. Such interpretations, however, are oblivious of the varying ways in which the realm of the sexual was linked to social hierarchies or to different notions about the gendered self. "Homosexual" in the present usually refers to men and women who exclusively have sexual desires for persons of their gender, while in Paul's times this was not the case. Males of certain status could have sex both with other males or females as long as certain protocols were observed: mainly, that the male of superior status was always the penetrator and never the penetrated, and that there was certain control over the passions involved.

Such scholarly agreement on the gap between past and present configurations of desire dissipates when it comes to evaluating Scripture's value for the present. Although contextualizing Pauline texts within ancient gender configurations in order to show how Paul's position is intrinsically linked to a hierarchical system where masculinity stands over femininity (Cosgrove 2002: 29), some scholars maintain that across-time condemnations of homosexuality are still scripturally grounded. Cosgrove, for instance, agrees that contemporary forms of homosexuality were not known to Paul, but, he maintains, the moral ban on homosexual relationships still applies by way of an extension of the basic rule.[21] Other authors, departing from the same premises, draw opposite conclusions: restoring the "biblical position" would imply reenacting a hierarchical social system based on misogyny, racism, and classism (Brooten 1996: 215–66; Martin 1996). In effect, since Romans 1 and 1 Corinthians 6 have become less of a window to ancient gender configurations and more of a mirror to contemporary concerns about the erotic, further reflection on the ideological use of the history of desires is called for.

One particular effect of contextualizing cultural constructions of gender and sexuality in antiquity has been that, ironically, many liberals and progressives—in church, academy, and politics alike—have paid little attention to the contextualization of cultural constructions in the present and, consequently, to the political, ideological, and religious effects of dis/identifying with the past. The debate known as the essentialism (Boswell 1981; 1994; Richlin 1992a, b; 2006) versus constructivism (Dover 1978; Williams 1998; Dunn 1998; Halperin 2002) argument highlighted the political stakes at play in the study of these issues.[22] On the one hand, by claiming that sexual identities are rooted in nature and, as such, are continuous across time and space, essentialism had the effect of enforcing Paul's indictments in the present but also provided the gay and lesbian movement basis to reappropriate the past ("we are everywhere"). On the other hand, by underscoring the cultural construction of any sexual identity, constructivism made it impossible to foreground in Antiquity contemporary moralizations of the sexual at the same time that it problematized the essentializing of identities, both gay and straight.

Both the Spanish Catholic Church and the government draw a straightforward link between the past and the present in terms of sexual identities. Both institutions for opposite purposes view "homosexuality" and "heterosexuality" as transhistorical identities. While the church does so in order to condemn any homosexual act, the government follows the same strategy in order to portray a history of oppression that needs to be accounted for and corrected. Such essentialist approach on both sides of the debate not only flattens configurations of desire across times and spaces but also obscures the varying ways in which diverse identities, desires, and behaviors play a role in the present. To the insights that queer theory offer in framing such debate I now turn.

As a queer theorist, David Halperin explores classical literature in order to expose the particularities of indigenous conceptions of the erotic in the past and their virtual utility for the present. The ideological outcome is the denaturalization of sexual regimes both in the present and in the past. Halperin shows that the "homosexual/heterosexual" divide that defines the contemporary sexual regime in Western societies is of recent vintage, and that the realm of "sexuality" understood in terms of individual erotic preferences has its origin in the scientific discourse starting in the nineteenth century. By underscoring the cultural dimensions of the sexual, queer theory criticizes essentialist accounts that understand the erotic as rooted in nature.

Halperin, in Foucauldian manner, also takes issue both with accounts seeking to pursue identifications in order to moralize the present and with explanations of the past aiming at foregrounding contemporary politics. If sexuality varies across times and spaces, any straightforward identification between the past and the present is undermined regardless of who makes such connections. Those who ground a moral indictment on homosexuality in ancient texts (Paul included) do not take sufficiently into consideration the ways in which our understanding of sexuality is alien to conceptions in classical and biblical times. In the same venue, to legitimate same-sex relations on the grounds of the past runs the risk of reenacting misogyny, racism, and pederasty (Halperin 2002: 32). The legitimation or condemnation of sexual acts depended on gender roles, status expectations, and social hierarchies. For instance, a man at the top of the social pyramid was allowed to penetrate their inferiors whether male or female without risking his masculine status. Masculinity was something men struggled to achieve, not a given biological fact. While in the present we understand homosexual acts as performed consensually between equal partners that have a given exclusive preference for members of the same gender, in the past, gender, consensus, and exclusive preferences were not the defining factors. In other words, males were allowed to have sex with, to put it bluntly, their property. Thus any appropriation of the past needs to account for the gender, age, class, and racial hierarchies contained in such sexual ideologies and practices.

Further, queer theorists have problematized the very attempt to draft taxonomies of desire because they obscure the ways in which subjects shape, live, and build their experience around the erotic[23] and because a classification of superseding systems visualizes history as a teleological enterprise (Menon 2008: 1–26). Queer theory, in the end, seeks to throw into relief the problems posed by pretending to know what "they were" and what "we are" in terms of the erotic. I have argued above that any contemporary reading of the past needs to account for its particularities and the gaps across historical periods. It is also important to notice that the present remains complex and obscure regarding sexual configurations, for as much as many individuals identify themselves along the lines of the homosexual/heterosexual divide, there are many others who do not see their identities reflected in those labels. There is a gap between the vocabulary at hand to describe the sexual and the way the sexual acquires continually new forms and practices. For instance, many self-identified "straights" have sex with other men for many reasons, not all of them sexual in nature; others do not define their sexuality in terms of the gender of their partner but on the basis of certain body types, age, and status differences, racial and ethnic preferences, and so on.

In contrast to these multifarious sexual configurations, the Catholic Church claims to have not only a pristine idea of what Paul meant by *arsenokoites* and *malakos* but also a knowledge of what is "queer" today. In its use of tradition, the government makes a similar claim by conflating present and past histories. Both the church and the state envision the homoerotic, and the sexual realm for that matter, as always referring to static identities. Further, the heterosexual bourgeois monogamous couple continues to be the model for any other possible and alternative erotic configuration (Warner 2002: vii–xxi). For the church, it provides the measuring rod to condemn homosexuality; for the government, the basis to extend legal rights. This common understanding obviates, however, that queer sex, both straight and gay, frequently skips the rule of complementarity presumed in such an ideal (Wittig 1992).[24] In brief, despite ecclesiastic and state attempts to reify identities, sexual practices, identities, configurations, and ideologies go beyond the labels imposed.

It is understandable that same-sex activity has been increasingly essentialized into an identity by churches, theologians and interpreters, activists, and governments. It is easier to moralize, theologize, theorize, claim rights, and legislate when labels are imposed and differing configurations fall under unambiguous concepts. At a global level, the path of congealing sexual acts into identities has been pursued either in order to condemn or grant rights ("Gay Rights in Developing Countries" 2010). To put it briefly: political activism and government prohibitions react to each other following a spiral pattern whereby "gay" becomes the place of contention between progressives/liberals, secularists/fundamentalists, left/right, and so on. Churches and states define the meaning of homosexuality in order to further their respective claims. Without denying the legitimacy of foregrounding the struggle for rights in terms of identities, I would like to end by pointing out the shortcomings of such an approach and by suggesting some hermeneutical keys in reading the biblical text in light of such insights.

CONCLUDING REFLECTIONS IN LIGHT OF THE NATIONAL CONTEXT

Stressing the political construction and the ideological function of sexual identities is not a dismissal of the "realness" with which peoples and communities experience those identities. The "gay" and "homosexual" labels are not only ideological placeholders; in many cases they faithfully mirror how people understand their identities and anchor political, social, and theological struggles. However, to call into question the shaping of sexual identities as they are played out in the national church-government debates implies that desire always skips categorization and identity fixation. Because desire is resistant to the rational, arguments tend to draw on alien discourses in order to show coherence. The case for procreation, marriage, and family can only be made by drawing on outdated scientific discourse and, more importantly, at the expense of important biblical traditions. Ironically, Christian Scriptures also offer a relativization of blood familial structures and a questioning of procreation and the marital bond that foregrounds the dominant model of the monogamous heterosexual couple.

On the side of the government, the law does not call into question but expands the ideology of the "straight family." By framing the debate around identities, both the government and the church have missed an opportunity to talk about the erotic beyond its social or religious configurations. The conflation of sexuality into homosexuality and heterosexuality is oblivious of actual sexual practices and identities that remain marginalized, less theorized or privileged by its invisibility. Self-identified straights that have sex with other males, people who do not configure their desire along the gender axis but across a variety of body types, ages, erogenous zones, nationalities, partner's self-identifications, and so on are unable to enter the debate due to the way it has been framed. Further, people who do not identify as male/female have no say in the straight/gay debate, and subjects seeking to make public commitments beyond the marriage contract find no voice. It is not coincidental that in the aftermath of the Spanish marriage bill, transgendered movements have protested against their increasing marginalization. In light of this, what role ought texts such as 1 Cor. 6:1-9 or Romans 1 (but also Genesis, Leviticus, or the Pastorals) to play in contemporary national political and religious debates around the sexual? I conclude with two hermeneutical suggestions that depart from the national context and seek to provide a common ground so the debate does not become sterile.

From the perspective of the religious/theological position, we can see Paul as arguing from a Jewish point of view against the idolatry (Romans 1) or the customary practices of the pagans (1 Corinthians 6). For Paul, "homosexuality" is a consequence of idolatry, not its cause. In Romans, the argument is related to the myth of the "fallen nature" (Martin 2006a), a doctrine that the Catholic Church has dismissed,[25] while in Corinthians the opposition to paganism is understood to shape the ethics of the community. Instead of reading Paul as embracing a blatant opposition to culture, it is better to understand his injunctions as a contextual response to a historical situation. His mission, in this reading, requires an opposition to cultural features hindering the expansion of the kingdom. By reading Paul as a purveyor of sexual norms, the church reenacts a morality that is not "radically democratic" (Schüssler Fiorenza 2009). Instead, envisioning Paul as a carrier of an ethics of love enables a relationship model in terms of Christian commitments (1 Corinthians 13). In light of this, "tradition" is not a chain of condemning statements but the place believers can mine in order to see how the Spirit has worked on queer lives.[26] When the "Letter to the Bishops of the Catholic Church on the Pastoral Care of Homosexual Person"[27] affirms that homosexuals cannot lead a happy life, not only is it making an empirically wrong statement,[28] but it is also dismissing queer life as a locus where the Spirit enriches church traditions (Bieringer 1997).[29]

From the perspective of the government, biblical texts need not be inserted within a tradition following a pattern of sexual oppression. Instead, Romans and 1 Corinthians are witnesses to queer conceptualizations of desire, not in order to restore native gender systems or power configurations but as instances of the virtually infinite ways in which subjects experience and express desire. In light of this interpretation, rather than being content with rescuing "gay and lesbians" from a history of oppression, the government should work toward a broader recognition of existing sexual desires that go beyond identities or that contest the very same idea of "sexual identity."

Notes

1. "Matrimonio," unlike "union de hecho," includes fiscal benefits and grants more than one thousand rights. It is important to notice that Spain has not passed a law "on gay marriage," but has amended the Constitution and the civil code. Where it previously read "women" and "men" ("hombres" and "mujeres"), it now reads "spouses."

2. Up to that point only Belgium and the Netherlands had taken such a step, although other countries have followed up since then: Canada (July 2005), Sweden (April 2009), Norway (May 2008), South Africa (November 2006), and Portugal (January 2010).

3. See also John Paul II 1994; Sacred Congregation for the Doctrine of the Faith 1975; 1986; 2003.

4. See also Conferencia Episcopal Española 2004: n2.

5. The underlining theology is found in John Paul II 1981.

6. See also Press Release in reaction to the legislation that puts homosexual unions at the same level as the marriage institution (May 5, 2005). Press Release about conscientious objection on a law that radically corrupts the essence of marriage (May 5, 2005). Press Release in reaction to the legislation that modifies the civil law code to establish that marriage is not between a man and a woman (June 30, 2005). Press Release about the European Parliament Resolution regarding 'homophobia' (May 11, 2006).

7. Ley 13/2005 de 1 de Julio, por la que se modifica el Código Civil en material de derecho a contraer matrimonio (Bill modifying the Civil Code in terms of marriage rights).

8. For the church, tradition is univocal, while for the Government, it must be revised in light of the history of marginalization.

9. For the church, natural law shapes society; for the government, it is rather the other way around.

10. There have been numerous church-state conflicts, ranging from politics on victims in the Civil War to the curricula in public and private schools.

11. I deliberately keep the words untranslated in order to stress the ambiguity of the terms and to avoid the ideological effects advanced by every available translation. See a presentation of this problem in Martin 1996.

12. It goes beyond the scope of the present contribution to reflect on philosophical developments in the last quarter of the twentieth century. As a brief note, hermeneutics has called into question any model in which the interpreter stands isolated from the tradition/context to which he or she belongs.

13. Notice the use of "Paul's intention" in the above-mentioned church documents.

14. See also Vander Stichele-Penner (2009). In his influential work, Jack Rogers considers that we must avoid a surface literalism, so we can escape the sort of subjectivism that brings our biases to the text. We must, instead, "take seriously the text as it is given to us and seek to understand it fully in its context" (Rogers 2009: 56). Further on, he insists that "to be faithful to the 'plain text' of Scripture, we must be very careful to understand the meaning of the text in its original context. Then we must be equally careful to discern if it is appropriate to apply that text in quite different, contemporary context" (57). Notice here how the author deploys a conception of meaning determined by "the original context."

15. Martin considers that the current demand to push churches toward a more gay-friendly politics is much less radical than the revolution brought about by the Puritans in the United States (Martin 2006b: 121).

16. The author reflects critically on recent anthologies that deal with "gay literature." It is beyond the scope of the present essay to consider to what extent selecting Romans 1 and 1 Corinthians 6 as central pericopes of analysis in debating same-sex issues is an appropriate strategy. My purpose is not to deal with the texts themselves but to analyze the rhetoric around them in a religious setting. To say it differently, choosing Romans and 1 Corinthians as sources in dealing with the sexual is, in itself, an ideological option.

17. 1 Corinthians is hardly ever analyzed by itself when dealing with sexuality. Romans 1 is cited as providing supporting evidence or as complementing the results obtained in the hermeneutical task.

18. In other words, the concern is gender not sexuality. See also Nissinen 1998.

19. In this interpretation, idolatry seems to be the cause rather than the effect of inappropriate sexual behavior. In this reading, homosexual behavior is condemned insofar as it is pursued against an idolatrous relationship with the divine. See Davies 1995. Leland White, in similar fashion, derives God's abandonment from the fact that pagans do not honor God: "Thus without honor, they act dishonorably, lacking control over their bodies" (White 1995: 23). Boswell emphasizes that, for Paul, the ideal is monotheism, and as a consequence, homosexuality derives from the gentile's rejection of this ideal (Boswell 1981: 108–9).

20. Rom. 11:24 seems to support this view. For the opposite view, see Gagnon 2001: 488.

21. Using a metaphor, a statute that prohibited "vehicles from entering the park" would include fire engines and ambulances, even if the city council did not mean to include emergency vehicles but simply forgot to consider them (Cosgrove 2002: 41).

22. For a presentation of the controversy, see Stein 1992.

23. See Butler 1990; 1993; 2004; Sedgwick 1990; Warner 1993; 1999.

24. For discussion on this topic, see Bersani 1995; 2010.

25. *Lumen Gentium* 16–17; *Gaudium et Spes* 58; *Nostra Aetate* 2; *Ad Gentes* 9.11.15.

26. For a historical study on the category of sodomy from Saint Augustine onward and a theological reappraisal of such history, see Jordan 1997; 2002.

27. "As in every moral disorder, homosexual activity prevents one's own fulfillment and happiness by acting contrary to the creative wisdom of God. The Church, in rejecting erroneous opinions regarding homosexuality, does not limit but rather defends personal freedom and dignity realistically and authentically understood" (n7).

28. For a theological reflection from a Catholic standpoint on the happy life of gay Christians, see Moore 2003: 151–76.

29. For an application of this conception of authority to the question of same-sex relationships, see Pizzuto 2008.

Bibliography

Aasgard, Reidar. 2004. *My Beloved Brothers and Sisters! Christian Siblingship in Paul.* JSNTSup 265. New York: T&T Clark.

Abdurraqib, Samaa. 2006. "Hijab Scenes: Muslim Women, Migration, and Hijab in Immigrant Muslim Literature." *MELUS* 31: 55–70.

Ackerman, Jane. 1995. "Stories of Elijah and Medieval Carmelite Identity." *History of Religions* 35: 124–47.

Adewale, S. A. 1988. *The Religion of the Yoruba: A Phenomelogical Analysis.* Ibadan, Nigeria: University Press.

Adewuya, J. Ayodeji. 2011. *Holiness and Community in 2 Cor. 6:14–7:1: Paul's View of Communal Holiness in the Corinthian Correspondence.* Reprint. Eugene: Wipf and Stock.

Agosto, Efrain. 2005. *Servant Leadership: Jesus and Paul.* St. Louis: Chalice.

———. 2008. *Corintios.* Minneapolis: Fortress Press.

Allinson, Robert E. 1989. *Chuang-Tzu for Spiritual Transformation: An Analysis of the Inner Chapters.* Albany: SUNY Press.

———. 2003. "On Chuang Tzu as a Deconstructionist with a Difference." *Journal of Chinese Philosophy* 30/3–4: 488–98.

Althusser, Louis. 1984. "Ideology and Ideological State Apparatuses (Notes towards an Investigation)." In *Essays on Ideology*, 1–60. London: Verso.

Anzaldua, Gloria. 1987. *Borderlands/La Frontera: The New Mestiza.* San Francisco: Spinters/Aunt Lute.

Apillera, Paraluman S. 2007. *Basic Tagalog for Foreigners and Non-Tagalogs.* Revised and Updated by Yolanda C. Hernandez. Hong Kong: Turtle.

Aune, David E. 2001. "Anthropological Duality in 2 Cor 4.16." In *Paul Beyond the Judaism-Hellenism Divide*, ed. T. Engberg-Pederson, 215–39. Louisville: Westminster John Knox.

Awolalu, J. Omosade. 1976. "Sin and Its Removal in African Traditional Religion." *JAAR* 44: 275–87.

Balz, H. 1990. "Sunerchomai." *EDNT* 3:304–305.

Barclay, J. M. G. 1996. "Neither Jew nor Greek: Multiculturalism and the New Perspective on Paul." In *Ethnicity and the Bible*, ed. M. G. Brett, 197–214. Leiden: Brill.

Barrett, C. K. 1965. "Thing Sacrificed to Idols." *NTS* 11: 138–53.

———. 1973. *A Commentary on the Second Epistle to the Corinthians.* New York: Harper & Row.

Bartman, Elizabeth. 2001. "Hair and the Artifice of Roman Female Adornment." *AJA* 105: 1–25.

Bartchy, S. S. 1973. *Mallon Chrēsai: First-Century Slavery and the Interpretation of 1 Cor 7:21.* Missoula, MT: Scholars.

Bauer, Walter, Frederick W. Danker, William F. Arndt, and F. Wilbur Gingrich. 2000. *A Greek-English Lexicon of the New Testament and Other Early Christian Literature,* 3rd ed. Chicago: University of Chicago Press.

Bauman, Richard A. 1992. *Women and Politics in Ancient Rome.* London: Routledge.

BeDuhn, Jason. 1999. "Because of the angels: Unveiling Paul's Anthropology in 1 Corinthians 11." *JBL* 118.2: 295–320.

Bell, Catherine. 1992. *Ritual Theory, Ritual Practice.* New York: Oxford University Press.

———. 1997. *Ritual: Perspectives and Dimensions.* New York: Oxford University Press.

Benoit, Pierre. 1970. "Resurrection: At the End of Time or Immediately After Death?" *Concilium* 10/6: 103–14.

Berger, Peter, and Thomas Luckmann. 1967. *The Social Construction of Reality: A Treatise in the Sociology of Knowledge.* Garden City, NY: Doubleday.

Bersani, Leo. 1995. *Homos.* Cambridge, MA: Harvard University Press.

———. 2010. *Is the Rectum a Grave? and other Essays.* Chicago: University of Chicago Press.

Betz, Hans Dieter. 1994. *Paulinische Studien.* Tübingen: Mohr Siebeck.

———. 2000. "The Concept of the Inner Human Being." *NTS* 46: 315–41.

Bieringer, R. 1994. "Die Gegner des Paulus im 2. Korintherbriefes." In *Studies on 2 Corinthians,* ed. R Bieringer and J. Lambrecht. Leuven: Leuven University Press.

———. 1997. "The Normativity of the Future: The Authority of the Bible for Theology." *ETL* 8: 52–67.

Bookidis, Nancy. 2005. "Religion in Corinth: 146 B.C.E. to 100 C.E." In *Urban Religion in Roman Corinth: Interdisciplinary Approaches,* ed. Daniel N. Schowalter and Steven J. Friesen, 141–64. Cambridge, MA: Harvard University Press.

Boswell, John. 1981. *Christianity, Social Tolerance, and Homosexuality: Gay People in Western Europe from the Beginning of the Christian Era to the Fourteenth Century*. Chicago: University of Chicago Press.

———. 1994. *The Marriage of Likeness: Same-Sex Unions in Pre-Modern Europe*. London: Fontana.

Bourdieu, Pierre. 1977. *Outline of a Theory of Practice*. Trans. Richard Nice. Cambridge: Cambridge University Press.

Boyarin, Daniel. 1993. "Paul and the Genealogy of Gender." *Representations* 41: 1–33.

———. 1997. *A Radical Jew: Paul and the Politics of Identity*. Berkeley: University of California Press.

Boyarin, Daniel, and Jonathan Boyarin. 1995. "Diaspora: Generation and the Ground of Jewish Identity." In *Identities*, ed. Kwame Anthony Appiah and Henry Louis Gates. Chicago: University of Chicago Press.

Braxton, Brad. 2000. *The Tyranny of Resolution: 1 Corinthians 7:17-24*. SBLDS 181. Atlanta: Society of Biblical Literature.

Brett, Mark. 1998. "Locating Readers: A Response to Frank Moloney." *Pacifica* 11/3: 303-15.

Brett, Paul. 1992. *Love Your Neighbor: The Bible as Christian Ethics Today*. London: Darton, Longman and Todd.

Briggs, S. 2000. "Paul on Bondage and Freedom in Imperial Roman Society." In *Paul and Politics: Ekklesia, Israel, Imperium, Interpretation: Essays in Honor of Krister Stendahl*, ed. Richard A. Horsley, 110–23. Harrisburg, PA: Trinity Press International.

Brooten, Bernadette J. 1996. *Love between Women: Early Christian Responses to Female Homoeroticism*. Chicago: University of Chicago Press.

Brun, Lyder. 1913. "'Um der Engel willen' 1 Kor 11,10." *ZNW* 14: 303–8.

Brunt, John C. 1981. "Love, Freedom, and Moral Responsibility: The Contribution of 1 Cor. 8–10 to an Understanding of Paul's Ethical Thinking." In *Society of Biblical Literature 1981 Seminar Papers*, ed Kent H. Richards, 19–33. Missoula, MT: Scholars.

———. 1985. "Rejected, Ignored, or Misunderstood? The Fate of Paul's Approach to the Problem of Food Offered to Idols in Early Christianity." *NTS* 31: 113–24.

Buell, Denise Kimber. 2001. "Rethinking the Relevance of Race for Early Christian Self-Definition." *HTR* 94/4: 449–76.

———. 2004. "The Politics of Interpretation: The Rhetoric of Race and Ethnicity in Paul." *JBL* 123/2: 235–51.

———. 2005. *Why This New Race? Ethnic Reasoning in Early Christianity.* New York: Columbia University Press.

Bultmann, Rudolf. 1951. *Theology of the New Testament.* Trans. Kendrick Grobel. New York: Charles Scribner's Sons.

———. 1985. *The Second Letter to the Corinthians.* Trans. Roy A. Harrisville. Minneapolis: Augsburg Publishing House.

Burton, Ernest De Witt. 1988. *A Critical and Exegetical Commentary on the Epistle to the Galatians.* Edinburgh: T&T Clark.

Büchsel, F. 1982. "εδωλον." In *Theological Dictionary of the New Testament,* ed. Gerhard Kittel, trans. Geoffrey W. Bromiley, 2:375–80. Grand Rapids: Eerdmans.

Butler, Judith. 1990. *Gender Trouble: Feminism and the Subversion of Identity.* New York: Routledge.

———. 1993. *Bodies That Matter: On the Discursive Limits of Sex.* New York: Routledge.

———. 2004. *Undoing Gender.* New York: Routledge.

Campbell, J. Y. 1965. "ΚΟΙΝΩΝΙΑ and Its Cognates in the New Testament." *JBL* 52: 352–80. Reprinted in *Three New Testament Studies,* 1–28. Leiden: Brill.

Campbell, W. S. 2008. *Paul and the Creation of Christian Identity.* T&T Clark Biblical Studies. London: T&T Clark.

Caraman, J. B. 1978. "Religions as a Problem for Christian Theology." In *Christian Faith in a Religiously Plural World,* ed. D. C. Dawe and J. B. Carman. Maryknoll, NY: Orbis.

Cargal, Timothy B. 1990. "The Generative Trajectory in Certain Non-Western Cultures." In Daniel Patte, *The Religious Dimensions of Biblical Texts: Greimas's Structural Semiotics and Biblical Exegesis,* 265–75. Atlanta: Scholars.

Carpenter, J. Estlin. *Comparative Religion.* London: William Norgate, n.d.

Cassidy, Edward Idris. 2005. *Ecumenism and Interreligious Dialogue: Unitatis Redintegratio, Nostra Aetate.* Rediscovering Vatican II. New York: Paulist.

Castelli, Elizabeth A. 1991. *Imitating Paul: A Discourse of Power.* Louisville: Westminster John Knox.

Charles, Jesse. 1988. "Chuang Tsu and the Problem of Personal Identity: A Study of Identity and Interrelatedness." Ph.D. diss., University of Hawaii.

———. 2003. "Comparative Philosophy: Its Aims and Methods." *Journal of Chinese Philosophy* 30/2: 259–70.

Chepey, Stuart. 2005. *Nazirites in Late Second Temple Judaism.* Leiden: Brill.

Cheung, Alex T. 1999. *Idol Food in Corinth: Jewish Background and Pauline Legacy.* JSNTSup 176. Sheffield: Sheffield Academic.

Clarke, L. 2003. "Hijab according to the Hadith: Text and Interpretation." In *The Muslim Veil in North America: Issues and Debates,* ed. Sajida S. Alvi, Homa Hoodfar, and Sheila McDonough. 214–86. Toronto: Women's Press.

Collins, Raymond F. 1999. *First Corinthians.* Collegeville, MN: Liturgical.

Comber, Leon. 1956. *Chinese Ancestor Worship in Malaya.* Singapore: Donald Moore Singapore.

Conferencia Episcopal Española (Comisión Permanente). 1994. Matrimonio, Familia y "Uniones Homosexuales."

Conferencia Episcopal Española (Comité Ejecutivo). 2004. En favor del verdadero Matrimonio.

Conzelmann, Hans. 1975. *1 Corinthians: A Commentary on the First Epistle to the Corinthians.* Philadelphia: Fortress Press.

Cope, Lamar. 1990. "First Corinthians 8–10: Continuity or Contradiction?" *ATR Supplementary Series* 11: 114–23.

Cosgrove, Charles H. 2002. *Appealing to Scripture in Moral Debate: Five Hermeneutical Rules.* Grand Rapids: Eerdmans.

———. 2006. "Did Paul Value Ethnicity?" *CBQ* 68: 268–90.

Craig, Erik. 2007. "Tao Psychotherapy: Introducing a New Approach to Humanistic Practice." *The Humanistic Psychologist* 35/2: 109–33.

Crossley, Nick. 2008. "Sociology." In *Merleau-Ponty: Key Concepts,* ed. Rosalyn Diprose and Jack Reynolds, 228–39. Stocksfield, UK: Acumen.

Cua, Anthony S. 1977. "Forgetting Morality: Reflections on a Theme in Chuang Tzu." *Journal of Chinese Philosophy* 4: 305–28.

Davies, Margaret. 1995. "New Testament Ethics and Ours: Homosexuality and Sexuality in Romans 1:26-27." *BibInt* 3/3: 315–31.

Dawes, G. W. 1990. "But If You Can Gain Your Freedom (1 Corinthians 7:17-24)." *CBQ* 52: 681–97.

De Guia, Katrin. 2005. *Kapwa: The Self in the Other: Worldviews and Lifestyles of Filipino Culture Bearers.* Pasig City, Philippines: Anvil.

De Mesa, José M. 1979. *And God Said, "Bahala na!" The Theme of Providence in the Lowland Filipino Context.* Maryhill Studies 2. Quezon City, Philippines: Jose M. de Mesa.

De Vos, Craig Steven. 1999. *Church and Community Conflicts: The Relationships of the Thessalonian, Corinthian, and Philippian Churches with their Wider Civic Communities.* SBLDS 168. Atlanta: Scholars.

Delling, F. 1964. "Prolambano." *TDNT* 4:14–15.

Deming, W. 1995. "A Diatribe Pattern in 1 Cor. 7:21-22: A New Perspective on Paul's Directions to Slaves." *NovT* 37/2: 130–37.

Derrida, Jacques. 1988. *Limited Inc.* Ed. Gerald Graff. Evanston: Northwestern University Press.

———. 1998. *Of Grammatology.* Trans Gayatri Chakravorty Spivak. Baltimore: Johns Hopkins University Press.

Dodd, Brian. J. 1996. *The Problem with Paul.* Downers Grove, IL: InterVarsity.

Douglas, Kelly Brown. 2005. *What's Faith Got to Do with It? Black Bodies/Christian Souls.* Maryknoll, NY: Orbis.

Douglas, Mary. 1966. *Purity and Danger: An Analysis of the Concept of Pollution and Taboo.* London: Routledge & Kegan Paul.

Dover, Kenneth James. 1978. *Greek Homosexuality.* London: Duckworth.

Dreyfus, Hubert L. 1991. *Being-in-the-World: A Commentary on Heidegger's Being and Time.* Cambridge, MA: MIT Press.

Duling, Dennis. 2008. "2 Corinthians 11:22: Historical Context, Rhetoric, and Ethnicity." *HvTSt* 64/2: 819–43.

Dunn, Laura A. 1998. "The Evolution of Imperial Roman Attitudes toward Same-Sex Acts." Paper from Department of Phililosphy, Miami University.

Eco, Umberto. 1983. "The Scandal of Metaphor: Metaphorology and Semiotics." *Poetics Today* 4: 217–57.

Egudu, R. H. 1972. "Can There Be Morality without Religion?" *Faith and Practice* 1/2: 10–11.

Ehrensperger, Kathy. 2004. *That We May Be Mutually Encouraged: Feminism and the New Perspective in Pauline Studies.* New York: T&T Clark.

Ellingworth, Paul, and Howard A. Hatton. 1994. *A Handbook on Paul's First Letter to the Corinthians.* New York: United Bible Societies.

Ellis, A. B. 1966. *The Tshi-Speaking Peoples of the Gold Coast of West Africa.* Reprinted. London: Frank Cass.

Ellis, E. Earle. 1960. "2 Corinthians 5:1-10 in Pauline Eschatology." *NTS* 6/3: 211–24.

Elliott, Neil. 1994. *Liberating Paul. The Justice of God and the Politics of the Apostle.* The Bible and Liberation 6. Maryknoll, NY: Orbis.

———. 2004. "The Apostle Paul's Self-Presentation as Anti-Imperial Performance." In *Paul and the Roman Imperial Order*, ed. Richard A. Horsley, 67–88. Harrisburg, PA: Trinity Press International.

Engberg-Pedersen, Troels. 1991. "1 Corinthians 11:16 and the Character of Pauline Exhortation," *JBL* 110: 679–89.

———. 2000. *Paul and the Stoics.* Louisville: Westminster John Knox.

Engles, Donald. 1990. *Roman Corinth: An Alternative Model for the Classical City.* Chicago: University of Chicago Press.

Enriquez, Virgilio. 1994. "*Kapwa* and the Struggle for Justice, Freedom and Dignity." In *Pamamaraan: Indigenous Knowledge and Evolving Research Paradigms*, ed. Teresita Obusan and Angelina Rodriguez, 1–18. Quezon City, Philippines: Asian Center.

Evans-Pritchard, E. E. 1956. *Nuer Religion.* London: Oxford University Press.

Fay, Ron C. 2008. "Greco-Roman Concepts of Deity." In *Paul's World*, ed Stanley E. Porter, 51–79. Leiden: Brill.

Feagin, Joe R. 2006. *Systemic Racism: A Theory of Oppression.* New York: Routledge.

Fee, Gordon. 1980. "Εἰδωλόθυτα Once Again: An Interpretation of 1 Corinthians 8–10." *Bib* 61: 172–97.

———. 1987. *The First Epistle to the Corinthians.* Grand Rapids: Eerdmans.

Fehl, Noah Edward. 1971. *Li: Rites and Propriety n Literature and Life: A Perspective for a Cultural History of Ancient China.* Hong Kong: The Chinese University of Hong Kong.

Finley, Moses I. 1980. *Ancient Slavery and Modern Ideology.* Exp ed. Princeton: Markus Wiener.

Finney, Mark. 2010. "Honour, Head-coverings and Headship: 1 Corinthians 11.2-16 in its Social Context." *JSNT* 33: 31–58.

Fisk, Bruce N. 1989. "Eating Meat Offered to Idols: Corinthian Behavior and Pauline Response in 1 Corinthians 8–10 (A Response to Gordon Fee)." *TJ* 10: 49–70.

Fitzmyer, Joseph A. 1990. "A Feature of Qumran Angelology and the Angels of 1 Cor 11:10." In *Paul and the Dead Sea Scrolls*, ed. Jerome Murphy-O'Connor and J. H. Charlesworth, 31–47. New York: Crossroad.

———. *First Corinthians. A New Translation with Introduction and Commentary.* New Haven: Yale University Press.

Fleming, Jesse. 1999. "Philosophical Counseling and Chuang Tzu's Philosophy of Love." *Journal of Chinese Philosophy* 26/3: 377–95.

Fotopoulos, John. 2003. *Food Offered to Idols in Roman Corinth: A Socio-Rhetorical Reconsideration of 1 Corinthians 8:1–11:1.* Tübingen: J. C. B. Mohr.

Fraser, John W. 1971. "Paul's Knowledge of Jesus: II Corinthians V.16 Once More." *NTS* 17/3: 293–313.

Friesen, Steven J. 2004. "Poverty in Pauline Studies: Beyond the So-called New Consensus." *JSNT* 26: 323–61.

———. 2005. "Prospects for a Demography of the Pauline Mission: Corinth among the Churches." In *Urban Religion in Corinth: Interdisciplinary Approaches*, ed. Daniel N. Schowalter and Steven J. Friesen, 351–70. Cambridge, MA: Harvard University Press.

Fung, Yiu-ming. 2010. "On the Very Idea of Correlative Thinking." *Philosophy Compass* 5/4: 296–306.

Furnish, Victor Paul. 1972. *The Love Command in the New Testament*. Nashville: Abingdon.

———. 1984. *II Corinthians*. AB. New York: Doubleday.

———. 1994. "The Bible and Homosexuality: Reading the Texts in Context." In *Homosexuality in the church: Both Sides of the Debate*, ed. Jeffrey S. Siker, 18–35. Louisville: Westminster John Knox.

Gagnon, Robert A. J. 2001. *The Bible and Homosexual Practice: Texts and Hermeneutics*. Nashville: Abingdon.

Garland, David E. 2003. *1 Corinthians*. Baker Exegetical Commentary on the New Testament. Grand Rapids: Baker Academic.

Gatumu, Kabiro wa. 2008. *The Pauline Concept of Supernatural Powers: A Reading from the African Worldview*. Milton Keynes, UK: Paternoster.

"Gay Rights in Developing Countries." 2010. *Economist*. May 27. http://www.economist.com/node/16219402?story_id=16219402.

Geertz, Clifford. 1973. *The Interpretation of Cultures*. New York: Basic.

Georgi, Dieter. 1986. *The Opponents of Paul in Second Corinthians: A Study of Religious Propaganda in Late Antiquity*. Philadelphia: Fortress Press.

———. 1997. "God Turned Upside Down." In *Paul and Empire: Religion and Power in Roman Imperial Society*, ed. Richard A. Horsley. 148–57. Harrisburg, PA: Trinity Press International.

Gerhart, Mary, and Allan M. Russell. 1984. *Metaphoric Process: The Creation of Scientific and Religious Understanding*. Fort Worth: Texas Christian University Press.

Gill, David. 1990. "The Importance of Roman Portraiture of Head-Coverings in 1 Corinthians 11:2-16." *TynBul* 41: 245–60.

Gillman, John. 1988. "A Thematic Comparison: 1 Cor 15:50-57 and 2 Cor 5:1-5." *JBL* 107/3: 439–54.

Gittlen, Barry M., ed. 2002. *Sacred Time, Sacred Place: Archaeology and the Religion of Israel*. Winona Lake, IN: Eisenbrauns.

Glancy, J. A. 2006. *Slavery in Early Christianity*. Reprint. Minneapolis: Fortress Press.

Glasson, Thomas Francis. 1990. "2 Corinthians 5:1-10 versus Platonism." *SJT* 43/2: 145–55.

Glasswell, M. E. 1990. "Ekdekomai." *EDNT* 1:407.

Gonzales, Dennis T., and Edward Mañalac. 1990. "Strengthening the Value of *Hating-Kapatid:* Strengthening the Value of Eucharistic Sharing." *Sanloob: A Philosophical-Theological Journal of Maryhill School of Theology* 5: 41–51.

González, Justo. 1996. *La Santa Biblia: Reading the Bible through Spanish Eyes.* Nashville: Abingdon.

Gooch, Peter D. 1993. *Dangerous Food: 1 Corinthians 8–10 in Its Context.* Waterloo, ON: Canadian Corporation for Studies in Religion/Corporation Canadienne des Sciences Religieuses by Wilfrid Laurier University Press.

Goodacre, Mark. 2011. "Does *Peribolaion* Mean 'Testicle' in 1 Corinthians 11.15?" *JBL* 130: 391–96.

Goudriaan, K. 1992. "Ethnical Strategies in Graeco-Roman Egypt." In *Ethnicity in Hellenistic Egypt,* ed. P. Bilde, T. Engberg-Pedersen, L. Hannestad, and J. Zahle, 74–99. Aarhus, Denmark: Aarhus University Press.

Graham, A. C. 1981. *Chuang-tzu: The Seven Inner Chapters and Other Writings from the Book Chuang-tzu.* London: George Allen and Unwin.

Green, Joel B. 2008. *Body, Soul, and Human Life: The Nature of Humanity in the Bible.* Grand Rapids: Baker Academic.

Grenholm, Cristina, and Daniel Patte. 2000. "Overture: Receptions, Critical Interpretations, and Scriptural Criticism." In *Reading Israel in Romans: Legitimacy and Plausibility of Divergent Interpretations,* ed. Cristina Grenholm and Daniel Patte, 1–54. Harrisburg, PA: Trinity Press International.

Guardiola-Saenz, Leticia. 1997. "Borderless Women and Borderless Text: A Cultural Reading of Matthew 15:21-28." *Semeia* 78: 69–82.

Gundry-Volf, Judith M. 1997. "Gender and Creation in 1 Corinthians 11:1-16: A Study in Paul's Theological Method." In *Evangelium, Schriftauslegung, Kirche,* ed. J Ådna et al., 151–71. Göttingen: Vandenhoeck & Ruprecht.

Haggerty, George E. 2000. "The Gay Canon." *American Literary History* 12; 1/2: 284–97.

Halbertal, Moshe, and Avishai Margalit. 1992. *Idolatry.* Trans Naomi Goldblum. Cambridge, MA: Harvard University Press.

Halperin, David M. 1990. *One Hundred Years of Homosexuality and other Essays on Greek Love.* New York: Routledge.

———. 2002. *How to Do the History of Homosexuality.* Chicago: University of Chicago Press.

Harland, Philip. 2003. *Associations, Synagogues, and Congregations: Claiming a Place in Ancient Mediterranean Society.* Minneapolis: Fortress.

Harrill, James Albert. 1994. "Paul and Slavery: The Problem of 1 Corinthians 7:21." *BR* 39: 5–30.

———. 1995. *The Manumission of Slaves in Early Christianity.* Tübingen: Mohr Siebeck.

———. 2003. "Paul and Slavery." In *Paul in the Greco-Roman World: A Handbook*, ed. J. Paul Sampley, 575–607. Harrisburg, PA: Trinity Press International.

———. 2006. *Slaves in the New Testament: Literary, Social, and Moral Dimensions.* Minneapolis: Fortress Press.

Harris, Murray J. 1974. "Paul's View of Death m 2 Corinthians 5.1-10." In *New Dimensions in New Testament Study*, ed. R. N. Longenecker and M. C. Tenney, 317–28. Grand Rapids: Eerdmans.

———. 2005. *The Second Epistle to the Corinthians.* Grand Rapids: Eerdmans.

Harrison, James R. 2008. "Paul and the Athletic Ideal in Antiquity: A Case Study in Wrestling with Word and Image." In *Paul's World*, ed. Stanley E. Porter, 81–109. Leiden: Brill.

———. 2011. *Paul and the Imperial Authorities at Thessalonica and Rome.* Tübingen: Mohr Siebeck.

Hawthrone, Gerald, Ralph Martin, and Daniel Reid, eds. 1993. *Dictionary of Paul and His Letters.* Downers Grove, IL: InterVarsity.

Hays, Richard B. 1989a. *First Corinthians.* IBC. Louisville: John Knox.

———. 1989b. *Echoes of Scripture in the Letters of Paul.* New Haven: Yale University Press.

———. 1997. *First Corinthians.* IBC. Louisville: Westminster John Knox.

Heckel, Theo K. 1993. *Der innere Mensch: Der paulinische Verarbeitung eines Platonishcen Motivs.* WUNT. Tübingen: Mohr Siebeck.

———. 2000. "Body and Soul in Saint Paul." In *Psyche and Soma: Physicians and Metaphysicians on the Mind-Body Problem from Antiquity to Enlightenment*, ed. John P. Wright and Paul Potter, 117–31. Oxford: Oxford University Press.

Heidegger, Martin. 1962. *Being and Time.* Trans. John Macquarrie and Edward Robinson. New York: HarperSanFranciso.

Henry, Carl F. H. 1985. *An Introduction to the Philosophy of Religion.* Englewood Cliffs, NJ: Prentice Hall.

Hettlinger, Richard Frederick. 1957. "2 Corinthians 5:1-10." *SJT* 10/2: 174–94.

Hock, Ronald F. 2008. "The Problem of Paul's Social Class: Further Reflections." In *Paul's World*, ed. Stanley E. Porter, 7–18. Leiden: Brill.

Hodge, Caroline Johnson. 2007. *If Sons then Heirs: A Study of Kinship and Ethnicity in the Letters of Paul.* New York: Oxford University Press.

Hollingshead, J. R. 1998. *The Household of Caesar and the Body of Christ: A Political Interpretation of the Letters from Paul.* Lanham MD: University Press of America.

Hooker, Morna. 1963. "Authority on Her Head: An Examination of 1 Cor 11:10." *NTS* 10: 410–16.

Horrell, David G. 1996. *The Social Ethos of the Corinthian Correspondence: Interests and Ideology from 1 Corinthians to 1 Clement.* Edinburgh: T&T Clark.

———. 1997. "Theological Principle or Christological Praxis? Pauline Ethics in 1 Corinthians 8.1–11.1." *JSNT* 67: 83–114.

———. 2001. "From ἀδελφοί το οἶκος θεου: Social Transformation in Pauline Christianity." *JBL* 120: 293–311.

———. 2005. *Solidarity and Difference: A Contemporary Reading of Paul's Ethics.* New York: T&T Clark.

Horsley, Richard. 1978. "Consciousness and Freedom among the Corinthians: 1 Corinthians 8–10." *CBQ* 40: 574–89.

———. 1997. "1 Corinthians: A Case Study of Paul's Assembly as an Alternative Society." In *Paul and Empire*, ed. Richard Horsley, 242–52. Harrisburg, PA: Trinity Press International.

———. 1998. *1 Corinthians.* ANTC. Nashville: Abingdon.

———. 2000. "Rhetoric and Empire and 1 Corinthians." In *Paul and Politics*, ed. Richard A. Horsley, 72–102. Harrisburg, PA: Trinity Press International.

———, ed. 2004. *Hidden Transcripts and the Arts of Resistance: Applying the Works of James C. Scott to Jesus and Paul.* Leiden: Brill.

Huh, C. H. 2004. "Introduction to Taopsychotherapy." In *Tao Psychotherapy and Western Psychotherapy: Congress Proceedings*, 6–18. Seoul: Korean Academy of Psychotherapists.

Hurd, John C. 1983. *The Origin of 1 Corinthians.* Macon GA: Mercer University Press.

Husserl, Edmund. 2002. *Ideas Pertaining to a Pure Phenomenology and to a Phenomenological Philosophy. Second Book: Studies in the Phenomenology of Constitution.* Trans. Richard Rojcewicz and André Schuwer. Dordrecht, Netherlands: Kluwer Academic.

Ibita, Ma. Marilou S. 2002. "'*Kain Tayo! Salo Na!*' Filipino Hospitality and the Vows." In *At Nanahan sa Atin: Coming Home to the Roots of the Filipino Religious*, ed. Querico T. Pedregosa, Gerard Francisco P. Timoner, and

Clarence Victor C. Marquez, 153–77. Quezon City, Philippines: Asia Pacific Dominican Formation Center.

———. 2005. "Dining with Jesus in the Third Gospel: Celebrating Eucharist in the Third World." *East Asian Pastoral Review* 42: 249–61.

Idowu, Bolaji. 1962. *Olodumare: God in Yoruba Belief.* London: SCM.

Ignacio, Louie. 2011. "Hating-Kapatid—GMA Christmas Short Film 2011." Youtube. http://www.youtube.com/watch?v=ZLsyvzvxmZY.

Irigaray, Luce. 1996. *I Love to You: Sketch for a Felicity within History.* Trans. Alison Martin. New York: Routledge.

Ivanhoe, Philip J. 1991. "Zhuangzi on Skepticism, Skill, and the Ineffable *Dao.*" *Journal of the American Academy of Religion* LX: 4:639–54.

Jacob, D. B. 1977. *A Text Book on African Traditional Religion.* Ibadan, Nigeria: Aromolaran.

Jervis, L. Ann. 1993. "'But I Want You to Know . . .': Paul's Midrashic Intertextual Response to the Corinthian Worshipers (1 Cor 11:1-16)." *JBL* 112: 231–46.

Jennings, Theodore W., Jr. 2009. "Paul against Empire: Then and Now." In *The Bible and the Hermeneutics of Liberation,* ed. Alejandro F. Botta and Pablo R. Andiñach, 147–67. Atlanta: Society of Biblical Literature.

Jewett, Robert. 2000. "The Social Context and Implications of Homoerotic References in Rom 1: 24-27." In *Homosexuality, Science, and the "Plain Sense" of Scripture,* ed. David L. Balch, 223–41. Grand Rapids: Eerdmans.

———. 2004. "The Corruption and Redemption of Creation: Reading Romans 8:18-23 within the Imperial Context." In *Paul and the Imperial Order,* ed. Richard A. Horsely, 25–46. Harrisburg, PA: Trinity Press International.

Jing, Xiao. 1899. "The Classic of Filial Piety." In *The Sacred Books of the East: The Texts of Confucianism.* Vol. 3, part 1, *The Shu King, The Religious Portions of the Shih King, The Hsiao King.* Trans. James Legge, 465–88. 2nd ed. Oxford: Clarendon Press, 1899. http://www.anselm.edu/homepage/athornto/xiaojing.htm.

John Paul II, Pope. 1981. *Familiaris Consortio: Apostolic Exhortation on the Role of the Christian Family in the Modern World.* Boston: Daughters of St. Paul.

———. 1994. *Letter to Families.* Gratissimam Sane. http://www.vatican.va/holy_father/john_paul_ii/letters/documents/hf_jp-ii_let_02021994_families_en.html.

Jones, James M. 1997. *Prejudice and Racism.* San Francisco: McGraw-Hill.

Jordan, Mark D. 1997. *The Invention of Sodomy in Christian Theology.* Chicago: University of Chicago Press.

———. 2002. *The Ethics of Sex*. Oxford: Blackwell.

Jung, C. G. 1958. "Psychology and Religion: West and East." In *The Collected Works of C. G. Jung, Volume 11*, R. F. C. Hull, trans. Princeton: Princeton University Press.

Kähler, Else. 1960. *Die Frau in den paulinischen Briefen*. Zurich: Gotthelf-Verlag.

Keener, Craig. 1991. *And Marries Another: Divorce and Remarriage in the New Testament*. Peabody, MA: Hendrickson.

———. 2005. *1–2 Corinthians*. Cambridge: Cambridge University Press.

Kelley, S. 2002. *Racializing Jesus: Race, Ideology and the Formation of Modern Biblical Scholarship*. Biblical Limits. New York: Routledge.

Kim, Yung Suk. 2008. *Christ's Body in Corinth: The Politics of a Metaphor*. Minneapolis: Fortress Press.

———. 2011a. "'Imitators' (*Mimetai*) in 1 Cor. 4:16 and 11:1: A New Reading of Threefold Embodiment." *HBT* 33: 147–70.

———. 2011b. *A Theological Introduction to Paul's Letters: Exploring a Threefold Theology of Paul*. Eugene, OR: Cascade.

Klauck, Hans-Josef. 1993. "Presence in the Lord's Supper: The Lord's Supper and the Lord's Supper Tradition: Reflections on 1 Corinthians 11:23b-25." In *One Loaf, One Cup: Ecumenical Studies of 1 Cor 11 and Other Eucharistic Texts*, ed. Ben F. Meyer, 57–74. New Gospel Studies 6. Macon, GA: Mercer University Press.

———. 2003. *The Religious Context of Early Christianity: A Guide to Graeco-Roman Religions*. Trans. Brian McNeil. Minneapolis: Fortress Press.

Klinghardt, Matthias. 1996. *Gemeinschaftsmahl und Mahlgemeinschaft: Soziologie und Liturgie frühchristlicher Mahlfeiern*. TANZ 13. Basel: Francke.

Knoblock, John. 1994. *Xunzi: A Translation and Study of the Complete Works*. Vol. 3, *Books 17–32*. Stanford: Stanford University Press.

Koehlinger, Amy. 2007. *The New Nuns: Racial Justice and Religious Reform in the 1960s*. Cambridge, MA: Harvard University Press.

Koch, Robert A. 1959. "Elijah the Prophet, Founder of the Carmelite Order." *Spec* 34: 547–60.

Kristensen, W. B. 1960. *The Meaning of Religion*. Translated by J. Carma. The Hague: Martins Nyhoff.

Kristeva, Julia. 2011. *The Severed Head and Capital Visions*. New York: Columbia University Press.

Kunio, Mugitani. 2004. "Filial Piety and 'Authentic Parents' in Religious Daoism." In *Filial Piety in Chinese Thought and History*, ed. Alan K. L. Chan and Sor-hoon Tan. 110–21. New York: Routledge.

Lafontaine, Laurene M. 2008. *Out of the Cloister.* Berkeley: University of California Press.

Lahav, Ran. 1995. "A Conceptual Framework for Philosophical Counseling: Worldview Interpretation." In *Essays on Philosophical Counseling,* ed. Ran Lahav and Maria da venza Tillmanns, 1–24. Lanham, MD: University Press of America.

Lakos, William. 2010. *Chinese Ancestor Worship: A Practice and Ritual Oriented Approach to Understanding Chinese Culture.* Newcastle upon Tyne: Cambridge Scholars Publishing.

Lambrecht, J. 1994. "The Nekrōsis of Jesus: Ministry and Suffering in 2 Corinthians 4:7-15." In *Studies on 2 Corinthians,* ed. J. Lambrecht and R. Bieringer. Leuven: Leuven University Press.

Lategan, Bernard C. 1977. "Scholar and Ordinary Reader: More Than a Simple Interface." *Semeia* 73: 243–55.

Legge, James. 1971. *Confucius: Confucian Analects, The Great Learning and the Doctrine of the Mean.* New York: Dover.

Leonard, A. G. 1906. *The Lower Niger and Its Tribes.* London: Macmillan.

Llewellyn-Jones, Lloyd. 2007. "House and Veil in Ancient Greece." *British School at Athens Studies* 15: 251–58.

Longenecker, Bruce W. 2009. "Exposing the Economic Middle: A Revised Economy Scale for the Study of Early Urban Christianity." *JSNT* 31: 243–78.

Lynch, Frank. 1968. "Social Acceptance." *Institute of Philippine Culture Paper* 2: 1–21.

Malherbe, Abraham J. 1987. *Paul and the Thessalonians: The Philosophic Tradition of Pastoral Care.* Minneapolis: Fortress Press.

Malina, Bruce J. 1993. *The New Testament World: Insights from Cultural Anthropology.* Louisville: Westminster John Knox.

Marion, Jean-Luc. 1991. *God without Being.* Trans Thomas A. Carlon. Chicago: University of Chicago Press.

———. 2011. "What We See and What Appears." In *Idol Anxiety,* ed. Josh Ellenbogen and Aaron Tugendhaft, 152–68. Stanford: Stanford University Press.

Marshall, Peter. 1987. *Enmity in Corinth: Social Conventions in Paul's Relations with the Corinthians.* Tübingen: Mohr.

Martin, Dale B. 1990. *Slavery as Salvation: The Metaphor of Slavery in Pauline Christianity.* New Haven: Yale University Press.

———. 1995. *The Corinthian Body.* New Haven: Yale University Press.

———. 1996. "Arsenokoitês and Malakos: Meanings and Consequences." In *Biblical Ethics and Homosexuality*, ed. Robert L. Brawley, 117–36. Louisville: Westminster John Knox.

———. 2006a. "Heterosexism and the Interpretation of Romans 1:18-32." In *Boswell Thesis*, ed. Mathew Kuefler, 130–51.Chicago: University of Chicago Press.

———. 2006b. *Sex and the Single Savior: Gender and Sexuality in Biblical Interpretation.* Louisville: Westminster John Knox.

Martin, Troy. 2004. "Paul's Argument from Nature for the Veil in 1 Corinthians 11:13-15: A Testicle Instead of a Head-Covering." *JBL* 123: 75–84.

Martinez, Aquiles Ernesto. 2003. *Después de Damasco: el Apóstol Pablo desde una Perspectiva Latina.* Nashville: Abingdon.

Marty, Martin E. 1982. "The Catholic Ghetto and All the Other Ghettos." *The Catholic Historical Review* 68: 185–205.

Martyn, J. Louis. 1997. *Galatians.* AB. New York: Doubleday.

Matera, Frank J. 2003. *II Corinthians: A Commentary.* NTL. Louisville: Westminster John Knox.

Mata, Roberto. 2010. "Beyond Socialization and Attrition: Border Pedagogy in Biblical Studies." In *Transforming Graduate Biblical Education: Ethos and Discipline*, ed. Elisabeth Schüssler Fiorenza and Kent Harold Richards, 247–66. Atlanta: Society of Biblical Literature.

May, Reinhard. 1996. *Heidegger's Hidden Sources: East Asian Influences on His Work.* London: Routledge.

MacDonald, Nathan. 2007. "Recasting the Golden Calf: The Imaginative Potential of the Old Testament's Portrayal of Idolatry." In *Idolatry: False Worship in the Bible, Early Judaism and Christianity*, ed. Stephen C. Barton, 22–39. New York: T&T Clark.

Maurer, C. 1964. "Skizo, skisma."*Theological Dictionary of the New Testament.* Gerhard Kittel and Gerhard Friedrich eds., G. W. Bromiley trans. 9 vols. Grand Rapids: Eerdmans.7:959–64.

McIntosh, Peggy. 1990. "White Privilege: Unpacking the Invisible Knapsack." *Independent School* 49/2: 32–35.

Meeks, Wayne. 1974. "The Image of the Androgyne: Some Uses of a Symbol in Earliest Christianity." *HR* 13: 165–208.

———. 1983. *The First Urban Christians: The Social World of the Apostle Paul.* New Haven: Yale University Press.

Meggitt, Justin J. 1994. "Meat Consumption and Social Conflict in Corinth." *JTS* 45: 137–41.

Menon, Madhavi. 2008. *Unhistorical Shakespeare: Queer Theory in Shakespearean Literature and Film.* New York: Palgrave Macmillan.

Merleau-Ponty, Maurice. 1969. *The Visible and the Invisible.* Ed. Claude Lefort. Trans. Alphonso Lingis. Evanston: Northwestern University Press.

———. 2005. *Phenomenology of Perception.* Trans. Colin Smith. New York: Routledge Classics.

Metuh, Emefie Ikenga. 1985. *African Religions in Western Conceptual Schemes: The Problem of Interpretation.* Bodija, Nigeria: Pastoral Institute.

Metz, Judith. 1996. "The Founding Circle of Elizabeth Seton's Sisters of Charity." *U.S. Catholic Historian* 14: 19–33.

Metzger, Bruce Manning. 1994. *Textual Commentary to the Greek New Testament.* 2nd ed. Stuttgart: Deutsche Bibelgesellschaft; London: United Bible Society.

Mignolo, W. D. 2007. Introduction. Coloniality of Power and De-Colonial Thinking. *Cultural Studies* 21(2-3): 155–67.

Mitchell, Margaret. 1989. "Concerning PERI DĒin 1 Corinthians." *NovT* 31/3: 229–56.

———. 1992. *Paul and the Rhetoric of Reconciliation: An Exegetical Investigation of the Language and Composition of 1 Corinthians.* Tübingen: J. C. B. Mohr.

Moffatt, James. 1929. *Love in the New Testament.* London: Hodder & Stoughton.

Moore, Gareth. 2003. *A Question of Truth: Christianity and Homosexuality.* New York: Continuum.

Murphy-O'Connor, Jerome. 1979. *1 Corinthians.* NTM 10. Dublin: Veritas.

———. 2009. *Keys to First Corinthians: Revisiting the Major Issues.* New York: Oxford University Press.

Newton, Derek. 1998. *Deity and Diet: The Dilemma of Sacrificial Food at Corinth.* JSNTSup 169. Sheffield: Sheffield Academic.

Neyrey, Jerome. 1986. "Body Language in 1 Corinthians: The Use of Anthropological Models for Understanding Paul and His Opponents." *Semeia* 35: 129–70.

———. 1990. *Paul, in Other Words: A Cultural Reading of His Letters.* Louisville: Westminster John Knox.

Ngugi wa Thiongo. 1986. *Decolonising the Mind: The Politics of Language in African Literature.* London: James Curry.

Nicholson, Suzanne. 2010. *Dynamic Oneness: The Significance and Flexibility of Paul's One-God Language.* Eugene, OR: Pickwick.

Niebuhr, Karl-Wilhelm. 1992. *Heidenapostel aus Israel: Die jüdische Identität des Paulus nach ihrer Darstellung in seinen Briefen.* Tübingen: J. C. B. Mohr.

Nissinen, Martti. 1998. *Homoeroticism in the Biblical World: A Historical Perspective.* Minneapolis: Fortress Press.

Norman, Corrie E. 2003. "Religion and Food." In *Encyclopedia of Food and Culture.* Vol. 3: *Obesity to Zoroastrianism, Index,* eds Solomon H. Katz and William Woys Weaver, 171–76. New York: Scribner/Thomson Gale.

Nouwen, Henri J. M. 1979. *Clowning in Rome: Reflections on Solitude, Celibacy, Prayer, and Contemplation.* Garden City, NY: Image.

Odell-Scott, David W. 1991. *A Post-Patriarchal Christology.* Atlanta: Scholars.

O'Neill, John. 1987. "The Absence of the 'In Christ' Theology in 2 Corinthians 5." *ABR* 35: 99–106.

Orr, W. F., and J. A. Walther. 1976. *1 Corinthians. A New Translation. Introduction with a Study of the Life of Paul, Notes, and Commentary.* AB 32. New York: Doubleday.

Osiek, Carolyn. 1992. "Slavery in the Second Testament World." *BTB* 22/4: 174–79.

———. 2005. "Family Matters." In *Christian Origins,* ed. Richard A. Horsley, 201–20. Minneapolis: Fortress Press.

Oster, Richard. 1988. "When Men Wore Veils to Worship: The Historical Context of 1 Corinthians 11.4." *NTS* 34: 481–95.

Ouspenksy, Leonid, and Vladimir Lossky. 1982. *The Meaning of Icons.* Trans. G. E. H. Palmer and E. Kadloubovsky. Crestwood, NY: St. Vladimir's Seminary Press.

"Ox Killed to Bless Stadiums." 2010. *Sport24.* May 25. http://www.sport24.co.za/WorldCup/NationalNews/Ox-killed.

Parkes, Graham, ed. 1987. *Heidegger and Asian Thought.* Honolulu: University of Hawaii Press.

Parrinder, E .G. 1949. *West African Religion.* London: Epworth.

Parry, R. 1916. *The First Epistle of Paul the Apostle to the Corinthians.* Cambridge: Cambridge University Press.

Patte, Daniel. 1983. *Paul's Faith and the Power of the Gospel: A Structural Introduction to the Pauline Letters.* Philadelphia: Fortress Press.

———. 1990a. *The Religious Dimensions of Biblical Texts: Greimas's Structural Semiotics and Biblical Exegesis.* Atlanta: Scholars.

———. 1990b. *Structural Exegesis for New Testament Critics.* Minneapolis: Fortress Press.

———. 1995. *Ethics of Biblical Interpretation: A Reevaluation.* Louisville: Westminster John Knox Press.

Patterson, Orlando. 1982. *Slavery and Social Death: A Comparative Study.* Cambridge, MA: Harvard University Press.

———. 1998. *Rituals of Blood: Consequences of Slavery In Two American Centuries.* Washington, DC: Civitas/CounterPoint.

Payne, Philip B. 2009. "Twelve Reasons to Understand 1 Corinthians 7:21-23 as a Call to Gain Freedom." Philip B. Payne personal website. http://www.pbpayne.com/wp-admin/1_Cor_7-21_escape_slavery.pdf.

Perkins, Pheme. 1982. *Love Commands in the New Testament.* New York: Paulist.

Perriman, Andrew C. 1989. "Paul and the Parousia: 1 Corinthians 15:50-57 and 2 Corinthians 5:1-5." *NTS* 35/4: 512–21.

Petersen, Norman. 1985. *Rediscovering Paul: Philemon and the Sociology of Paul's Narrative World.* Philadelphia: Fortress Press.

Phua, Richard Liong-Seng. 2005. *Idolatry and Authority: A Study of 1 Corinthians 8.1-11.1 in the Light of the Jewish Diaspora.* New York: T&T Clark.

Pizzuto, Vincent A. 2008. "God Has Made It Plain to Them: An Indictment of Rome's Hermeneutic of Homophobia." *BTB* 38: 163–83.

Pobee, John S. 1997. "Bible Study in Africa: A Passover of Language." *Semeia* 73: 161–79.

Polaski, S. H. 2005. *A Feminist Introduction to Paul.* St Louis: Chalice.

Pollmann, Karla. 2005. "Marriage and Gender in Ovid's Erotodidactic Poetry." In *Satiric Advice on Women and Marriage from Plautus to Chaucer*, ed. Warren S. Smith, 92–110. Ann Arbor: University of Michigan Press.

Porter, Stanley. 1993. *Verbal Aspect in the Greek of the New Testament with Reference to Tense and Mood.* New York: Peter Lang.

———. 1995. *Idioms of the Greek New Testament.* 2nd ed. Sheffield: JSOT Press.

Punt, Jeremy. 2007. "Popularising the Prophet Isaiah in Parliament: The Bible in Post-Apartheid, South African Public Discourse." *R&T* 14/2: 206–23.

———. 2009. "Post-Apartheid Racism in South Africa. The Bible, Social Identity and Stereotyping." *R&T* 16/3–4: 246–72.

———. 2010a. "Paul, Power and Philemon: Knowing Your Place: A Postcolonial Reading." In *Philemon in Perspective: Interpreting a Pauline Letter*, ed. F Tolmie, 223–50. BZNW 169. New York: Walter De Gruyter.

———. 2010b. "Power and Liminality, Sex and Gender, and Gal 3:28. A Postcolonial, Queer Reading of an Influential Text." *Neot* 44/1: 140–66.

Räisänen, Heikki. 1983. *Paul and the Law.* Tübingen: Mohr.

Ray, Benjamin C. 1976. *African Traditional Religions: Symbol, Ritual and Community*. Englewood Cliffs, NJ: Prentice Hall.

Rhee, D. 1995. "The Tao and Western Psychotherapy." In *Psychotherapy East and West: Integration of Psychotherapies*, 162–68. Seoul: Korean Academy of Psychotherapists.

Richlin, Amy. 1992a. *Pornography and Representation in Greece and Rome*. New York: Oxford University Press.

———. 1992b. *The Garden of Priapus: Sexuality and Aggression in Roman Humor*. New York: Oxford University Press.

———. 2006. *Marcus Aurelius in Love*. Chicago: University of Chicago Press.

Robbins, Vernon K. 1996. *Exploring the Texture of Texts: A Guide to Socio-Rhetorical Interpretation*. Harrisburg, PA: Trinity Press International.

Rogers, Jack. 2009. *Jesus, the Bible, and Homosexuality: Explode the Myths, Heal the Church*. Louisville: Westminster John Knox.

Roloff, J. 1990. "Ekklesia." *EDNT* (Exegetical Dictionary of the New Testament. Horst Balz and Gerhard Schneider eds. 3 Vols. Grand Rapids: Eerdmans. 1:410–15.

Rudolph, David J. 2011. *A Jew to the Jews: Jewish Contours of Pauline Flexibility in 1 Corinthians 9:19-23*. Tübingen: Mohr Siebeck.

Ruiz, Jean-Pierre. 2009. "The Word Became Flesh and the Flesh Becomes Word: Notes toward a U.S. Latino/a Theology of Revelation." In *Building Bridges, Doing Justice: Constructing a Latino/a Ecumenical Theology*, ed. Orlando O. Espin, 47–68. Maryknoll, NY: Orbis.

Runesson, A. 2008. "Inventing Christian Identity: Paul, Ignatius, and Theodosius I." In *Exploring Early Christian Identity*, ed. B Holmberg, 59–92. WUNT 226. Tübingen: Mohr Siebeck.

Sacred Congregation for the Doctrine of the Faith. 1975. *Persona Humana. Declaration on Certain Questions Concerning Sexual Ethics*. Washington, DC: Office of Publishing Services, United States Catholic Conference.

———. 1986. *Letter to the Bishops of the Catholic Church on the Pastoral Care of Homosexual Persons*. Washington, DC: Office of Publishing Services, United States Catholic Conference.

———. 2003. *Considerations Regarding Proposals to Give Legal Recognition to Unions between Homosexual Persons*. Washington, DC: Office of Publishing Services, United States Catholic Conference.

Sanders, E. P. 1983. *Paul, the Law, and the Jewish People*. Philadelphia: Fortress Press.

Santiago, Carmen. 1976. "The Language of Food." In *The Culinary Culture of the Philippines*, ed. Gilda Cordero-Fernando, 133–39. Manila: Bancom Audiovision.

Savage, Timothy. 1996. *Power Through Weakness: Paul's Understanding of the Christian Ministry in 2 Corinthians.* New York: Cambridge University Press.

Sato, Masayuki. 2003. *The Confucian Quest for Order: The Origin and Formation of the Political Thought of Xun Zi.* Leiden: Brill.

Schlier, H. "Airesis." *TDNT* 1:180–83.

Schmidt, Brian B. 1996. *Israel's Beneficent Dead: Ancestor Cult and Necromancy in Ancient Israelite Religion and Tradition.* Winona Lake, IN: Eisenbrauns.

Schmithals, Walter. 1970. *Gnosticism in Corinth: An Investigation of the Letters to the Corinthians.* Nashville: Abingdon.

Schneider, Johannes. 1964. s.v. "συνέρχομαι." In *Theological Dictionary of the New Testament*, ed. Gerhard Kittel, trans. Geoffrey W. Bromiley, 2:666–84. Grand Rapids: Eerdmans.

Schowalter, Daniel N. 2010. "Seeking Shelter in Roman Corinth: Archaeology and the Placement of Paul's Communities." In *Corinth in Context: Comparative Studies on Religion and Society*, ed. Steven J. Friesen, Daniel N. Schowalter, and James C. Walters, 327–41. NovTSup 134. Leiden: Brill.

Schüssler Fiorenza, Elisabeth. 2009. *Democratizing Biblical Studies: Toward an Emancipatory Educational Space.* Louisville: Westminster John Knox.

Schweitzer, A. 1968. *The Mysticism of Paul the Apostle.* Trans. W Montgomery. 2nd ed. New York: Macmillan.

Schweizer, E. 1972. "σάρξ, σαρκικός, σάρκινος." In *Theological Dictionary of the New Testament*, ed. Gerhard Kittel, trans. Geoffrey W. Bromiley, 8:125–35. Grand Rapids: Eerdmans.

Scott, James C. 1990. *Domination and the Arts of Resistance: Hidden Transcripts.* New Haven: Yale University Press.

Sechrest, Love. 2009. *A Former Jew: Paul and the Dialectics of Race.* London: T&T Clark.

Sedgwick, Eve Kosofsky. 1990. *Epistemology of the Closet.* Berkeley: University of California Press.

Segovia, Fernando. 1992. "Two Places and No Place on Which to Stand: Mixture and Otherness in Hispanic American Theology." *List* 27: 26–40.

———. 1994. "Reading the Bible as Hispanic-Americans." In *New Interpreter's Bible.* Vol. 1, *General and Old Testament Articles, Genesis, Exodus, Leviticus*, ed. Leander Keck, 167–73. Nashville: Abingdon.

———. 1995. "Toward a Hermeneutics of the Diaspora: A Hermeneutics of Otherness and Engagement." In *Reading from This Place*. Vol. 1., *Social Location and Biblical Interpretation in the United States*, ed. Fernando F. Segovia and Mary Ann Tolbert, 57–73. Minneapolis: Fortress Press.

———. 2000. *Decolonizing Biblical Studies: A View from the Margins*. Maryknoll, NY: Orbis.

———. 2009. "Toward Latino/a American Biblical Criticism: Latin(o/a)ness as Problematic." In *They Were All Together in One Place? Toward Minority Biblical Criticism*, ed. Randall C. Bailey, Tat-siong Benny Liew, and Fernando F. Segovia, 193–223. Atlanta: Society of Biblical Literature.

Simoons, Frederick J. 1991. *Food in China: A Cultural and Historical Inquiry*. Boca Raton: CRC.

Singer, Irving. 1984. *The Nature of Love, 1: Plato to Luther*. Chicago: University of Chicago Press.

Sirat, Colette. 1990. *A History of Jewish Philosophy in the Middle Ages*. Cambridge: Cambridge University Press.

Skogemann, P. 1986. "Chuang Tzu and the Butterfly Dream." *Journal of Analytical Psychology* 31: 75–90.

Smith, Dennis E. 2003. *From Symposium to Eucharist: The Banquet in the Early Christian World*. Minneapolis: Fortress Press.

Smith, W. Robertson. 1914. *The Religion of the Semites*. London: A & C Black.

Social Weather Stations. 2011. "Fourth Quarter 2011 Social Weather Survey." http://www.sws.org.ph/pr20111222.htm.

Socias, James, ed. 2004. *Daily Roman Missal*. Chicago: Midwest Theological Forum; Schiller Park, IL: World Library.

Song, Choan-Seng. 1991. *Third-Eye Theology: Theology in Formation in Asian Settings*. Rev. ed.. Maryknoll, NY: Orbis.

Spicq, Ceslaus. 1958–59. *Agapè dans le Nouveau Testament: Analyse des Textes*. Ètudes Bibliques 3 vols. Paris: Librairie Lecoffre.

Spinelli, Ernesto. 1994. *Demystifying Therapy*. London: Constable.

Stanley, C. D. 1996. "Neither Jew nor Greek: Ethnic Conflict in Graeco-Roman Society." *JSNT* 64: 101–24.

Stein, Edward. 1992. *Forms of Desire: Sexual Orientation and the Social Constructionist Controversy*. New York: Routledge.

Sterckx, Roel. 2011. *Food, Sacrifice, and Sagehood in Early China*. New York: Cambridge University Press.

Stowers, Stanley. 1998. "Paul and Slavery: A Response." In *Slavery in Text and Interpretation*, ed. A. D. Callahan, R. A. Horsley, and A. Smith, 295–311. *Semeia* 83/84. Atlanta: Society of Biblical Literature.

Sumney, Jerry. 1990. *Identifying Paul's Opponents: The Question of Method in 2 Corinthians.* Sheffield: Sheffield Academic.

Sundlker, Bengt G. M. 1961. *Bantu Prophets in South Africa.* 2nd ed. London: Oxford University Press.

Surburg, Mark P. 2006. "The Situation at the Corinthian Lord's Supper in Light of 1 Corinthians 11:21: A Reconsideration." *Concordia Journal* 32: 17–37.

Tan, Yak-hwee. 2005. "Judging and Community in Romans: An Actions within the Boundaries." In *Gender, Tradition and Romans: Shared Ground, Uncertain Borders*, ed. Cristina Grenholm and Daniel Patte, 39–60. New York: T&T Clark.

Tatum, Beverly. 1997. *"Why Are All the Black Kids Sitting Together in the Cafeteria?" And Other Conversations about Race.* New York: Basic.

Taussig, Hal. 2009. *In the Beginning Was the Meal: Social Experimentation and Early Christian Identity.* Minneapolis: Fortress Press.

Teiser, Stephen F. 1996. "Introduction: The Spirits of Chinese Religion." In *Religions of China in Practice*, ed Donald S. Lopez Jr., 3–37. Princeton: Princeton University Press.

Thielman, Frank. 1989. *Plight to Solution: A Jewish Framework for Understanding Paul's View of the Law in Galatians and Romans.* Leiden: Brill.

Theissen, Gerd. 1975. "Die Starken und Schwachen in Korinth: Soziologische Analyse eines theologisches Streites." *EvT* 35: 155–72.

———. 1982. *The Social Setting of Pauline Christianity: Essays on Corinth.* Edinburgh: T&T Clark.

———. 1983. *The Social Setting of Pauline Christianity: Essays on Corinth.* Trans. J Schütz. Philadelphia: Fortress Press.

———. 2001. "The Social Structure of Pauline Communities: Some Critical Remarks on J. J. Meggitt, *Paul, Poverty and Survival*." *JSNT* 84: 65–84.

Thiselton, Anthony C. 2000. *The First Epistle to the Corinthians: A Commentary on the Greek Text.* NIGTC. Grand Rapids: Eerdmans.

———. 2006. *First Corinthians: A Shorter Exegetical and Pastoral Commentary.* Grand Rapids: Eerdmans.

Thrall, Margaret E. 1994. *The Second Epistle to the Corinthians.* 2 vols. Edinburgh: T&T Clark.

Tomson, Peter J. 1990. *Paul and the Jewish Law: Halakha in the Letters of the Apostle to the Gentiles.* Minneapolis: Fortress Press.

Troeltsch, Ernst. 1981. *The Social Teaching of the Christian Churches*, vol. 1. London: Allen and Unwin, 1931; reprint, Chicago: University of Chicago Press.

Tsai, Kathryn Ann, trans. 1994. *Lives of the Nuns: Biographies of Chinese Buddhist Nuns from the Fourth to Sixth Centuries.* A translation of the *Pi-chu'iu-ni chuan*, comp. Shih Pao-ch'ang. Honolulu: University of Hawaii Press.

Ukpong, Justin S. 1996. "The Parable of the Shrewd Manager (Luke 16:1-13): An Essay in Inculturation Biblical Hermeneutic." *Semeia* 73: 189–210.

Van der Toorn, Karel, ed. 1997. *The Image and the Book: Iconic Cults, Aniconism, and the Rise of Book Religion in Israel and the Ancient Near East.* Leuven: Uitgeverij Peeters.

Vander Stichele, Caroline, and Todd Penner. 2009. *Contextualizing Gender in Early Christian Discourse: Thinking Beyond Thecla.* New York: T&T Clark.

Vena, O. D. 2000. "My Hermeneutical Journey and Daily Journey into Hermeneutics: Meaning-making and Biblical Interpretation in the North American Diaspora." In *Interpreting beyond Borders*, ed. Fernando F. Segovia, 84–106. Sheffield: Sheffield Academic.

Wadud, Amina. 1999. *Qur'an and Woman: Rereading the Sacred Text from a Woman's Perspective.* New York: Oxford University Press.

Walker, William O., Jr. 1975. "1 Corinthians 11:2-16 and Paul's Views Regarding Women." *JBL* 94: 94–110.

Walker, Christopher, and Michael B. Dick. 1999. "The Induction of the Cult Image in Ancient Mesopotamia: The Mesopotamia *mīs pi* Ritual." In *Born in Heaven, Made on Earth: The Making of the Cult Image in the Ancient Near East*, ed. Michael B. Dick, 55–121. Winona Lake, IN: Eisenbrauns.

Walls, Neal H., ed. 2005. *Cult Image and Divine Representation in the Ancient Near East.* Boston: American Schools of Oriental Research.

Warnach, Viktor. 1951. *Agape: Die Liebe als Grundmotiv der neutestamentlichen Theologie.* Düsseldorf: Patmos-Verlag.

Warner, Michael, ed. 1993. *Fear of a Queer Planet: Queer Politics and Social Theory.* Minneapolis: University of Minnesota Press.

———. 1999. *The Trouble with Normal: Sex, Politics and the Ethics of Queer Life.* New York: Free Press.

Watson, Burton. 1968. *The Complete Works of Chuang Tzu.* New York: Columbia University Press.

Watts Henderson, Suzanne. 2002. "'If Anyone Hungers . . .': An Integrated Reading of 1 Cor 11:17-34." *NTS* 48: 195–208.

Weeks, Stuart. 2007. "Man-made Gods? Idolatry in the Old Testament." In *Idolatry: False Worship in the Bible, Early Judaism and Christianity*, ed. Stephen C. Barton, 7–21. New York: T&T Clark.

Westfield, Lynn, ed. 2008. *Teaching Black, Being Black.* Nashville: Abingdon.

Westermann, D. 1949. *The African Today and Tomorrow.* London: Oxford University Press.

Wheeler, Stephan M. 1995. "Imago Mundi: Another View of the Creation in Ovid's Metamorphoses." *AJP* 116: 95–121.

White, Leland J. 1995. "Does the Bible Speak About Gays or Same-Sex Orientation? A Test Case in Biblical Ethics." *BTB* 25/1: 14–23.

Whitehead, James D and Evelyn Eaton Whitehead. *Holy Eros: Recovering the Passion of God.* Maryknoll: Orbis.

Williams, Craig A. 1998. *Roman Homosexuality: Ideologies of Masculinity in Classical Antiquity.* New York: Oxford University Press.

Willis, Wendell. 1985. *Idol Meat in Corinth: The Pauline Argument in 1 Corinthians 8 and 10.* Chico, CA: Scholars.

———. 2007. "1 Corinthians 8–10: A Retrospective after Twenty-Five Years." *ResQ* 49: 103–12.

Wink, Walter. 1984. *Naming the Powers: The Language of Power in the New Testament.* Philadelphia: Fortress Press.

Winter, Bruce W. 1978. "The Lord's Supper at Corinth: An Alternative Reconstruction." *RTR* 37: 73–82.

———. 2001. *After Paul Left Corinth: the Influence of Secular Ethics and Social Change.* Grand Rapids: Eerdmans.

———. 2003. *Roman Wives, Roman Widows: The Appearance of New Women and the Pauline Communities.* Grand Rapids: Eerdmans.

Wire, Antoinette Clark. 1990. *The Corinthian Women Prophets: A Reconstruction through Paul's Rhetoric.* Minneapolis: Fortress Press.

Witherington, Ben, III. 1993. "Not So Idle Thoughts about Eidolothuton." *TynBul* 44/2: 237–54.

———. 1995. *Conflict and Community in Corinth: A Socio-Rhetorical Commentary on 1 and 2 Corinthians.* Grand Rapids: Eerdmans.

Wittig, Monique.1992. *The Straight Mind and Other Essays.* Boston: Beacon.

Wu, Kuang-ming. 1982. *Chuang Tzu: World Philosopher at Play.* New York: Crossroad.

Xunzi. 2003a. "A Discussion of Heaven." In *Xunzi: Basic Writings.* Trans. Burton Watson, 83–92. New York: Columbia University Press.

———. 2003b. "A Discussion of Rites." In *Xunzi: Basic Writings*. Trans. Burton Watson, 93–114. New York: Columbia University Press.

———. 2003c. "Improving Yourself." In *Xunzi: Basic Writings*. Trans. Burton Watson, 25–33. New York: Columbia University Press.

Yang, C. K. 1961. *Religion in Chinese Society: A Study of Contemporary Social Functions of Religion and Some of Their Historical Factors*. Berkeley and Los Angeles: University of California Press.

Yearley, Lee H. 2005. "Daoist Presentation and Persuasion: Wandering among Zhuangzi's Kinds of Language." *JRE* 33/3: 503–35.

Yeo, K. K. 1994. "The Rhetorical Hermeneutic of 1 Corinthians 8 and Chinese Ancestor Worship." *BibInt* 2: 294–311.

———. 1995. *Rhetorical Interaction in 1 Corinthians 8 and 10: A Formal Analysis with Preliminary Suggestions for a Chinese, Cross-Cultural Hermeneutic*. Leiden: Brill.

PRESS RELEASES

Reaction to the legislation that puts homosexual unions at the same level as the marriage institution (May 5, 2005) [http://www.almendron.com/politica/comentarios/com0004.pdf]

Conscientious objection on a law that radically corrupts the essence of marriage (May 5, 2005) [http://www.conferenciaepiscopal.es/index.php/documentos-ejecutivo/900-acerca-de-la-objecion-de-conciencia-ante-una-ley-radicalmente-injusta-que-corrompe-la-institucion-del-matrimonio.html]

Reaction to the legislation that modifies the civil law code to establish that marriage is not between a man and a woman (June 30, 2005) [http://aica.org/aica/documentos_files/Otros_Documentos/Varios/2005_06_30_CEE.htm]

European Parliament Resolution regarding 'homophobia' (May 11, 2006) [http://www.europarl.europa.eu/sides/getDoc.do?language=ES&pubRef=-//EP//TEXT+TA+P6-TA-2006-0018+0+DOC+XML+V0//ES]

Author Index

Scripture Index

195

198 | 1 and 2 Corinthians

Ancient and Other Extra-Biblical Sources Index